NONFICTION, THE TEACHING OF WRITING, AND THE INFLUENCE OF RICHARD LLOYD-JONES

Practices & Possibilities

Series Editors: Aimee McClure, Mike Palmquist, and Aleashia Walton
Series Associate Editor: Jagadish Paudel

The Practices & Possibilities Series addresses the full range of practices within the field of Writing Studies, including teaching, learning, research, and theory. From Richard E. Young's taxonomy of "small genres" to Patricia Freitag Ericsson's edited collection on sexual harassment in the academy to Jessie Borgman and Casey McArdle's considerations of teaching online, the books in this series explore issues and ideas of interest to writers, teachers, researchers, and theorists who share an interest in improving existing practices and exploring new possibilities. The series includes both original and republished books. Works in the series are organized topically.

The WAC Clearinghouse and University Press of Colorado are collaborating so that these books will be widely available through free digital distribution and low-cost print editions. The publishers and the series editors are committed to the principle that knowledge should freely circulate and have embraced the use of technology to support open access to scholarly work.

Other Books in the Series

Linda Adler-Kassner and Elizabeth Wardle, *Writing Expertise: A Research-Based Approach to Writing and Learning Across Disciplines* (2022)

Michael J. Faris, Courtney S. Danforth, and Kyle D. Stedman (Eds.), *Amplifying Soundwriting Pedagogies: Integrating Sound into Rhetoric and Writing* (2022)

Crystal VanKooten and Victor Del Hierro (Eds.), *Methods and Methodologies for Research in Digital Writing and Rhetoric: Centering Positionality in Computers and Writing Scholarship, Volumes 1 and 2* (2022)

Heather M. Falconer, *Masking Inequality with Good Intentions: Systemic Bias, Counterspaces, and Discourse Acquisition in STEM Education* (2022)

Jessica Nastal, Mya Poe, and Christie Toth (Eds.), *Writing Placement in Two Year Colleges: The Pursuit of Equity in Postsecondary Education* (2022)

Natalie M. Dorfeld (Ed.), *The Invisible Professor: The Precarious Lives of the New Faculty Majority* (2022)

Aimée Knight, *Community is the Way: Engaged Writing and Designing for Transformative Change* (2022)

Jennifer Clary-Lemon, Derek Mueller, and Kate Pantelides, *Try This: Research Methods for Writers* (2022)

Jessie Borgman and Casey McArdle (Eds.), *PARS in Practice: More Resources and Strategies for Online Writing Instructors* (2021)

NONFICTION, THE TEACHING OF WRITING, AND THE INFLUENCE OF RICHARD LLOYD-JONES

Edited by Douglas Hesse and Laura Julier

The WAC Clearinghouse
wac.colostate.edu
Fort Collins, Colorado

University Press of Colorado
upcolorado.com
Denver, Colorado

The WAC Clearinghouse, Fort Collins, Colorado 80523

University Press of Colorado, Denver, Colorado 80202

© 2023 by Douglas Hesse and Laura Julier. This work is released under a Creative Commons Attribution-NonCommercial-NoDerivatives 4.0 International license.

ISBN 978-1-64215-200-5 (PDF) | 978-1-64215-201-2 (ePub) | 978-1-64642-571-6 (pbk.)

DOI 10.37514/PRA-B.2023.2005

Library of Congress Cataloging-in-Publication Data

Names: Hesse, Douglas Dean, editor. | Julier, Laura, 1952– editor.
Title: Nonfiction, the teaching of writing, and the influence of Richard Lloyd-Jones / Edited by Douglas Hesse and Laura Julier.
Description: Fort Collins, Colorado : The WAC Clearinghouse; University Press of Colorado, [2023] | Series: Practices & possibilities | Includes bibliographical references.
Identifiers: LCCN 2023026019 (print) | LCCN 2023026020 (ebook) | ISBN 9781646425716 (paperback) | ISBN 9781642152005 (adobe pdf) | ISBN 9781642152012 (epub)
Subjects: LCSH: English language—Rhetoric—Study and teaching (Higher). | Creative nonfiction. | Lloyd-Jones, Richard, 1927–2014—Influence. | LCGFT: Essays.
Classification: LCC PE1404 .N66 2023 (print) | LCC PE1404 (ebook) | DDC 808/.0420711—dc23/eng/20230803
LC record available at https://lccn.loc.gov/2023026019
LC ebook record available at https://lccn.loc.gov/2023026020

Copyeditor: Andrea Bennett
Designer: Mike Palmquist
Cover Image: "Richard Lloyd-Jones at the Spring Green Motel 2010," by John Lloyd-Jones.
Series Editors: Aimee McClure, Mike Palmquist, and Aleashia Walton
Series Associate Editor: Jagadish Paudel

The WAC Clearinghouse supports teachers of writing across the disciplines. Hosted by Colorado State University, it brings together scholarly journals and book series as well as resources for teachers who use writing in their courses. This book is available in digital formats for free download at wac.colostate.edu.

Founded in 1965, the University Press of Colorado is a nonprofit cooperative publishing enterprise supported, in part, by Adams State University, Colorado State University, Fort Lewis College, Metropolitan State University of Denver, University of Alaska Fairbanks, University of Colorado, University of Denver, University of Northern Colorado, University of Wyoming, Utah State University, and Western Colorado University. For more information, visit upcolorado.com.

Land Acknowledgment. The Colorado State University Land Acknowledgment can be found at https://landacknowledgment.colostate.edu.

Dedication

To Jix, for all that he was, all that he did, all that he stood for.

Contents

Acknowledgments ix

Introduction. A Fifty-Year Trajectory of Creative Nonfiction 3
    Douglas Hesse and Laura Julier

Part One. Nonfiction and Richard Lloyd-Jones: A Legacy

Chapter 1. Reflections on a Legacy: The Practice of Wisdom 19
    Kathleen Blake Yancey

Chapter 2. With Jix. 33
    Margaret Finders

Chapter 3. Detours of Intention 45
    Tom Montgomery Fate

Chapter 4. Letter to Jix. 49
    David Hamilton

Chapter 5. Among the Ruins of Bethsaida: Reflections on Thirty Years of
Teaching Creative Nonfiction. 57
    John T. Price

Part Two. Teaching Creative Nonfiction: Practices and Values

Chapter 6. A Compositionist Teaches Creative Nonfiction 71
    Bruce Ballenger

Chapter 7. A Harmony of Variables 85
    Robert Root

Chapter 8. Making Matters. 93
    Nancy DeJoy

Chapter 9. On Failure: Notes Toward a Pedagogy of Risk 113
    Jocelyn Bartkevicius

Chapter 10. Personal Essays as a Path to Effective Transactional Writing,
or No, You Haven't Always Wanted to Be a Doctor. 123
    Rachel Faldet

Chapter 11. Redefining Preparation: The Need for Creative Nonfiction in High School 141
 Nicole B. Wallack

Chapter 12. Creative Nonfiction Accents the National Day on Writing . . . 157
 Douglas Hesse

Chapter 13. How Young Can You Go? Age and Experience and the Personal Essay's Limbo Pole 175
 Jenny Spinner

Chapter 14. I Am Going to Write About You 187
 Kerry Reilly

Chapter 15. The Next Anthology: The Personal Essay in the Digital Age . . . 193
 Ned Stuckey-French

Chapter 16. Why I Write, Read, Teach, Edit Nonfiction 205
 Laura Julier

Afterword. Richard "Jix" Lloyd-Jones: A Biographical Note 217
 Carl H. Klaus

Appendix. Word and Focus 219
 Richard Lloyd-Jones

Appendix. Poesis: Making Papers 229
 Richard Lloyd-Jones

Contributors 235

Acknowledgments

We want foremost to acknowledge and celebrate the late Carl Klaus, teacher and mentor to both of us. It was his idea for this collection, and many pieces here benefit from Carl's deep expertise in the essay. We also appreciate the encouragement of Jean Lloyd-Jones, an esteemed leader in Iowa politics and women's rights. Jean and Jix made a wonderful, formidable partnership.

We want to acknowledge the patience of the contributors to this volume, who endured some false starts and delays on our part yet stuck with the project with great generosity.

Thanks to Mike Palmquist, publisher, and the staff of the WAC Clearinghouse and the University Press of Colorado.

We're grateful to Emily Kirkpatrick, Colin Mucray, and Lisa Avetesian for permission to reprint material previously published by NCTE; to James McCoy, director of the University of Iowa Press; to Steve Semken, publisher and founder of Ice Cube Press; and to William Sewell, David Masiel, and John Boe, editors over the years at the wonderful journal *Writing on the Edge*. Elizabeth Stuckey-French supported us in bringing Ned's draft work to its final form. We wish Ned were here for its publication.

We appreciate the patience and insights of our spouses, Becky Bradway and Kate Carroll de Gutes, each themselves nonfiction writers.

Finally, we want to acknowledge the English Department of the University of Iowa for having played such an important role in our educations—and the educations of so many of this book's contributors. From the 1970s, when creative nonfiction was a dim glowing ember in American universities, Iowa has blown insistent breath on the genre, lighting and warming its readers and writers.

NONFICTION, THE TEACHING OF WRITING, AND THE INFLUENCE OF RICHARD LLOYD-JONES

Introduction. A Fifty-Year Trajectory of Creative Nonfiction

Douglas Hesse
UNIVERSITY OF DENVER

Laura Julier
MICHIGAN STATE UNIVERSITY

How might we understand the past and promise of creative nonfiction in contemporary writing classes? We've gathered sixteen authors, editors, and teachers to explore facets of a question that's more intricate and important than it may initially seem. Many explain how they developed as writers themselves, and several note the influence of a prominent figure in American writing, Richard Lloyd-Jones, chair of the University of Iowa English department at a pivotal time, as well as chair of the Conference on College Composition and president of the National Council of Teachers of English. We'll say more shortly about Jix (as he was popularly known). Nonfiction's large landscape includes the personal essay and memoir, of course, but also literary journalism, forms of nature writing, profiles, travel, and place writing, lyric essays, and swaths of story-driven advocacy and cultural analysis. This vast terrain is inflected—and often impelled—by a creative sensibility, designed to provide enjoyment as well as deliver information, ideas, or arguments. The magazine *Creative Nonfiction* maps this landscape as "true stories, well told" (to cite just one definition among many, some of which are offered throughout the essays in this collection), which may be simplistic and problematic but which underscores the aesthetic/artful dimension of works whose style and craft matter as much as its content.

We ask about the place of creative nonfiction in the context of broad disagreements about the nature and purpose of writing in academic settings. As we'll explain—and as the essays in this book illustrate—one area of contention has been the role of "creative" writing versus "expository" or "academic." In the past few decades, creative writing (historically, mostly fiction and poetry) has been assigned mainly to elective courses, with required courses having a more "practical" purpose. But that purpose is debated. Is it to foster personal growth and engagement? to learn writing conventions valued in the academy? to acquire rhetorical skills for argument? to develop critical faculties? Robert Connors documented how, ever since composition started becoming a formal college subject in the 1870s, writing courses have been driven as much by convenience and tradition as by research and reflection. Even engaged teachers, those guided more by scholarship than by casual expedience, disagree about the content of required writing, as illustrated by volumes like *A Guide to Composition Pedagogies* (Tate).

In any case, there's mostly been a boundary between creative writing and composition, the former claiming the fictional/imaginative/aesthetic, the latter holding truthful/purposive/rhetorical. The increasing visibility of academic creative nonfiction in recent decades has scuffed this division. Lee Gutkind claims to have coined the term in the early 1990s, though he discovered it no more than Columbus discovered America. After all, creative nonfiction has manifested for centuries, in early essays by Montaigne and Addison and Steele; in place writings like Mary Russell Mitford's *Our Village* or Henry David Thoreau's *Walden*; in travel writings like Su Shi's daytrip essays, Mark Twain's *Roughing It*, or Rebecca Solnit's *A Book of Migrations: Some Passages in Ireland*; in essayists like Virginia Woolf, George Orwell, Christa Wolf, Victoria Ocampo, Gabriela Mistral, James Baldwin, Joan Didion, Audre Lorde, and June Jordan; in the literary journalism of John McPhee and Susan Orlean; and on and on. Lynn Bloom documented how personal essays were circulated and canonized through first-year writing textbook anthologies throughout the 20th century, with Orwell, E.B. White, and Didion being the most frequently represented. Clearly, creative nonfiction has long been present in required writing courses, although some of its more belletristic expressions have occluded since the 1980s and 1990s, even as creative writing programs grew happy to claim this enterprise. Doug has explored that key transitional period in essays including "Who Owns Creative Nonfiction?" and "The Place of Creative Writing in Composition Studies." In this volume, Bruce Ballenger narrates with both analytic and deeply personal skill what's at stake in departments where custody of creative nonfiction becomes contested in creative writing's divorce from English departments.

For the most part, creative nonfiction appeared in 20th century composition as examples of narration or description, two of the four modes of discourse (the others being exposition and argument), in a long-discredited (if convenient) pedagogy steeped in a reductive notion of the mind operating through distinct faculties. That pedagogy taught fundamental cognitive operations by having students emulate prose models, with the idea that these operations would transfer to other writing situations. E.B. White's much-anthologized "Once More to the Lake" was used to teach narrative and descriptive technique rather than, say, how a writer might invest memory and plain experience with literary interest, for reasons meaningful to the writer.

Those practices, with their implications for creative nonfiction, are evident as early as 1902 in Charles Sears Baldwin's *A College Manual of Rhetoric*. Baldwin divided "prose composition" into "logical composition (persuasion and exposition)" (vii) and "literary composition (narration and description)" (ix), devoting three chapters to each. His key (and perhaps controversial) assertion was that what he called "literary composition" was, in fact, part of rhetoric, a location claimed a century earlier by Hugh Blair's *Rhetoric and Belles Lettres*. Baldwin framed the distinction in terms of Thomas De Quincey's "literature of knowledge and literature of power," a basis that Ross Winterrowd would elaborate in his 1986 book about the essay genre, *The Rhetoric of the Other Literature*. The idea that creative nonfiction might have persuasive and critical force is one to which we'll return in the last section of this introduction, where we'll provide three additional reasons for teaching creative nonfiction.

It's striking, then, to see creative nonfiction largely disappear from the field of rhetoric/composition and required writing courses starting in the late 1980s, with a modest resurgence of late. The reasons are complex. The most mundane is simply curricular space. As research and theory have amply demonstrated the complex situatedness of writing, especially through genre, activity theory, and the intricacies of audience in rhetorical situations, not all types and tasks can win teaching attention. Genres like the personal essay and memoir were rendered especially vulnerable by political critiques in the 1990s, through influential attacks on aesthetics and poetics. For example, James Berlin's work amplified ideological critiques of what too-glibly got called "expressivism"; many people faulted first-person writing and genres like the personal essay as Romantically simplistic, classist, and indulgent, wasting vital time that should be spent in more important writing activity: important both politically (in Berlin's views) and personally. Students are better served, the argument went, by understanding and practicing various traditions of academic discourse or learning how to analyze and emulate various practical genres. In an iconic debate, preserved in 1995 *College English* articles, Peter Elbow and David Bartholomae exchanged positions, the former calling for general, open writing practices, the latter calling for practice joining academic conversations and conventions (Elbow, Bartholomae). Bartholomae's ideas ultimately won out, at least by the scorecard of what writing journals mainly published and writing conferences mainly featured: rhetoric and argument, academic discourses, and cultural analysis. There were prominent exceptions, of course. A 2001 symposium on "The Politics of the Personal" explored "our excitement as well as frustrations" about personal narratives, generally supporting those practices but analyzing "uncritical celebration" (Brandt et. al, 41–42). In 2003, Doug guest-edited a special issue of *College English* on Creative Nonfiction, which included essays by Wendy Bishop, Lynn Bloom, Bronwyn Williams, Robert Root, and Harriet Malinowitz (Special).

Creative nonfiction authors appeared as CCCC presenters through the 1980s. However, their presence dwindled through the 1990s, with only sporadic panels about the essay and literary journalism occurring since then. Rhet-comp scholars did give narrative, essayistic talks and their essayistic articles were published by the profession's journals, but those writers tended largely to be already well-established in the field, figures like Lynn Bloom or Nancy Sommers, whose 2010 CCCC panel with Kathleen Blake Yancey and Doug Hesse later won the Donald Murray Prize for creative nonfiction. A group of teacher/writers started hosting a CCCC workshop on writing nonfiction in the 1990s, an annual event continuing to the present, now under the aegis of the Creative Nonfiction Special Interest Group, which continues to organize the Murray Prize. Creative nonfiction continues to sprinkle the CCCC program each year. In the main, however, composition studies' forfeit of creative nonfiction was creative writing's gain, fueling courses, programs, and degrees, undergraduate to MFA. First-year writing programs, once home to belletristic genres as well as to more "practical" ones, moved much of creative nonfiction's furniture to the curb.

By the 2020s, three traditions dominate most required writing curricula. The first teaches writing conventions that are deemed important in future courses: the get-them-ready curriculum. Its light version postulates a generic kind of academic discourse, generally thesis and support, with some kinds of library-based research and attention to citation and documentation styles; its heavy version attends to the different types of academic discourse, manifested in genres, styles, epistemologies, and so on; this version aspires to build analytic skills to figure out conventions required in different disciplines. A second dominant curricular tradition is argument, a focus on convincing readers to adopt beliefs or actions. While the site of argument is sometimes the academy, more often it's the public sphere, where student rhetors learn to apply strategies (generally evidence-driven logical appeals, after Aristotle, Toulmin, or Rogers) to popular arguments, in courses perhaps organized around statis theory, perhaps around genres or topics. The third dominant tradition is organized primarily around topics or themes: food or food security, sustainability or climate, homelessness, or popular culture (horror movies, hip hop or hipster culture, reality television, etc.) and so on. In terms of writing, such courses are variously justified, sometimes as a light academic discourse version, sometimes as popular discourse, and sometimes as simply epistemic, a pedagogy of engagement, grounded in write-to-learn principles for first-year composition.

Required and Nonrequired Writing

Beyond these current traditions are a complex of assumptions about the nature of college writing and its function. Consider four dichotomous views of instruction that have variously waxed and waned, waned and waxed over those years. First: "Writing is a basic skill that every student should acquire by college—or at least in a first-year college course" versus "Writing is a complex art that can be mastered by relatively few, usually by virtue of their innate talent and intense dedication." Or second: "Students should learn writing as a practical tool for transacting the worlds of school and work" versus "Students should learn writing as a means of personal expression and civic participation." Or third: "Some writing (the kind most importantly taught in schools) is highly conventional and learned by practicing strict rules, forms, and models" versus "Other writing (the kind that authors do) is complexly creative and learned through apprenticeship among other aspiring authors." Or fourth: "There are fundamental characteristics of all writing situations, types, and genres, and learning some basic strategies will transfer widely" versus "Writing is so varied and context-specific, both in production and features, that beyond a surprisingly low level, basic strategies are fairly useless."

There's some truth—and plenty of oversimplifying—in these dichotomies, of course, owing to the casual way we use the complex term "writing." When

Newsweek's Merrill Sheils in 1975 infamously explained "Why Johnny Can't Write," he neglected to distinguish whether Johnny (or Jenny or Jaunita) was failing as student, journalist, accountant, poet, attorney, screenwriter, or grammarian. In the decades since, a fertile growth of research and knowledge has made clear that writing is variously "good" for variously different audiences, purposes, and genres. Mapping the dappled landscape of writing onto a curriculum, let alone a course or two, is complicated by the ascendancy of higher education as an individual economic good rather than a social good, no less as an experience for intellectual, ethical, or spiritual growth.

What does it mean for some genres of writing (and their purposes and epistemologies) to find academic sponsorship in elective or major courses, while others, more instrumental or practical, are required for all? What assumptions about the nature of writing underlie these relegations? About how students should experience and understand it? About writing's role in lives beyond work and school?

It's tempting to answer such questions with "It depends," forfeit everything to fracture, and just let writing get sorted among fiefdoms and their sponsors. But the writers in this volume offer a different path. They prize identities for students that are grounded in possibility and connection, not limit and separation. Writing is a technical art, yes, but also a liberal art. It's an instrument for getting things done, of course, but also an instrument for reshaping the world and the writer within it, for readers who sometimes want surprise and innovation as much as they want predictability and information. Writing teachers are

> the ones at the center who reach to all other disciplines and to all other people. We synthesize knowledge and unite people. By our force, we draw from the wisdom of other disciplines and in making it ours, transform it by combining it in new ways. The instrument of language which we play . . . opens the secret places and weds the separate selves. (49)

Writing these lines some forty years ago was Richard Lloyd-Jones, known widely as Jix, whose influences inform this volume. Jix championed and embodied a view of writing that remains vitally resonant. Writing is a skill, surely—but not only a skill. Lloyd-Jones's view suffused writing cultures at The University of Iowa, where he taught more than 40 years, and his view circulated across the national landscape of writing instruction, pre-K through grad school, through his leadership roles in the National Council of Teachers of English (NCTE) and the Conference on College Composition and Communication (CCCC).

Jix, Creative Nonfiction, and Iowa, 1970–2000

Between 1970 and 2000, The University of Iowa English department sponsored an expansive view of writing where teachers and students traveled, largely without passport, between literature and writing, between "creative" writing and "other" writing, variously nonfiction, expository, or rhetorical. There was a fundamental belief that language was worth intensively studying and practicing across the whole sweep of English. Iowa provides an interesting case study because, at a time when nonfiction writing at most colleges was reductively relegated to first-year composition, there it was taken as a matter of interest and importance, part of the whole palette, arguments to personal essays, reports to poems to novels. We won't claim that the Iowa English department was unique during this period, let alone "responsible" for nonfiction's rise. We're simply explaining how the department, as part of a capacious view of writing, sponsored nonfiction, to use Deborah Brandt's technical term for how certain institutions and individuals sponsor various literate practices.

By 1974, Iowa was offering over thirty writing courses, from various workshops in fiction, poetry, playwriting, and translation to multiple courses in expository writing, science writing, writing for social action, and others. Five additional courses in nonfiction prose included The Tradition of the Essay, The Art of the Essay, and a Survey of Non-Fiction Prose (University, *General 1974–76*). This count doesn't include general education rhetoric courses, offered in a separate program shared by English and Communication. The extensive curriculum illustrated the department's affirmation that "The broad purpose of the major in English is to provide a program of humane learning focused on the study of language and literature and the discipline of writing" (61). Twenty years later, Iowa offered over 40 courses in writing. Among significant changes was a shift in nomenclature, with expository (a common term to contrast with "creative writing" from the mid–20th century) being replaced by nonfiction. More telling were delineations of nonfiction. By 1994, Iowa offered both Essay Writing Workshop and Nonfiction Writing Workshop, both Forms of the Essay and Forms of Nonfiction—and introductory and advanced levels of each (University, *General 1994–96*, 127).

Marking this curricular expansion was the nation's first English department graduate degree in nonfiction writing, initiated in 1976 as the Master of Arts with Emphasis in Expository Writing (shorthanded as the M.A.W.), a degree that twenty years later became an M.F.A. in Nonfiction. As the degree changed, so did its nature and spirit. At its formation, the M.A.W. emphasized "the theory, analysis, practice and teaching of expository writing. It is designed to meet the needs of students who wish to become teachers or critics of expository writing, students who wish to become professional writers, or students who have no specific career objectives but still wish to improve their writing" (University, *General 1976–78*, 59). Students wrote a thesis that was "an extended piece of expository writing." With its transformation to M.F.A. in Nonfiction in 1996, the degree was then characterized as "broadly devoted to literary nonfiction, with special opportunities for work in essay and prose. It is designed primarily for persons who wish to become nonfiction writers but also may be appropriate for those who wish to teach." The M.F.A. thesis was now defined as "a single extended piece of nonfiction, a collection of shorter nonfiction pieces, or a collection of essays" all "expected to be of publishable quality" (University, *General 1996–98*, 133.)

The 2022 Iowa catalog lists seven learning outcomes for the M.F.A., following recent contemporary trends in higher education that every course and degree program must specify learning outcomes. Those for the Iowa M.F.A. in Nonfiction include understanding "forms such as the essay, lyric essay, memoir, journalism, and experimental writing," practicing a range of narrative strategies and styles, and understanding "the practical aspects of a writer's professional life" (University, "English").

The Iowa nonfiction M.A./M.F.A. emerged from a rich landscape for writing, in an English department long known through the famous Iowa Writers Workshop, founded in 1936. (Iowa had been accepting creative Ph.D. dissertations since 1922.) We emphasize that the Nonfiction Writing Program and the Writers Workshop are deliberately separate entities; whether the workshop, either at Iowa or elsewhere, is a healthy, let alone ideal, place to incubate one's craft, especially for writers of color, is quite another matter, as writers like Felicia Rose Chavez or Lan Samantha Chang have compellingly illustrated (Neary).

Our broader point is that during the 20th century, Iowa took writing seriously in all its manifestations, including creative nonfiction and most prominently the essay. Whether this wide embrace was unique across the U.S., we won't venture, but the record of Iowa English supports claims in general catalogs going back to 1976 that "For the past 50 years, the University of Iowa has been a national leader in virtually all areas of the teaching of writing . . . [and] also a leader in the area of nonfiction writing and rhetorical theory" (University, *General 1996–98*, 133).

In this context, we introduce a prominent figure in the centrality of writing at Iowa and in the US: Richard Lloyd-Jones. Obviously, it's unreasonable to claim that Jix was a singular force for creative nonfiction; vital contributions and energies came from many people. But during much of that time he served as chair of the English Department and Director of the School of Letters. Recognition for Jix's contribution to nonfiction at Iowa is embodied in the Lloyd-Jones Institute for Outreach, a program whereby M.F.A. students offer free master classes in writing across the state of Iowa, with more recent forays around the country. This broad interest in writing and developing writers is characteristic of Jix's career as scholar, teacher, and servant.

With Iowa colleagues Richard Braddock and Lowell Schoer, Jix had authored the landmark 1963 study, *Research in Written Composition*. Iowa developed one of the first Ph.D.s in rhetoric and composition, and in the late 1970s its faculty had organized and hosted an influential National Endowment for the Humanities Institute that brought writing program directors from around the country to Iowa City. *Time* magazine described the Institute at length, explaining that "In some ways, Iowa is the nerve center of writing reform" and quoting Jix and his colleague David Hamilton, whose essay about that experience appears in this book ("Letter to Jix"). Even required first-year rhetoric courses were inflected by a spirit of writing as exploration, creation, and craft, with large numbers of those courses taught by graduate students who had come to study writing not only from famous authors in the Workshop but also from writers and scholars of writing such as Carl Klaus, Susan Lohafer, Carol de St. Victor, Paul Diehl, Lou Kelly, Cleo Martin, and Brooks Landon.

Nationally, Jix chaired CCCC, the nation's largest and oldest professional association of college and university writing teachers, which awarded him its first Exemplar Award, for lifetime achievement. Later, Jix was elected president of NCTE, then a 75,000-member organization of K–16 teachers. His contributions extended to schools nationally but also intensively in the state of Iowa. He helped Jim Davis create the Iowa Writing Project, which supported teachers across the state in three-week workshops, emphasizing them as writers. The IWP, similar in concept to the Bay Area/National Writing Project, focused on pedagogy and scholarship part of the time but also provided time for teachers to write (Jensen 10). Through all his professional work, classroom to department to campus to profession, Jix advocated a broad view of writing as an activity alternatively practical and aesthetic, intensely important for the social good, deeply humanizing. He taught and valued technical writing for engineers, even as he sometimes hired famous poets to teach them, as he explains in an essay we've reprinted at the end of this volume. He wrote policy statements and contributed to public arguments, most famously drafting the controversial *Students' Right to Their Own Language* with Geneva Smitherman (Jensen 27–28), even as he also wrote poems and letters, personal essays, and memoirs, calling on others to do the same. Several writers in this volume explain Jix's contributions. His longtime colleague Carl Klaus provides a view of the man and his accomplishments. Robert Root describes Jix's influences growing out of *Research on Written Composition*, including on creative nonfiction. Kathleen Blake Yancey characterizes his larger national contributions to writing and English studies. Tom Fate and Margaret Finders take us directly into Jix's classrooms. Jocelyne Bartkevicius traces how she extends a teaching approach from a course on style he taught to her own course, Studies in Contemporary Nonfiction.

Why Nonfiction Now

We live in the age of data analytics, when algorithms trace trends among inputs and extracts, shaping decisions and investments. Among products that programmers are creating—and marketers aspiring to sell—are ones devoted to writing. For example, by 2010, companies like Narrative Science (since acquired by Salesforce and absorbed into Tableau) were marketing AI tools that touted "writing human stories at machine speeds," with the further promise that "our technology application requires no human authoring or editing" (Narrative). Traditional media like *The Washington Post* have used bot applications like Heliograf to produce routine stories about such events as elections or high school football games "to successfully automate the creation of articles based [on] compiling data in templates" that judges found "eloquently written and backed" (WashPostPR). The internet is full of AI writing tools: Jaspar, SEO, Ai Writing, Rytr, to name just a few, with Chat GPT exploding on the scene in late 2022. Across a series of articles since 2019, *The New*

Yorker has examined the writing prowess of AI text generators like GPT-3. These apps appeal to some hope to get writing out of the way, sparing people for activities more important or interesting than turning information into prose.

But we also live in a renewed age of makers and artisans, where craft finds value in process, not only product, from the imperfect tries of home brewers to the polished creations of expert vintners. In *The Revenge of Analog,* David Sax documents a renewed interest in everything from vinyl records to print books, from board games to film. We've seen cooking acquire prominence as a leisure activity, even entertainment, beyond a necessary evil to be overcome via the frozen dinner aisle. Even old-fashioned scrapbooking has had a renaissance. Perhaps these maker movements are just fashionable dabbling, status-marking ways of spending time—or perhaps they mark a desire to participate more fully in efforts that require agency and human ingenuity. Our digital age may be influencing how we shape and share personal essays, as Ned Stuckey-French explores in his piece, but these emerged technological practices are enhancing, not effacing, the impulse to write.

The essays in this book present a view of writing that is neither luddite nor romantic. There are surely useful kinds of writing that conform to highly conventionalized, routine forms, writing that prizes transparency and efficiency. These kinds are worth teaching, and it's worth exploring how technologies might facilitate drafting them. But other subject matters, ideas, and experiences resist convenient codification. They require—and reward—authorial curiosity and presence, inviting writers to analyze, synthesize, interpret, and render with insight and craft, in modes variously narrative and essayistic. Such engagements make deep and serious writers who experience writing not only as something that has to be done and endured but as something that also gets to be done and pursued, creating artifacts that others read not only out of obligation but out of desire. This is the province of creative nonfiction. In their content and style, all these essays exemplify writing as rewarding exploration and craft. This volume includes several examples, among them these two: John Price weaves his daily routine with musings of archaeological knowledge, including such knowledge as embodied in first-generation teachers of nonfiction. And Kerry Reilly explores both the reward and challenge—even the discomfort and confusion—of writing about others, implicating oneself in so doing.

Creative nonfiction needs little promotion or help, including within the academy, where its courses and programs are supported by a host of craft books, anthologies, and guides, including those by Brenda Miller, Phillip Gerard, Becky Bradway and Doug Hesse, and Robert Root, to name but a sliver of the array. The scholarly literature is extensive, from early collections like *Essays on the Essay* (Butrym) and *Literary Nonfiction: Theory, Criticism, Pedagogy* (Anderson) to 2022 *Edinburgh Companion to the Essay* (Aquilina). Literary magazines include nonfiction, and many of them focus on it solely, most venerably *Fourth Genre* (of which Laura was editor) but also *Hippocampus, River Teeth, Brevity, Under the Gum Tree, Creative Nonfiction,* and so on. Our slick magazines (*The New Yorker, Atlantic, Harper's*) publish it to larger readerships, and essays appear regularly as columns and features of national newspapers. Consider, for example, *The New York Times*' long-running Modern Love column. All these tributaries support a burgeoning industry of annual Best American nonfiction series (Travel Writing, Science and Nature Writing, Food Writing, Sports Writing, Spiritual Writing), starting with the *Best American Essays*, now in its fourth decade. Several writers in this volume regularly contribute essays to that literature, including recent books by Ned Stuckey French, John Price, Tom Fate, and essays by Jocelyn Bartkevicius.

We call for something in addition to all this activity: recognition for creative nonfiction's importance to writing studies, which should embrace anew a tradition it recently abjured. We're not insisting on a spot of priority or pre-eminence. But a more complete house of writing and writing courses should welcome creative nonfiction's staircases and living rooms, kitchens and parlors, its genres not simply shelved as curios and bric-a-brac. Such a house might take its architecture from Richard Lloyd-Jones's work at Iowa and in the national neighborhoods of English. Beyond welcoming the dimension of writing as a liberal art, one essentially human and humanizing, we offer four reasons why the citizens of not only AWP but also CCCC should teach and write creative nonfiction as part of their broad practice.

First, it offers alternative rhetorical approaches in an historical moment when traditional logocentric strategies are falling short. While thesis plus evidence may remain compelling in the well-regulated discourses of academic disciplines, it's sadly clear that facts alone have less purchase in public discourses, where ideologies frame, filter, and fracture reasons and reasoning. In contrast, locating information in narrative approaches, placing ideas in and against experience and observation with the force of ethos and the logic of entailment, at least garners attention. Corporations have understood the need to tell stories (sometimes cynically or badly, mind you), embedding products, services, and profit motives in trajectories that unfold from character and context, from human agency. Literary journalism and personal essays place ideas and observations in the lived experience of character and craft rather than a frontal propositional assault readily dismissed as ideology. Readers can be engaged by elements of the telling, and if the craft is good, they'll at least engage views they may ultimately reject.

Second, there is important identity work being done in writing studies, efforts especially valuing diversity and inclusivity. Creative nonfiction well suits this goal, given how it makes central and visible an author's narrative lens and consciousness.

The field has recognized that knowledge, rather than being objectively produced with implications immutable to all, is often situated. Different histories, experiences, and contexts shape the meaning of meaning. We invite often-silent or suppressed voices to write themselves in. Of course, creative nonfiction can be as prone as other writing pedagogies (notably, those historically in first-year writing) to work against including multiple voices. Felicia Rose Chavez's important book *The Anti-Racist Writing Works: How to Decolonize the Creative Classroom* has vital perspectives for the nonfiction classroom as well as the poetry or fiction classroom, recommending practices that all writing teachers should adapt. Even as creative nonfiction's ethos seeks to value, amplify, and complicate identities, not suppress them, its teachers must recognize the continued presence and practice of long exclusionary legacies. With that important caveat, we note that at one level, a current motivation in teaching writing is expansive: build larger and nuanced knowledges inclusive of race, class, gender, ability, among other identities. At another level, the motivation is epistemological. Significance and meaning come through the interpretive lenses of lived experience and individual formation, burnished by membership in various communities. This idea already has correlatives in composition studies. For example, the common practice of asking students to write literacy narratives has them tell and analyze their experiences as readers and writers, usually in relation to others or to scholarship on schooling, home life, and literacy development. A second connection comes through autoethnography, the increasingly popular research methodology that shares much with personal essays. In fact, in using reflection to narrate experience, connecting it to wider cultural formations and belief, autoethnography might be understood as reframing the long tradition of the essay under a new disciplinary guise. Third, one tradition of writing-to-learn, a now 40-year mainstay of writing across the curriculum, draws on James Britton's conception of expressive discourse as writers making sense of things for themselves, perhaps independent from but often prior to sharing that knowledge with others. Primary is finding how to integrate new knowledge and concepts with one's own experience. Writing to learn also underpins some invention practices, encouraging writers first to draft in terms that make sense to themselves, and only later to revise to accommodate readers' needs and expectations. At that juncture of revising toward other readers, the creative nonfiction choice would turn toward making an interesting artifact, one that carries the writer's voice and trace rather than effacing it by disciplinary convention.

That choice raises a third broad value of creative nonfiction for composition studies practice and pedagogy: the challenge and reward of creating writing that people aren't compelled to read but rather choose to. The challenge is cognitive, rhetorical, and aesthetic: how to render experience and insight in ways interesting not only to the writers and people close to them (which is hardly a trivial reason) but also to a wider readership. The charge that creative nonfiction is impractical compared to academic discourse or civic argument might be true in the sense of it not meeting preexisting exigencies. But in addition to the important kinds of writing that wait for a turn in a decorous Burkean parlor, to cite a well-used metaphor, there's an important place for writing that introduces new threads, writing that's acceptable not because it makes a sanctioned move within an established discursive channel, but because the skilled performance of a writerly sensibility makes new subject matters interesting through craft. Alternatively, perhaps creative nonfiction is just another type of parlor, a vast gallery of smaller salons in which authorial presence, story, and style might render interesting and worthy a host of topics, events, and experiences.

Several essays in this volume explore carefully and reflectively complex matters of teaching. Nancy DeJoy and Rachel Faldet each illustrate how and, as importantly, why and with what effect one might bring creative nonfiction to the center of college required writing courses. Nicole Wallack argues for that same attention in high school writing instruction, even against active calls for "practical" transferrable skills. Jenny Spinner explores and theorizes the implications of age for writing nonfiction, critiquing assumptions that the essay is a middle-aged or old genre by explaining why the genre matters for young writers, too. Doug provides a history of one such foray, a high-profile but short-lived set of national creative nonfiction contests for high school and undergraduate writers, co-sponsored by NCTE and a prominent aspect of an ambitious National Day on Writing. Laura narrates her own experiences as an early reader and student of nonfiction, which informed all her later experiences as writer, teacher, and ultimately editor of nonfiction, reflecting on the ways in which the influence of the University of Iowa under Jix's leadership shaped her understanding of how to engage writers in teaching and in editing one of the first journals dedicated to various forms of creative nonfiction.

Our point is that writing studies—composition as well as creative—benefits from fully engaging the many manifestations of writing, with creative nonfiction as a centrally valuable component. That's the example and enduring message of Jix Lloyd-Jones, who sought in his own teaching, curricular designs, and national leadership to foster deep facility with and appreciation for writing as an activity valuable not only for what it could do instrumentally (after all, Jix was molded first as a teacher of technical writing) but also what it could do liberally, through a broad writing sensibility. Jix offered one more example, imperative, and license: Teachers themselves should be writers. Teacher writing is inevitable through syllabi, student comments, reports, and the rest of workaday text-making. Beyond that, of course, are pieces for scholarly publication. But there are writing spaces yet beyond these, writing where teachers put their own lives and insights at the center, pursuing interests beyond the disciplinary and academic. You'll see much of this in the pieces that follow. These essays are variously historical and reflective, philosophical and political, mapping classroom possibilities and writing lives. Some authors explore their own practices, suggesting teaching implications. Others reflect more explicitly on students. All embody in style and voice a focus on the full arts of written language, their authors owing at least an increment of their practice, whether directly or obliquely, to the contributions of Richard Lloyd-Jones.

Works Cited

Aquilina, Mario, Nicole B. Wallack, and Bob Cowser, Jr., editors. *The Edinburgh Companion to the Essay*. Edinburgh UP, 2022.

Bradway, Becky, and Doug Hesse. *Creating Nonfiction*. St. Martin's, 2009.

Anderson, Chris. *Style as Argument: Contemporary American Nonfiction*. Southern Illinois UP, 1987.
Bartholomae, David. "Writing with Teachers: A Conversation with Peter Elbow." *College Composition and Communication*, vol. 46, no. 1, Feb. 1995, pp. 62–71.
Bartkevicius, Jocelyn. "Gun Shy." *Waveform: Twenty-First-Century Essays by Women*, edited by Marcia Aldrich. U of Georgia P, 2016, pp. 96–113.
Berlin, James. *Rhetorics, Poetics, and Cultures: Refiguring English Studies*. National Council of Teachers of English, 1996.
Blair, Hugh. *Lectures on Rhetoric and Belle-Lettres* (1785), edited by Linda Ferreira-Buckley. Southern Illinois UP, 2005.
Bloom, Lynn. "The Essay Canon." *College English*, vol. 61, no. 4, Mar. 1999, pp. 401–30.
Braddock, Richard, Richard Lloyd-Jones, and Lowell Schoer. *Research on Written Composition*. National Council of Teachers of English, 1963.
Brandt, Deborah. *Literacy in American Lives*. Cambridge UP, 2001.
Brandt, Deborah, Ellen Cushman, Anne Ruggles Gere, Anne Herrington, Richard E. Miller, Victor Villanueva, Min-Zhan Lu, and Gesa Kirsch. "The Politics of the Personal: Storying Our Lives Against the Grain." *College English*, vol. 64, no. 1, Sep. 2001, pp. 41–62.
Britton, James, Tony Burgess, Nancy Martin, Alex McLeod, and Harold Rosen. "An Approach to the Function Categories." *The Development of Writing Abilities, 11–18*. National Council of Teachers of English, 1978, pp. 74–87.
Chavez, Felicia Rose. *The Anti-Racist Writing Workshop: How to Decolonize the Creative Classroom*. Haymarket Books, 2021.
Connors, Robert. *Composition-Rhetoric: Backgrounds, Theory, and Pedagogy*. U of Pittsburgh P, 1997.
Elbow, Peter. "Being a Writer vs. Being an Academic: A Conflict in Goals." *College Composition and Communication*, vol. 46, no. 1, Feb. 1995, pp. 72–83.
Fate, Tom Montgomery. *The Long Way Home: Detours and Discoveries*. Ice Cube Press, 2022.
Gerard, Phillip. *Creative Nonfiction: Researching and Crafting Stories of Real Life*. Waveland Press, 2017.
Hesse, Douglas. "Who Owns Creative Nonfiction?" *Beyond Postprocess and Postmodernism: Essays on the Spaciousness of Rhetoric*, edited by Theresa Enos and Keith D. Miller. Erlbaum, 2003, pp. 251–66.
———. "The Place of Creative Writing in Composition Studies." *CCC*, vol. 62, no. 1, Sept. 2010, pp. 31–52.
Jensen, Julie. "Interview of Richard Lloyd-Jones." 28 February 1991. Archives of the National Council of Teachers of English, "Commissions, Committees, and Task Forces, Box 2," University of Illinois Library.
Lloyd-Jones, Richard. "A View from the Center." *Views from the Center: The CCCC Chairs' Addresses, 1977–2005*, edited by Duane Roen. Macmillan, 2006, pp. 45–53.
Miller, Brenda. *A Braided Heart: Essays on Writing and Form*. U of Michigan P, 2021.
Narrative Science. "Writing Human Stories at Machine Speeds." Narrativescience.com, 2010. web.archive.org/web/20100326134027/http://narrativescience.com/, accessed 7 July 2020.

Neary, Lynn. "In Elite MFA Programs, the Challenge of Writing While 'Other.'" NPR, 19 Aug. 2014. https://www.npr.org/sections/codeswitch/2014/08/19/341363580/in-elite-mfa-programs-the-challenge-of-writing-while-other.

Price, John. *All Is Leaf: Essays and Transformations*. U of Iowa P, 2022.

Sax, David. *The Revenge of Analog: Real Things and Why They Matter*. Public Affairs, 2016.

Sheils, Merrill. "Why Johnny Can't Write." *Newsweek*, vol. 86, no. 23, 8 Dec. 1975, pp. 58, 60–62, 65.

Special Issue: Creative Nonfiction, Guest Ed. Douglas Hesse. *College English*, vol. 65, no. 3, January 2003.

Tate, Gary, Amy Rupiper Taggart, Kurt Schick, and H. Brooke Hessler, eds. *A Guide to Composition Pedagogies, 2e*. Oxford UP, 2013.

"The Righting of Writing: From Kindergarten on Up, Americans Are Wrestling with the Word," *Time*, vol. 115, no. 20, pp. 88–92.

Root, Robert. *The Nonfictionist's Guide: On Reading and Writing Creative Nonfiction*. Rowman and Littlefield, 2008.

Sears, Charles Baldwin. *A College Manual of Rhetoric*. Norwood Press, 1902.

Spinner, Jenny. *Of Women and the Essay: An Anthology from 1655 to 2000*. U of Georgia P, 2018.

Stuckey-French, Ned. *One by One, the Stars: Essays*. U of Georgia P, 2022.

Su Shi. "Red Cliff 1" and Six other Pieces. *Inscribed Landscapes: Travel Writing from Imperial China*. Richard E. Strassberg, ed. and trans. U California P, 1994, pp. 183–194.

Tate, Gary, Amy Rupiper Taggart, Kurt Schick, and H. Brooke Hessler, eds. *A Guide to Composition Pedagogies*, 2nd edition. Oxford UP, 2013.

University of Iowa. *General Catalog, 1974–76*. University of Iowa Libraries, Iowa Digital Library, digital.lib.uiowa.edu/islandora/object/ui%3A26731, accessed 20 June 2022.

———. *General Catalog, 1976–78*. University of Iowa Libraries, Iowa Digital Library, digital.lib.uiowa.edu/islandora/object/ui%3A26732, accessed 20 June 2022.

———. *General Catalog, 1994–96*. University of Iowa Libraries, Iowa Digital Library, digital.lib.uiowa.edu/islandora/object/ui%3A26741, accessed 20 June 2022.

———. *General Catalog, 1996–98*. University of Iowa Libraries, Iowa Digital Library, digital.lib.uiowa.edu/islandora/object/ui%3A26742, accessed 20 June 2022.

———. "English (nonfiction writing), M.F.A." *General Catalog 2022–23*. catalog.registrar.uiowa.edu/liberal-arts-sciences/english/english-nonfiction-writing-mfa/, accessed 20 June 2022.

Wallack, Nicole B. *Crafting Presence: The American Essay and the Future of Writing Studies*. Utah State UP, 2017.

WashPostPR. "The Post's Heliograf and ModBot Technologies Take First Place in 2018 Global BIGGIES Awards." WashPost PR Blog, 23 March 2018. www.washingtonpost.com/pr/wp/2018/03/23/the-posts-heliograf-and-modbot-technologies-take-first-place-in-2018-global-biggies-awards/, accessed 28 June 2022.

Winterowd, W. Ross. *The Rhetoric of the Other Literature*. Southern Illinois UP, 1990.

Part One. Nonfiction and Richard Lloyd-Jones: A Legacy

Chapter 1. Reflections on a Legacy: The Practice of Wisdom

Kathleen Blake Yancey
Florida State University

Of Welsh ancestry, Richard Lloyd-Jones in his professional life consistently invoked values he associated with the Welsh, among them the need for community, the integral relationship between language and identity, and the wisdom of acting together for the common good. In calling on that heritage, he enriched his professional community, sounding notes relevant both then and today.

A legacy

Legacies come in different forms.

We often hope our children and grandchildren will carry on our legacy, enacting and commemorating the formal and the informal: holiday traditions, graduations, a picnic in the sun. My friend Bud makes his mother's potato salad every summer; he can't remember which holiday it belongs to, so each year he makes it three times—for Memorial Day, July 4th, and Labor Day. Late in November, I send my two children identical Advent calendars, a reminder of the calendar windows they lifted open every December day through Christmas Eve, another reminder of my own childhood December windows in a snowy Frankfurt-am-Main.

We sometimes hope for a professional legacy. I used to wonder if I'd have one; if I did, what it would look like. As I walked from one building to another on the UNC Charlotte campus, not 50 years old in 1995, I'd look at building names: would I want to be remembered with a Yancey Hall? Or perhaps a Yancey Scholarship, for the most inventive writer or the most promising, someone who bent the conventions, who made us pay attention, who made us want to read that writing and write ourselves.

Richard Lloyd-Jones—Jix—carried on a personal legacy also infusing the many professional legacies he left the field of rhetoric and composition. His heritage was Welsh, which he drew on tacitly and explicitly, perhaps most vividly in a 2010 YouTube video of his talk at a family reunion hosted at a chapel built by earlier family members, now preserved by their children's children. That site, he acknowledged, originally represented a different kind of community, but, he said, it is the maintenance of the community, even as it may change, that matters:

> There is a union among us, perhaps not exactly the same bonds or union that the people found when they built the chapel, but another kind that may be a little closer to what the Welsh would

call *cefinder*, cousinship, what their nation is. It transcends age, it transcends political opinions, it transcends occupation, it transcends level of wealth and status. It says we belong to each other, there is a kind of otherness about it.

Jix's legacy is about *belong*[ing] *to each other*, about a *cefinder* that *transcends*.

Exemplars

Jix was the first Exemplar named by the Conference on College Composition and Communication (CCCC), a group whose members refer to each other as the college writing folk.

An exemplar is a wonderfully paradoxical designation; it's either a typical example, so nearly mundane, or it's excellent, extraordinary. And it's complicated in other ways: a person could be typical in one domain of activity and exemplary in another. By most accounts, Jimmy Carter wasn't particularly effective as a president, but as a human being, he is exemplary. You don't campaign to be exemplary, though you do for elected office. Like all presidents, Carter wanted to win his two presidential contests: a person running for a presidential election is all about winning, no small task. There's setting the goal, raising money, fielding a staff, raising more money, developing a plan, raising more money. By way of contrast, one doesn't plan or aim to be either an exemplar or an Exemplar; you just sort of do what you do, and perhaps someone notices. Or perhaps that's naïve: there may well be a difference between *being* an exemplar and being *named* an Exemplar. In Jix's case, it's easy to see how the two are one.

The CCCC Exemplar Award was created in 1989, its announcement buried in a CCCC Secretary's Report, itself buried at the back of an issue of the journal *College Composition and Communication*, specifically in item 10 of over 20 motions passed: "To establish a CCCC Executive Committee Exemplar Award." The call for nominations, published a year later, defined the Exemplar as "representing the highest ideals of scholarship, teaching, and service to the entire profession. Because the Exemplar Award seeks to recognize individuals who set the very best examples for the rest of us, representing what the ideal teacher/scholar/ colleague can be at her or his best, service should be national or international in scope." It's not a low bar.

The Exemplar is honored by accepting the award at the CCCC conference opening General Session and giving a talk, the Exemplar Address. Jix's address, the first, was published the following year in the organization's journal, setting a pattern for the Exemplars to come. In this 1991 address, "Who We Were, Who We Should Become," Jix sounded several of the same notes as he did in that chapel 19 years later, emphasizing especially how important it is that CCCC members "hav[e] a place in a community, family." That CCCC community had changed, he observed, and the task he'd set himself in the address was to narrate that change in the context of what the future might offer: "Let me for a few moments engage the questions of who we have been, who we are, and who we might become" (487). Although his historical account of the field is recognizable to those in it, his emphases were his own. Referring to faculty teaching writing at mid-century, he noted their "corporate identity ... [as] ad hoc problem solvers looking for survival" (487). Then, as now, he said, the community is inclusive: "We are fellows, companions with each other and with our students" (488). He identified CCCC's "special interests as social and ethical" and lauded the work of community colleges, where the "faculties ... included a disproportionate number of reformers and oddly credentialed people, hard to handle" (489), this last a compliment. He praised the 1974 CCCC Position Statement "The Students' Right to Their Own Language," one he had a hand in creating, in large part for bringing together what he called the House of the Intellect with a commitment to social diversity as a means of enacting change:

> The statement had an intellectual base in sociolinguistics, but its energy came from support of social diversity. It forced a reconsideration of "correctness." It implied a model of language as "transactional" rather than as artifact. Behind the anger of the political oratory was acceptance of a thesis about the nature of language.
>
> That redefining of the study of language echoed a re-emphasis on rhetoric, no longer seen as "empty" or "mere," but rather understood as the means by which language identifies discourse groups and negotiates truth among their members. (490)

He worried about the disenfranchised faculty teaching composition and about the disengagement of more senior faculty from that process. He worried about the relative dearth of faculty in rhetoric and composition in English departments, and he worried about composition being taught and directed by people ignorant of the complexity of those tasks. He also understood CCCC as a community oscillating between its own goals and tasks assigned to it by others, with CCCC consequently "straddle[ing] the issues of utility and vision, of servility and liberation of mind" (493). Jix also understood that this oscillation could be adjusted and re-arranged: "I have sometimes argued that we promise utility to open the door and then once inside we work to liberate the spirit of our writers" (493).

Jix closed his Exemplar Address by exhorting the field toward two ends: to continue working at being a community—"we need even more efforts to be *simultaneously* many and one" (496)—and to claim its rightful place in the academy. Observing that such efforts are unlikely to "polish our vitaes," Jix pointed again to the family community as the force making not only education but life itself meaningful: "Just possibly, we are the best hope for a family voice emerging from an efficient academic machine, and we should say so" (496).

Community had been Jix's legacy; he passed it forward to CCCC.

Writing Assessment

Writing assessment, and assessment more generally, doesn't really excite people. As a general matter, we don't really like testing or evaluation or assessment—until we do. If my child, after being tested, fails to be identified as a gifted student, that feels like two failures in one: the experience of being labeled as not gifted (a.k.a., a kind of failure), especially when the failure is wrong, that is, itself a failure. If the aircraft we are about to board has failed a test, we may think twice about the need to travel. Of course, that depends on the test: if one of the passenger lights doesn't work, we'll fly; if the aircraft's hydraulic system fails a functionality test, we begin to look at train schedules. If we plan to buy a new refrigerator, we happily consult *Consumer Reports*, which is basically a compilation of assessments; and many people, especially those of a certain (younger) age, consult various social media as part of routine decision-making processes. Seeing a movie? Check Rotten Tomatoes, a site of aggregated movie and TV assessments (a.k.a., reviews). Going out for dinner? Consult Yelp for multiple crowdsourced reviews (a.k.a., assessments). Thinking of a vacation? Try Travel Advisor.

So, assessment? It's complicated.

In the 1970s, writing assessment was called evaluation of writing, and among certain faculty in the burgeoning field of rhetoric and composition, it was an exciting enterprise. Seeing beyond the contemporaneous testing mechanisms, most of them taking the form of so-called objective measures, these faculty devised a different way of thinking about assessment, their purpose in part to develop new methods of writing assessment that would compete, and possibly defeat, the multiple choice tests—so prevalent then, still popular today—that by definition distort writing and fail students multiply, the last a point on which Jix was both lucid and eloquent:

> A common test used for college entrance and many English achievement or "exit" examinations is a test of conventional usage and manuscript mechanics: Recent discussion about its misuse has centered on its billing as a test of writing skill. It is, of course, a test of social conformity, of how well a person recognizes the language forms most commonly used by those in authority in America. The test undoubtedly sorts out the people who will succeed in college, but that does not make it a test of skills in discourse. ("Primary Trait Scoring" 34)

Giving this kind of test its due, Jix doesn't mistake it as a valid measure; he aims to enhance both the value of a writing test and its validity by bringing writing back into the practice of a writing evaluation tilted toward evaluation. To do that, he claims, you need a theory of writing. Interestingly, in contributing to a (new) theory and practice of writing assessment, Jix also theorized writing. He does so, first, by way of critique. The "methods perfected by ETS [Educational

Testing Service] assume that excellence in one sample of one mode of writing predicts excellence in other modes," Jix says (37); put simply, that approach sees writing as universal: "good writing is good writing." But not to Jix: he observes that good writing is not the same across tasks and genres, but rather different, a point he makes with wonderfully commonsense examples: "the writer of a good technical report may not be able to produce an excellent persuasive letter to a city council" (37). Given the ways the field of rhetoric and composition understands genre now—and indeed the way people listening to different genres of music and watching different genres of movies now understand and practice genre, at least tacitly—it's difficult to appreciate how much before its time Jix's observation about differences in rhetorical situations and genre is. Aims related to genre, he says, matter: purposes related to rhetorical situations, they matter.

But a model of discourse—a.k.a., a theory of writing—is about more than critique; it's also about how people write, as Jix explains:

> In order to report precisely how people manage different types of discourse, one must have a model of discourse which permits the identification of limited types of discourse and the creation of exercises which stimulate writing in the appropriate range but not beyond it. The three-part model that Klaus and I selected was based on the purpose (goal, aim) of the discourse and reflected whether the character of the writing grew out of a focus on the writer, the audience, or the subject matter. (Perhaps we show the influence of Aristotle and his interpreters, and we will take any credit we can earn by that allusion.) ("Primary Trait Scoring" 37–38)

In other words, a model of discourse includes several key concepts: a governing purpose and three domains, the writer, the audience, and the subject matter. Put in today's terms, Jix was providing a writing construct defining writing; it's not, as ETS assumed, a global construct in which good writers are good writers and good writing is good writing, but rather—as we understand it today—a differentiated construct sensitive to differences in writers as in writing situations. Jix's construct of writing was important for several reasons, among them that it helped set the stage for portfolio assessment, which, beginning from the same premise about writing as a differentiated activity, includes multiple texts representing different genres for a fuller representation of writing.

As important, Jix stipulated what we might call standards for designing a test, standards that also entail a set of ethics, and again, his statement is prescient.

If one decides that a valid (or publicly acceptable and persuasive) test requires both a sample of discourse and a human reaction, then one must elect some holistic system, precisely defining the segment of discourse to be evaluated. The writing sample must reflect the writer's choices rather than the testmaker's choices; the critical response must be affective as well as cognitive, and must interpret unconventional and creative language as well as report conventional devices.

Here, in this version of a test, the writer is center stage: the writer's choices are paramount; writing is about emotion as well as intellect; language that is unconventional and creative counts—as it does in non-testing situations. And interestingly today, in the age of machine scoring of writing, Jix reminds of the value of a human reaction.

Jix also explains the system that he, collaborating with others, created: Primary Trait Scoring, a writing assessment keyed to the primary defining feature(s) of a given genre. Doing so required a sequence of steps: "to define the universe of discourse, to devise exercises which sample that universe precisely, to ensure cooperation of the writers, to devise workable scoring guides, and to use the guides" (37). As he noted, Primary Trait Scoring, although a kind of holistic scoring, differed from its cousins; they, like ETS, understood writing, and writers, as universalized; Primary Trait understood writing in terms of different tasks, each one "a unique situation" with its own evaluative criterion/a. Methodologically, the scoring guide was built inductively, from the bottom up:

> A writing task is composed and set in a full rhetorical context. After consideration of a very large number of responses to the task, a Scoring Guide is written which identifies and de- scribes a key characteristic or primary trait which is crucial to success with the writing task. Readers then evaluate responses by placing them in categories based on the designated primary traits. (37)

And to show how this process worked in practice, Jix shared two tasks and a wide range of responses to them: one task, called simply, "[A] 'Woman's Place' Essay," was familiar and conventional, as its title suggests:

> Some people believe that a woman's place is in the home. Others do not. Take ONE side of this issue. Write an essay in which you state your position and defend it. (60)

What was allowed in terms of development, however, was less conventional, more aligned with Jix's notion of unique writers: composers could employ various kinds of evidence, among them historical, legal, analogical, experiential.

The second task, less conventional and familiar, had a large name: "Imaginative Expression of Feeling through Inventive Elaboration of a *Point of View*." In writing assessment circles, it was known more colloquially, as the boat task:

> Primary Trait Scoring—the boat
>
> Look carefully at the picture. These kids are having fun jumping on the overturned boat. Imagine you are one of the children in the picture. Or if you wish, imagine that you are someone standing nearby watching the children. Tell what is going on as he or she would tell it. Write as if you were telling this to a good friend, in a way that expresses strong feelings. Help your

friend FEEL the experience too. Space is provided on the next three pages.

The rationale for this task is also, as the title Primary Trait suggests, quite specific: "The test is whether a writer can project him/herself into a situation, find a role and an appropriate audience, and then reveal an attitude toward the material in relation to the role—a complex writing task." As important, such a writer might be 6 or 16. (48)

As the history of writing assessment attests, Primary Trait Scoring did not prevail: a more universalized holistic scoring did. The rationale for Primary Trait may have been too sophisticated for its time, the labor too intensive and specific, the boat task too unconventional—it's hard to know. But it laid the groundwork for much of what faculty in numerous disciplines take as axiomatic today: writing differs across contexts; writing requires a human reaction; writing assessment should reflect the writer's choices; writing criteria should represent the task.

Service

Tenure-line faculty in the academy tend to think of our work through the three lenses of teaching, research, and service, with service, perhaps not surprisingly, being the least prestigious. That perception is built into the academy in two ways, at least. Departments with higher profiles—offering Ph.D.s in research institutions or promising majors in liberal arts colleges—aren't thought of in terms of service, while departments who focus on general education, or who don't offer majors or graduate degrees, are thought of in terms of service, and often in those terms only, often labeled as such collectively: as service departments. Working in a service department, or in a service program like first-year composition (FYC) in a non-service department, regardless of how noble the teaching, how significant the faculty's research, can feel a bit like working second-class: supporting students until they do real academic work, in their majors, in their graduate degrees. And even in departments with shiny graduate degrees and award-bedecked research profiles and without a particular service role, the message about service is, again, delivered very clearly, very consistently, especially in performance reviews: in my department's annual review procedure, service is worth a whopping 5%. And in case that annual reminder wasn't sufficient, I once had a colleague tell me that I suffered because of my service ethic. Although he meant ethic in a different sense, I appreciated the unintentionally ironic juxtaposition of suffer, service, and ethic.

Such a view of service can be especially sensitive for faculty in rhetoric and composition, whose role has historically focused quite precisely on the classic service course, first-year composition—in part, it should be noted because sometimes, at some institutions, faculty in rhetoric and composition have been, and still continue to be, confined by others to that service course, that service mission.

All of which provides an intriguing context for considering Jix's relationship to service. He was quite aware of the tension between status and service, as he suggested in his Exemplar Address. Although he confessed, at one time, to believing in the "useful fictions" promoted by vitae-building, he encouraged his colleagues to see such status-building as a "polite lie":

> Given the present climate of quantification of status, when we take on a few more advisees or make a talk to the Rotary Club, we hurry to the computer to add an item to the vitae, as though it really made any difference to who we are. Oh, it may make a difference in what we get paid, or even in our academic rank in some schools, or to our "mobility," but we all know that the vitae is a polite lie, a list of achievements made for the convenience of academic managers. (486)

Being in community, he reminded his listeners and readers, brings with it "the obligations of our positions and the expectations of the community," even if it is imperfect, even if "some of the brothers and sisters and cousins took on more than their share of the chores and maybe took away more of the family goods, too" (486). Which, of course, is a very different way of understanding service, not as the bottom rung on a hierarchy with no mechanism for academic mobility, but rather as a kind of participation a community requires and rewards, those rewards a function of the community itself.

The many service roles that Jix inhabited, and typically for very long stretches, speak to his enactment of this philosophy, one defining academic service as community participation. Important, too, are the number and kinds of communities he served. In listing only some of them, as I do below, I've made rhetorical choices. Should I separate departmental service from collegiate, disciplinary from institutional? How I arrange these service roles, in other words, invents Jix anew. They are not partitioned, but rather presented together, as he must have experienced them, all of the moment:

> Member, University of Iowa Faculty Council, 1957
> Chair, University of Iowa Faculty Senate
> Director, General Education Program in Literature, 1965–1969
> Member, CCCC Students' Rights to Their Own Language Committee
> Consultant, CCCC Committee on Testing, 1977–79
> Director of Undergraduate Studies, 1965–1976
> Consultant, National Assessment of Educational Progress (NAEP)
> Assistant Chair, Associate Chair, Chair, Past Chair, CCCC, 1975–1978

Chair, Department of English, 1976–1985
Director, School of Letters, 1976–1985
Associate Director of the NEH Iowa Institute on Writing, late 1970s–early 1980s
Vice President, President-Elect, President, Past President, NCTE, 1984–1987
Chair, (numerous NCTE commissions)
Chair, University Undergraduate Scholarship Committee
Chair, Human Rights Committee
Chair, University Budget Committee
Chair, University Committee on Public Relations
Member, Liberal Arts Executive Committee
Member, Educational Policy Committee
Secretary, Liberal Arts Assembly
Member, CCCC Language Policy Committee

Perhaps most poignantly, Jix donated his body to the University of Iowa's College of Medicine's Department of Anatomy: even in death, he contributed to community.

Language

Much like Irish, Welsh wasn't a language favored, or at times even permitted, by the British government. In the 19th century, Welsh students—much like students in Ireland and on U.S. Native American land—were forbidden to speak their native tongue. Of course, every prohibition is local: students who were found to be speaking Welsh had to wear a NOT WELSH (NW) sign around their neck, which they could pass on to another student speaking Welsh. The student wearing the NW at the day's end was beaten, an intimidatingly brutal policy promising at least one good beating a day.

During the 20th century, Britain relaxed some of its grasp on Wales, while Wales asserted some of its educational and linguistic authority, and by the end of the century, some of that authority spoke to the right to practice Welsh. In 2011, with the Welsh Language Measure passed by the Welsh Assembly, that right was guaranteed: Welsh was officially equal to English. Although only a quarter of today's Welsh population speak Welsh, all schoolchildren until the age of 16 now learn it in school, and as an official statement of Wales proclaims, "Welsh is a living language, which means it is part of the Welsh identity."

Language was in some ways the centerpiece of Jix's life, which is especially intriguing given that it was hard for him to hear it—he literally lived with a lifelong hearing loss—and his dyslexia meant that seeing its written form could also be a challenge. Such challenges Jix saw as "work[ing] to my advantage." Despite the hearing loss, he was able to listen in class, he said,

> rearranging material in my own structures and then possessing it. It was a response to my dyslexia and also a response to the hearing . . . It has encouraged a habit of my mind that tends to run from association to association. (Quoted in Finders 502)

Fascinated by language, Jix understood its power: students are, he said, "controlled by language as much as they control the language" (Finders 502). His philosophy of language, located in metaphor, was sensual: "metaphor requires you to have an insight. You have to see it—literally see it"; language is "more than just the words. It's the way the word is elaborated. The word is the vehicle for the metaphor. The meaning that we draw out of it is the tenor." A teacher of writing, Jix said, "must love language and be a writer" (Finders 503).

My theory is that Jix was especially sensitive to the relationship between language and identity because of his Welsh background. He certainly understood that linkage when he participated in composing the 1974 Students' Right to Their Own Language document, which was revolutionary in its time, and for some, still revolutionary today. As its title suggests, it affirms students' rights to language, the same kinds of linguistic rights denied to Welsh children.

We affirm the students' right to their own patterns and varieties of language-the dialects of their nurture or whatever dialects in which they find their own identity and style. Language scholars long ago denied that the myth of a standard American dialect has any validity. The claim that any one dialect is unacceptable amounts to an attempt of one social group to exert its dominance over another. Such a claim leads to false advice for speakers and writers, and immoral advice for humans. A nation proud of its diverse heritage and its cultural and racial variety will preserve its heritage of dialects. We affirm strongly that teachers must have the experiences and training that will enable them to respect diversity and uphold the right of students to their own language.

Geneva Smitherman recalls that two successive committees worked on the statement and that, at times, the work was contentious. Jix, she said, played an outsized role:

> Credit for blending the multiple writing styles into a readable document goes to the talented editorial hand of Richard Lloyd-Jones and the skillful diplomacy of the late Melvin Butler, linguist and committee chair, whose untimely death prevented him from witnessing the fruits of his labor. (362)

Smitherman also makes it clear why a talented editorial hand and skillful diplomacy were needed. When the statement was proposed,

> [t]he fall-out was tremendous. Stringent, vociferous objections were put forth. There were calls for the resolution to be rescinded

and the background document recalled. Some blasted CCCC for abdicating its responsibility and pandering to "wide-eyed" liberals in the field. Others accused CCCC of a "sinister plot" to doom speakers of "divergent" dialects to failure in higher education by telling them that their stigmatized language was acceptable. A few simply said that CCCC had done lost they cotton-pickin minds.

On the other hand, there were many who embraced the spirit of the resolution. They thanked CCCC for the supporting document, which many found extremely helpful, even as they acknowledged its flaws. Some complimented the organization for its "moral and professional courage." Others stepped to the challenge of developing writing assignments to "tap the potential" of their marginalized students. A few simply asked CCCC why it took yall so long. (362)

The Statement passed 79–20; an entire issue of *College Composition and Communication* (*CCC*) was devoted to what CCCC chair Richard Larson called "this perceptive statement" so that CCCC members could have it "in durable form," could understand it, could read literature supporting it, could learn how to teach with it.

Jix's office on the university campus included on one wall "an old green chalkboard, blank except for an inch-high yellow chalk message: Y GWIR YN ERBYN Y BYD" (Finders 498). A Welsh expression, it translates as "The truth against the world," and is typically followed by A OES HEDDWCH, which translates as "Will you bring peace?" Idiomatically, it means something like this: you can speak your mind, so that/be assured there will be peace; we cannot have a real peace without truth.

Jix was committed to truth and peace, and to their relationship to each other, especially as expressed through language.

Legacy

Most people in rhetoric and composition, I think, associate Richard Lloyd-Jones with the 1963 Braddock Report. That document, formally titled *Research in Written Composition*, demonstrated empirically that if we want students to write better, we can stop teaching grammar: it doesn't help. But the Braddock Report had as a larger goal identifying what might help students and more specifically what we could claim based on empirical evidence about how to best teach composition. It was somewhat surprising for Jix to co-author an empirical report: he saw himself as a rhetorical theorist, not an empiricist; as someone who valued more than the empirically demonstrated since he also valued "experiential knowledge" and "crafts." But he co-authored the Braddock Report with his two colleagues, and in some ways that research project set the stage for his later work in writing assessment.

Even now, it's difficult to overstate its value of the Braddock Report. The Hillocks Report, a meta-analysis of research on written composition that followed some twenty years later, began by paying homage to the Braddock Report. When people ask about the value of teaching grammar at all, the Braddock Report is invoked. In histories of the field, the Braddock Report is often cited as one document marking rhetoric and composition's beginning. Perhaps so, but what that report in fact reported, using a now-famous comparison between chemistry and alchemy, was that rhetoric and composition was having a rather inauspicious beginning:

> Today's research in composition, taken as a whole, may be compared to chemical research as it emerged from the period of alchemy: some terms are being defined usefully, a number of procedures are being refined, but the field as a whole is laced with dreams, prejudices, and makeshift operations. Not enough investigators are really informing themselves about the procedures and results of previous research before embarking on their own. Too few of them conduct pilot experiments and validate their measuring instruments before undertaking an investigation. Too many seem to be bent more on obtaining an advanced degree or another publication than on making a genuine contribution to knowledge, and a fair measure of the blame goes to the faculty adviser or journal editor who permits or publishes such irresponsible work. And far too few of those who have conducted an initial piece of research follow it with further exploration or replicate the investigations of others.
>
> Composition research, then, is not highly developed. (5)

Still, in part because of the Braddock Report, in part because of his leadership of the Iowa NEH Writing Institute, in part because of the numerous roles he played in CCCC and NCTE, Jix is often credited as one of the founders of rhetoric and composition. He was, I think, foundational in founding a discipline, but he was also wary about a disciplinarity too oriented to *vitae polishing*, very wary about a disciplinarity that would divide. It's not that he didn't see adversaries, but he saw them only as adversaries, and he located them not inside the community, but outside.

What's also remarkable is how prescient Jix was, the ways he related issues of status to issues of meaning, the ways he saw language and social justice and intellect interwoven. He seemed to understand that the issues linking language and identity and social action never really go away; they are addressed, another topic or crisis emerges, and we shift our attention. But fundamentally, they return.

Likewise, his view of a community—as one in which *we belong to each other*, a community *simultaneously many and one*—isn't so much aspirational but possible. Reading about these ideas in his scholarship, hearing his talks through his written word, evokes something Jix-like, something straightforward, something humane, some new approach serving the common good, some new means of sounding a common cause *simultaneously [for] many and one*. Years ago, I wrote about how we might understand community as a kind of plural commons, as a site like the Boston Commons in its ability to welcome many and include them as one. Rhetoric and composition doesn't have a site, a physical place: in that sense, it's what scholars call a social imaginary, but Jix conceptualized the field as a site, an enduring place for all, where *we belong to each other*.

In bringing all this to rhetoric and composition, he also, and perhaps most importantly, brought a kind of wisdom, something like what in ancient rhetoric is called phronesis, a practical wisdom infused with the ethical and often revealed in narrative. In Welsh, which holds community and identity as prime virtues, the term for wisdom is DOETHINEB. Jix had, I think, both kinds, one rhetorically oriented, one community based. Those wisdoms marked his contributions to the field, to the world.

And all of us—in rhetoric and composition and out of it—are his beneficiaries.

Works Cited

Finders, Margaret. "With Jix." *College Composition and Communication*, vol. 43, no. 4, Dec. 1992, pp. 497–507.

Hillocks, George. *Research on Written Composition: New Directions for Teaching*. ERIC Clearinghouse on Reading and Communication Skills. National Conference on Research in English. National Institute of Education (ED), Washington, D.C.

Larson, Richard. "To Readers of CCC: Resolution on Language." *College Composition and Communication*, vol. 25, no. 3, Special Issue on Students' Right to Their Own Language, autumn 1974.

Lloyd-Jones, Richard. "Primary Trait Scoring." In *Evaluating Writing: Describing, Measuring, Judging*, edited by Charles R. Cooper and Lee Odell, NCTE, 1977, pp. 33–66.

———. "A View from the Center." *College Composition and Communication*, vol. 29, no. 1, Feb. 1978, pp. 24–29.

———. "Who We Were, Who We Should Become." *College Composition and Communication*, vol. 43, no. 4, Dec. 1992, pp. 486–496.

Smitherman, Geneva. "CCCC's Role in the Struggle for Language Rights." *College Composition and Communication*, vol. 50, no. 3, Feb. 1999, pp. 349–376.

Chapter 2. With Jix

Margaret Finders
AUGSBURG UNIVERSITY

A teacher is one who is present when learning takes place.

– Eskimo proverb

"I don't think a journalist has the right to disappear." When Professor Richard Lloyd-Jones speaks, his words have a haunting quality about them.[1] They hover over students, rematerializing at the library, over a cup of coffee, in front of the television set. His writing classes have a way of sneaking up on students who will be nodding off, envisioning a late afternoon brew, when his words seep in. Students are often out the door and two steps from the stairs when his words filter through, drawing them back. Rushing to catch Professor Lloyd-Jones before he leaves the classroom, they stop him in the doorway, asking, "So you're saying you can't hide behind words? There's no way around it? There is no neutral?" "All language is persuasive? Even the layout is manipulative?" And to these students, Lloyd-Jones responds, "It's all an illusion."

Lloyd-Jones has been orchestrating scenes like this one on the University of Iowa campus since his arrival in 1952. His work has been pressing on our assumptions about writing for decades. Preparing to unclutter his office after forty years in the profession, he's certainly left a mark on the page, a trail of influence in the teaching of writing: *Research in Written Composition*, written with Richard Braddock and Lowell Schoer, a term as chair of the Conference on College Composition and Communication, another as president of the National Council of Teachers of English, numerous articles and essays, the first of CCCC's Exemplar Awards honoring "a person who has served as an exemplar for the organization and represented the highest ideals of scholarship, teaching, and service to the entire profession." Codesigning primary-trait scoring, collaborating on the CCCC Statement on "The Students' Right to Their Own Language," working as Director of the University of Iowa School of Letters for ten years, serving in other administrative duties for eighteen more—Lloyd-Jones has compiled more than one lifetime's work.

Lloyd-Jones's works and words drew me up to the fourth floor of the English-Philosophy Building. I plodded up toward his office, his words colliding in my mind. "When does persuasion become coercion? Choosing and not choosing are both choices. You can't hide behind words. It's all illusion."

---

1. This article originally appeared in *College Composition and Communication*, vol. 43, no. 4, Dec. 1992, pp. 497–507. It is republished with permission of National Council of Teachers of English.

I hesitated at the top of the stairs, pausing to collect my breath and my nerve. At the end of the hallway Lloyd-Jones's door stood open, light spilling out into the dim corridor. I inhaled, walking toward the office door. Then, momentarily relieved to find his office empty, I exhaled.

Actually this office wasn't empty at all. Floor-to-ceiling bookcases lined the walls, stacks of books teetered precariously from floor to window ledge. Books surrounded the room, crowded his computer and cluttered his desk top. Two red, white, and blue political banners stating "I'm another Jean Lloyd-Jones fan" clung to the slats in the window blind, and many more lay scattered on top of his desk beside the white telephone, nearly hidden among the papers and folders and journals and books. One of two grey metal chairs just inside the door served as a small desk, piled with print. The other was scooted back under an old green chalkboard, blank except for an inch-high yellow chalk message—Y GWIR YN ERBYN Y BYD—and a map of the British Isles scotch-taped beside it, perfectly square.

I stood at the doorway, thinking about Lloyd-Jones, how he had shaped writing and the teaching of writing in the nation. Although I had met him only one semester prior, Lloyd-Jones had been influencing my teaching for the past fourteen years. When I was troubled over standardized tests, primary trait scoring came into play. When I struggled with correct language usage in my classroom, I turned to his work on students' right to their own language. Many, many times I returned to pages in *The English Coalition Conference: Democracy through Language*, a collaborative report Lloyd-Jones and Andrea Lunsford edited to represent the work of sixty teachers from kindergarten through college.

From his writing, I knew him well, but he knew me only from a semester's coursework. So I stood peeking into his office, nervously waiting for Professor Lloyd-Jones, Jix as just about everybody knew him.

He appeared from around the corner, walking toward me, wearing one of his guayaberas, a long, square cotton shirt embroidered down the front, trimmed out with a New Mexican silver and turquoise string tie that I had come to expect each day in rhetorical theory class.

Jix is an extraordinary teacher, I thought as he strolled toward me, though I hadn't thought so at the beginning of last semester. Jix had these annoying habits. Not really teaching, just puttering around. He reminded me of my grandfather shuffling about in his garden, moseying from the peas to the war to a little lecture about matches. Never finishing one thing before halfway into the next.

I remember how irritated I had been in rhetorical theory class. Jix arrived early, taking a seat at the end of the table in front of the window. The rest of us wandered in, all distressed over some reading. Jix never started class. It began like an opening scene from a play, with actors not quite rehearsed, voices tentative and staccato.

Students politely argued with each other, Jix watching, not saying a word. "I think as editors, Bizzell and Herzberg just threw in those Renaissance women because it is the politically correct thing to do."

"No, I think they represent a tradition that the preachers of the Middle Ages were trying to suppress."

"Oh, Christine de Pizan and Laura Cereta were included to interrupt the male-dominated discourse."

"The oral tradition of courtly love served as a defense of liberal voices. Look on page 497."

"No, I don't read it as a defense."

Jix sat, silent, his chair slid back away from our table, his large frame resting back against the window, arms folded across his chest, one foot tapping. He glanced at his large turquoise and silver watch and removed his glasses to wipe a cotton cloth across the tinted lenses. Taking off the thick rubber band that held our papers together, he sorted them out, each one folded vertically and arranged alphabetically, fanning them across the table in front of him. But mostly he looked directly at us, leaning back against the window, appearing almost ready to slip out, tapping his outstretched foot and smiling. He watched and waited.

A high-pitched whistle from his hearing aids jarred us to attention. He fiddled with them and in a low, deliberate whisper said, "These darn things. You know, I can't tell if they're whistling unless you people jump.

"You know, I was watching the news last night," he began almost in a whisper. "Did any of you see that commercial with the young soldier in Saudi Arabia saying, 'I would like to say hello to my mother and my brother in West Virginia'? Notice that he would like to say. Why would he choose to use indirect speech? What's going on here?" Lloyd-Jones's questions were followed by silence. He assumed his position against the window. Silence surrounded us. Beside me, Barb browsed through her own six-page Aristotle outline, underlining a phrase here and there. Jix offered up to the silence, "Where are we being driven and by what means?"

Prefacing my answer with a retractable hedge, I began, "Could it be that they want to create a greater distance? The inability to even speak directly?"

Jix grabbed hold of my comment, pinching it, then giving back a particle: "They?"

"The political filters," Ken jumped in. "The military directly imposing upon network television to sway the general public toward a neutral stance."

"Neutral?" Jix waited. Silence slowly and uncomfortably filled up the room. Students studied the ceiling, scratched phrases in their notebooks, frowned at their shoes.

Jix held up a University of Iowa publication that he had just received in campus mail. "Meet Hunter Rawlings," he read the royal-blue copy. "Look at the layout. Notice the quality of the paper. In classical terms, the delivery. How are we to receive this?"

Barb scowled and flipped to Cicero. I looked at the bold blue, the sheen from this slick copy, jotting down invention, arrangement, delivery into my notes. The light glared, making the message invisible. I struggled to remember the other elements. Five. I knew classical rhetoric had five. What were they? I leaned toward Barb. Someone was mentioning economic factors, the expense of printing. Again silence crept in.

Lloyd-Jones cleared his throat and paused, using his hands to orchestrate movement. "You know you have to begin reading as two readers, as a modern and also as a contemporary to the author, always playing at least two positions. Let's look at St. Augustine." He began reading aloud, enchanting us with quiet, soothing rhythms. As if from a pulpit, his voice embraced the room.

> To them that love God, all things work together unto good, to such as according to His purpose, are called. For whom he foreknew, he also predestined to be made conformable to the image of His Son: that he might be the Firstborn among many brethren.

Then abruptly, Jix raised his hand as if to signal that he was tagging one of us with some unstated question. He leaned back into the windowsill, crossed his arms, watching attentively as we tried to untangle the material. Sunlight folded in around his shoulders as he watched the discussion play itself out before him.

A hesitant voice, "Would that be considered grand style?" More voices: "The style represents the text as truth." "Before the Enlightenment?" "Truth, with a capital T, existed within the text."

As the discussion died, Jix leaned forward, asking, "What do you make of this?" pointing toward the blackboard, reading the white chalk text:

> The whole duty of a writer is to please and satisfy himself, and the true writer always plays to an audience of one. Let him start sniffing the air or glancing at the trend machine, and he is as good as dead although he may make a nice living. (E. B. White)

My notes for that class looked like some strange worn rag rug. Bits held together by broken threads. Page numbers jotted against fragmented references. Pieces of stories knotted to textual analysis. Ends of sentences left dangling.

I came to expect long silences interwoven with a steady stream of story about television or text or his sons or his wife's re-election to the Iowa Senate. Silence became an entity, no longer an absence but a rich presence that surrounded the language and called for connections. I found myself more willing to interrupt the talk, always holding the silence as sacred. Thinking back about that class and seeing Jix walking toward me in the hallway of the English-Philosophy Building, his round, Welsh face smiling, I relaxed.

"Howdy do," he greeted me at his door. "What can I do for you today?" He scooped up the papers from the chair and tossed them with others on the computer table. Between the screeches of his chair, I fumbled about, explaining my plan to capture him on paper, inviting myself into his writing classes—SW:131 Writing for Public Policy and SW:10 Expository Writing—and asking to visit with him and his students regularly. Jix replied, "You're welcome any time. It's an honor to be asked."

I spent several hours listening to Jix talk about teaching, about writing, about the limits of language. I visited the two classes he was teaching, often forgetting myself, struggling to keep quiet when Jix would toss out something like, "Why do you think some people resist the validity of metaphor as a way of knowing?" His writing classes meandered about, lingering here and there whenever a topic struck someone's fancy.

The baseball cap with the ponytail noticed me first as I entered SW:131 Writing for Public Policy: "So you gonna take a test drive with Lloyd-Jones?"

"Yes, I'm interested in seeing how he teaches."

"Better sit close. Lloyd-Jones is hard to hear." I sat down beside this young man. "If you're gonna tape, you better move closer to the window." I got up and sat beside a red-headed woman with her area of tabletop piled with books.

"God, you're not taping us, are you?" She slid her notebook away from me, uncapped a pen, and recrossed her arms.

Jix appeared in the doorway, a large three-ring notebook tucked under his arm. He moved to the end of the table, taking a seat in front of the window. Opening up the notebook, he removed a stack of papers and spread them out across the table. Students casually arrived, taking seats around the long rectangular table.

"Well, actually, I'm taping Lloyd-Jones, but . . ." Jix cleared his throat, and the woman began taking notes before a word was uttered.

Papers rustled, chairs creaked, The Cubs cap looked up from digging in his faded green backpack and groaned, "It's the rain. This isn't conducive to discussion. Not gonna have much to say."

"Something may boil up if it gets hot enough in here," Jix replied, handing out a revised schedule, explaining the next "amusement," Jix's word for each writing assignment. Students studied the mimeographed handout while Jix explained the task. "It's a potential reader stand. That is to say, it's a kind of examination we've been stumbling around with. It's a way of making a guess about what your likely readers know, understand, and believe. It's a way of controlling the knowledge rather than being controlled by it."

Students worked to wrap this next task around their semester project. They wrestled with possibilities. Panic flickered across the red-headed woman's face. She struggled to connect the assignment to her project on the fading interest of Americans to volunteer. "VA hospitals depend on voluntarism. My point is that we are no longer a nation of volunteers." She hesitated. There was just a hint of question in her statement. Jix answered her unstated questions. Other students posed concerns for the group. Jix encouraged students to reshape the task to fit their needs. He suggested that one student ignore the task altogether and proceed with his own plan.

Turning attention back to paper seven, Jix suggested looking at student work. "Go, man," the Cap coaxed his buddy who began reading from his handscrawled paper. "One way our opinions are altered is one-to-one speech, cocktail party and kegger talk . . ." He continued reading from his wrinkled page.

"Reactions? Reactions?" Jix invited discussion with a wave of his arm.

Students remained silent. Jix, too. One woman studied her fingernails. The man beside her reread his paper, crossing out phrases and drawing lines in the margins. Finally the reader took a stab at it. "I believe something from a friend. I believe what a friend tells me."

"Are you thinking of a particular incident? A particular friend?" Silence. Students looked at Jix and waited. The man beside the Cubs cap frowned and squinted. The reader shuffled through the pages of his copy.

The red-headed woman entered the conversation. "If my friend has some incredible statistics, and I know more, I'm not going to believe my friend."

Jix looked directly at her and leaned forward, asking, "How do you know you're going to believe your information?"

She cocked her head. Her mouth dropped open. Her pen froze. "What?" she whispered.

Lifting his right arm to dismiss them for the day, Jix repeated his question exactly: "How do you know you're going to believe your information?" Sending them off on a side trip, curving back roads, touring one of his "amusements," the daily writing tasks, designed to take away the "big deal" of any one paper.

"It's an issue of facility," he told me later. Seated near Jix in his office, beside the 1930 proposed map of the campus, across from the wooden coat rack holding one black fur cap, surrounded by texts, the words of his friends and colleagues, I came to know print differently. Text with ink not quite dry, smudged and erasable. Voices pressed onto paper, still wriggling.

I sat there, scrounging about the room visually: a draft of Peter Elbow's new book, *What Is English?*, someone's M.A. thesis, a roll of maps, the university's 1992 possible building sites. Jix's voice interrupted my canvassing: "The one thing I want any writing class to do, even a graduate theory class to do, is to make people conscious of the problematic element about the knowledge that they are so sure of. That they are, in fact, controlled by language as much as they control the language."

He explained to me that what he wanted that young man to do in class today with his issue of a friend's opinion was to bring the abstractions down to a concrete somebody affected by concrete incidents. "Since one way or another the thing human beings retell to each other is their sense of abstraction: how they control the world, how they shape it. You can't do it if you don't present the detail, but the thing that you are presenting is the world view, the structure." And so Jix was always playing those questions, twisting them slightly. In expository writing, students had been conceptualizing a job. One student had divided his income into categories: entertainment, car, beer. Jix asked, "What do those categories represent?" Several voices replied, "Expenses."

"Yes, but I wonder if that's the best term." He paused. "I wonder if you think of it as the value. You create categories that represent things that are important to you. When you organize a budget, what you are really doing is organizing a reality." Jix folded his hands at his mouth as if in prayer. "You have promised the reader a structure," he said through his hands, opening them out, palms up. "What do you mean by balanced budget?" His hands swayed to indicate imbalance, always leaving them with a question, complicating the seemingly simple.

When I ask him after class how students in Writing for Public Policy would be able to do the next assignment, which was to explain the basic idea of their project using metaphor, Jix leaned back into his squeaky, old chair and smiled. "They won't."

Now it was my turn to pause. I glanced first to my notes and then to my tape recorder, the small red light indicating the recorder was on. "You see," he continued, "when they adopt a different language, they adopt different imperatives about what they know and don't know and how they handle it. Metaphor really requires you to have an insight. You have to see it—literally see it."

At that moment, I realized another reason for this interviewing project, the selfish pleasures of being in the presence of a language lover. Over the telephone, Jix had told me once but then again in his office, making sure that it was recorded on tape, "A teacher of writing must love language and be a writer." And Jix satisfied both of his own categories. When we were talking about research, about empirical data and qualitative studies, Jix used the word "joy," reminding me why I was really here, engaged in graduate studies in rhetorical theory. "We talk about the political but not about the importance of language as play." It wasn't fancy theory but fancy, I think, that positioned Jix as a leader in the field.

Jix was preparing to retire after nearly half a century, here in this office on the fourth floor of the English-Philosophy Building, not because he had made a conscious decision to become a teacher of writing, but rather because he, like many of us, "fancied himself a poet." He told me that he had always favored the idea of college teaching because his two uncles and two aunts had all taught in college. "My father was the only one who didn't, and my mother had no siblings, so that all the exposure led me to believe that teaching in college was a good idea. It never dawned on me that it might not be an appropriate thing to do, so I sort of slipped into it."

He had slipped into writing by accident, he said. When he got out of the army, the Veterans Administration did testing to "rehabilitate this medically unfit person." Jix expressed interest in English or philosophy. The VA people said, "Nobody wants to hire a philosopher." So, having no real quarrel with that, Jix studied literature with an emphasis in philosophy. Through a secretary in the art department who was giving piano lessons to his wife, Lloyd-Jones landed an assistantship, teaching business writing in the commerce college. The next year he shifted to technical writing in the engineering college.

When Jix talked about his younger days, I could hardly imagine him a school boy in rural Iowa, participating in debate with dyslexia and hearing loss. As an active member of his high school's debate team, Jix always elected to be last.

Without notes, he would listen carefully and prepare his delivery in his head. "I have a very hard time making marks on the page," Jix said. "I leave out words. I leave out pieces of words. I will suddenly be into the next word and a word will begin one way and end another." However, he had very little negative experience with writing in school, mostly because "there wasn't any." Working with debate, he perfected systems of discourse without ever "having the irritation of producing manuscripts." He succeeded all the way through college and graduate school without ever taking notes. "I simply used the system of listening in class," he said, "rearranging material in my own structures and then possessing it. It was a response to my dyslexia and also a response to the hearing. It could have been a limitation but actually it worked to my advantage. It has encouraged a habit of my mind that tends to run from association to association. I think you said that digression does not exist in my world."

I denied it, laughing, wondering if I could have been the one who said it first. I asked Jix about his first writing teacher. A long line of my own writing teachers, ones like Mrs. Brown, the kind, nurturing type, and Mr. Till, the harsh you'll-thank-me-one-day type, and Jix, all paraded before me. "Well," he leaned back into his chair and studied the air. "Actually, I was essentially my first writing teacher—or rather my colleagues were." Sharing a classroom with his colleagues, Jix watched their classes in operation. They watched Jix. Their office, a row of desks in the back of their classroom, became a teaching lab. They shared materials, texts, and observations. Craft was a part of the daily routine of sharing. "It was a master-apprentice relationship," Jix said. "And when it was my turn, I had to be more conscious of what I was doing to pass it on."

Jix lectured in Writing for Public Policy one day, a rare occurrence. He began the class from the end of the table. "I'm going to do a little filibustering today. You'll notice on your papers today, I've been a little too grandfatherly. Giving you more advice than you probably want, and you can always choose to ignore that. But many of you have latched onto a slogan." He continued, explaining about generalizations and commitments and passion.

Students looked bored. One young man stretched out, closing his eyes, his head resting back against the wall. Marsha sat, slumped back away from the table, her notebook closed, her head down, waiting for class to end. With materials crammed in her book bag, Marsha rushed for the door. I stopped her in the hallway. "You know he was talking to me today," she mumbled as we paused by the drinking fountain. "I don't have a focus. I wasn't interested in welfare, but it seemed like something I could do. All these assignments. It's like some giant puzzle, but you have no clue. You can't make out the picture." She headed down the stairs.

"I was talking to Marsha today and folks like Marsha," Jix caught up with me on the stairs. "She'd latched onto a slogan, and now she is finding that slogan to be inaccurate. She'll be able to look beyond the slogan next time. Or we hope she will."

He paused at the top of the stairs. "Most students want to connect the dots with straight lines. I don't know why they can't connect them like this," he said, extending his fingers, looping his hands, designing s's and /'s and o's in the air. Students often claimed that Jix leaves them hanging in the wind. I confronted him with this accusation. "I do leave them hanging in the wind," he said, "but it is my hope that they will learn to enjoy hanging out there. The desire for certainty and closure is a mistaken academic ideal."

Arriving at his office door, Jix dug in his pocket for the key. I teased, "I always imagine you carrying around a pocketful of stories, ready to be flipped out like quarters."

"Well, I guess I do, ones that have worked in the past, ones that illustrate a particular point. But of course, new ones emerge." We entered the office, Jix switched on the light, and I clicked on the tape recorder.

"Stories," I said. I really preferred to listen rather than talk. "You just never know what may turn up," Jix had said weeks earlier. Most of the time, I didn't like to interfere, waiting to see what would turn up, allowing a full silence to surround his stories.

I especially enjoyed hearing Jix retell a piece of Hamlet in one class. It was clear that he wanted students to understand how the metaphor, the structure, the single word could alter how a reader would receive an entire piece.

Once again around the large table, students were whispering, chattering about spring break, complaining about the work. "Florida, how rad. I'm just gonna go to Des Moines."

"Finally got assignment number 16 done. I'm caught up." "I'm behind three papers, you jerk."

Lloyd-Jones' classes all looked the same. I checked my calendar to determine which class I was in. It was the 26th so it had to be Writing for Public Policy.

Jix waited and then began, "One reason that women feel uncomfortable in the business world is that they are constantly exposed to male metaphors. Rather than talk about abstract theory, which I love to do, mind you, I'll bring up a few instances." Jix cleared his throat, retelling the story of Laertes and Ophelia. "One of the things we are told about Ophelia is that she has not so large a tether as her brother. What do you understand about Ophelia when you are told she has not so large a tether?"

"She's on a shorter leash than her brother."

"Where do you ordinarily associate a leash?"

"A dog. Something to be dominated."

"Just dogs?" Jix pushed.

"Animals."

"All animals?" Jix wouldn't let go. "Just domesticated animals."

Circling back, Jix asked, "What are we supposed to understand about Ophelia?"

Discussion took off. Many voices. Cows, pigs, dogs, mavericks as metaphors. They moved on through Gulliver's Travels. Jix led them to the less visible. He collected slivers of thoughts, melding them together like an alchemist. "So what you're saying is," he paused, "it's more than just the words. It's the way the word is elaborated. The word is the vehicle for the metaphor. The meaning that we draw out of it is the tenor."

Back in his office he told me, "The teacher must be able to hear the question the student is asking when the student isn't able to ask it very well. When the student gives an opinion, the teacher needs to get them to go beyond their response. You have to listen, anticipate the moves of fifteen to twenty students." His voice intensified. "But it's dangerous. It's bullying. When I reshape their words, students must be able to recognize them as their own." And I sat and wondered if Jix will mind my working over his words.

On my next visit, I found Jix at his desk, working through students' papers, writing tiny words in the margins with a black pen. Interrupting him from his task, I asked how he felt about all of this interviewing stuff. "After however long I've been doing this business and after reading things that people have written about what I have allegedly said, I've become quite philosophical about what gets stated," he laughed. "That's not wholly fair. Whatever one says is going to be transmuted. By definition there is no way you can say anything that will not be transmuted."

Later, after sorting through stacks of notes and Jix's writing tasks, journal articles and books and tapes, I once again climbed the stairs for some kind of wrap-up. The room was brighter, a bit tidier. "Ah, you're moving out."

"Well, the stacks are smaller."

"More light," I replied, surveying the room once again, detecting this time what was not there. The fans were missing. The chairs empty. Some books had disappeared. The computer table clear. I plopped myself down. Jix swiveled his chair out away from his desk, his grey sweater blending with the chair. I clicked on the tape.

"I look at that slogan up there," he motioned to the old green chalkboard, "and I think that represents the kinds of uncertainty and posturing and a few other things. That was the product of an eighteenth-century Welsh slate mason who revived the Eisteddfod, the great song fests of Wales, and created the Gorsedd, the contest of bards. This guy was a poet who took the bardic name of Iolo Morgannwg. His real name was Edward Williams. It roughly translates 'truth against the world.' It is one of those phrases that in a way doesn't mean a damn thing, but there's a certain kind of self-righteousness in it. Probably the world in this case meant people in general. Y BYD, the great world, common opinion, and the truth is a little hard to be sure of. Very Unitarian, I guess, in its insistence on truth. In a way, it's a rallying cry."

Silence.

"Our value systems cannot survive unless we have education because education will enlarge your sense of who you are as a human being, but it will also make you more effectively part of a community that has to carry on the life we all have to lead. There was a time when the church provided that commonality. A time when patriotism provided that commonality."

Silence.

"In the humanities in general, and in writing in particular, where you are always trying to deal with the most complex thing that the language can represent, you're always blurring out into those other areas. So I can josh about being a grandfather or a bully, which in a sense is joshing about roles, relationships. You can't solve the writing problems until you have sorted out the content. Which is to say in most cases, you couldn't make some sense of what it means until you have sorted out your place in society. Your relationship to some other human being in society. I was consciously making a commentary about human roles."

Silence.

"You can't even walk through a room without making somebody different for the fact that you walked through the room. The stakes are multiplied many times over every time you go into a classroom. And the context is always larger because when you go into a classroom, all of the receptors in that classroom have already been anesthetized by previous receptions, expectations. They've set up filters. They're tired. They only see or hear you a small fraction of the time. They don't pay attention, but it's a little broader than that. They've been anesthetized. They simply cannot receive unless you break through that stereotype, and you never quite do. You are always their stereotype. You are who they make you, and so I think one of the roles you play is constantly trying to get them to recategorize you. And sometimes you succeed, and sometimes you don't. It's the sand in the oyster. You don't want to have so much sand that you kill the oyster, but you want enough to have a pearl every now and then."

Silence.

"A little disruption is not a bad thing." Jix leaned forward. "You ought to be upsetting."

Chapter 3. Detours of Intention

Tom Montgomery Fate
College of DuPage

In 1984, I enrolled in the only graduate nonfiction writing program in the country, even though I wasn't sure what "nonfiction" actually meant.[1] It was blurry back then—not yet "creative" or "literary" or the "fourth genre." But I assumed it included journalism, and that's what mattered. I wanted to write about the war in Nicaragua. The Reagan Administration was trying to destroy the Sandinista government, and in the depths of my twenty-something naiveté and idealism, I thought that writing about it could make a difference. That words could impact the world. That the art of the writer was also a form of activism.

On the first day of my first class—Advanced Expository Writing—a know-it-all student from New York, a self-identified "working journalist," began jabbering about George Orwell's "rare ability to bridge fact and truth." I had no idea what he was talking about. Since it actually was 1984, a discussion then arose about the modern relevance of the novel, which I pretended that I'd read. The whole first semester was like that—lots of pretending and posing. Thankfully, our teacher, Jix Lloyd-Jones, was smart and kind, and seemed to expect the stark differences in our backgrounds.

In the next class session, with a thin stick of chalk, Jix scratched the word "essay" on the blackboard, and added the origin (*essai*) and root meanings ("trial" or "attempt"). Then he said that the personal essay was the nonfiction equal of a short story. This startled me, because I thought the word "essay" meant the dry, academic writing that had been required in all my prior schooling. But I loved short stories, and soon became hooked on the personal essay, a nonfiction genre that was making a comeback. I liked the essay because it felt so much like life, an unending series of attempts, or what I later called "detours of intention," which can be read two ways: sometimes you choose the route, but more often it chooses you. That's how writing/teaching/life is. You don't always know where you're going.

~~~

In that course, we read fifteen essays in our anthology. But three of them stuck with me. These writers focused on neo-colonialism (George Orwell), family and parenthood (E. B. White), and race and identity (James Baldwin).

The first two pieces Jix assigned for contrast. One was quite political, looking more outward at the world, and the other deeply personal, looking more inward at

---

1. This essay originally appeared in a longer form in Tom Montgomery Fate, *The Long Way Home: Detours and Discoveries*, Ice Cube Press, 2022. It is reprinted with permission.

the self. George Orwell's "Shooting an Elephant" (1921) did read like a short story: a clear plot with an emotional climax. Orwell, a member of the Imperial Police in Burma, had to kill a huge elephant "solely to avoid looking a fool." Uneasy with his unearned authority, and confused by Burmese culture, he botched the killing, and the animal died a slow, excruciating death. The essay is a critique of British colonialism. Orwell was trapped: he detested the British Empire he represented, yet was also hated by the locals he was supposed to protect.

One line in the essay would later haunt me: "when the white man turns tyrant it is his own freedom that he destroys." In a few years, I would find strands of Orwell's story in my own—in Nicaragua and Guatemala and the Philippines and other sites of U.S. colonialism, where I would work and write and struggle to fit in, and to undo Euro-American privilege. Mostly I failed. In an interview, Ernesto Cardenal, the Nicaraguan Minister of Culture, once told me "You don't have to save the world, you just have to see it." It was a question Jix would later raise: does a writer's seeing (the art) precede and enable the saving (the activism)? Are they necessarily separate or different processes?

While Orwell's essay was fast-paced and political, E.B. White's "Once More to the Lake" (1941) was slow, intensely personal, and did not read like a short story. When White was a kid, each summer his father took their family to a lake in Maine for vacation. The essay is about a nostalgic return trip he makes decades later to the same lake with his own young son, who had never been there.

Some students in the class liked the piece, but others found White's endless memories and reflections self-absorbed. Exhibit A: White kept imagining himself as his own father and his boy as himself a few decades earlier. "I began to sustain the illusion," he writes, "that he was I, and therefore, by simple transposition, that I was my father." Such middle-aged insights didn't connect with the younger students. I didn't love the essay, but I didn't mind it. Maybe just because I liked to fish.

But twenty years later White's story would become my own. And that line—"that he was I"—would return to me when my son was born. So would the "simple transposition that I was my father" when my father later died from Alzheimer's. These events revealed to me something Jix knew: the essayist stops time for his or her readers, so that the words and images, like fresh leaves of mint in a steaming pot of water, can steep into deeper and deeper colors and flavors of meaning.

Back then I didn't fully understand this, nor the comforting lures of nostalgia. Probably because I didn't yet know that time moves faster as you age. That it's not a delusion. When you're five years old, a single year is one-fifth of your entire life. But when you're 50, one year is one-fiftieth of your life. So there are a few million more things to remember, and forget—college, marriage(s), children, broken bones and hearts, a leaking roof, a friend's death from cancer. Or maybe shooting an elephant or going fishing with your kid.

Which moments matter? Can the reader find their story in yours? These were the unspoken questions that Jix always seemed to be asking, and that I still carry.

The third essay, James Baldwin's "Notes of a Native Son," was intensely personal and political. There was no choice. His art and activism—amid the Harlem renaissance and resistance—were woven into one life, one perpetual struggle for social justice, and survival. In the class, Baldwin balanced Orwell: the colonial story told by the colonized, by the silenced, the invisible. Baldwin was teaching us how to see in a new way.

So how could a white, small-town Iowa kid in 1984 connect to the suffering of an angry gay black man in New York City forty years earlier? I'm not sure, but the narrative voice was more honest and self-revelatory than any essay I'd yet read. More so than White or Orwell. While I could not comprehend the violation and violence a black person felt in 1943 (nor in 2020), Baldwin's essay moved me. His belief in the spiritual and political power of writing sparked my own. And perhaps like Orwell, despite the depth of my white privilege, I wanted to believe that writing could somehow diminish the unbearable "weight of white people in the world" that Baldwin carried and despised.

Baldwin captures two pivotal days from his life with sobering clarity. On July 29, 1943, his stepfather died and his sister was born. Four days later, on August 3, he turned 19 and they buried his father amid the exploding Harlem riots. These events came to represent not only Baldwin's life in crisis, but a nation in crisis.

Jix used the essay to teach a basic writing move: the "framing" of an arresting image or charged moment in order to both limit and invite the reader's attention while introducing a theme. Late in the essay Baldwin frames a moment of rage. A white waitress in a fancy hotel rejects him—"We don't serve Negroes here"—and he explodes in anger, throws a glass at her, then realizes the danger he is in and runs. The moment captures Baldwin's vulnerability, his longing to be seen/visible, but need to be unseen/invisible in order to survive.

After this essay, we went back and reviewed parallel framed moments in Orwell and White. This basic strategy and model would become central to my writing and teaching. At the time I needed help or tools—some simple models for how to see and read my life like a writer. And now I had one: the camera. But this was in the pre-digital era, film was expensive, and there was no auto focus. So you really had to learn how to pay attention, how to see, how to frame and focus the image, and recognize the emotional nuance of the light and darkness in the language—how to invite and limit your reader.

When I left that class I'd just begun to understand the chaos and beauty of the perpetual trial of the essay, of writing, of seeing a life, and teaching others how to do it. And I'd begun to get my head around a core idea that was likely self-evident to everyone else: out of the millions of moments and images that we perceive, and that constantly buzz through the wild circuitry of our brain, we can only ever retain and frame a few. That's what Jix was always getting at. What do you choose to see? Where are you focused? In your language, but also in your life. What few precious moments will you choose to frame, and turn into art—into a handful of stories—that will once more change you, and the reader, and the world?

Chapter 4. Letter to Jix

David Hamilton
University of Iowa

For Noel Heermance, who will know why.

It's not easy to write of Richard (Jix) Lloyd-Jones, who chaired our department nine of my first ten years here.[1] Not only was Jix a mysterious man, but, through many years as his colleague, we were in key ways opposites. His instinct was to step back, and sometimes up, as if to a precipice, survey the scene, and strive to grasp the whole of it. Mine was to find my footing within it and venture forays from there. When Jix spoke to our department, he prided himself on speaking without notes, and he practiced several mnemonic strategies to keep his words in order. I admired that and felt one should not be overprepared for informal and semiformal occasions. I relied less and less on notes for my classes, too, but I never made the effort to know, much less master, the mnemonic strategies Jix favored. Sometimes I suffered for it.

Beyond all that, we had two further things in common. Jix had damaged lungs and I asthma, so when he paused on a landing of our building, wheezing, I knew the feeling well. Inhalers kept mine at bay. Jix was less fortunate. He had worse than severe asthma always and stopped at every landing. Also, we were both closet poets.

When I appeared in Iowa suddenly, by desperate chance, as a possible replacement for his closest colleague and friend, Richard Braddock, it must have been disorienting, though I was blithely ignorant of it. For years those two had collaborated on, and eventually published, *Research in Written Composition,* brought out while I was in graduate school. They were way ahead of whatever game I had, and suddenly Braddock was gone, killed in a traffic accident while on sabbatical in Australia. Otherwise, I wouldn't have been invited to speak to the English department and be considered for a position within it. I came armed only with what I knew, which did not include their book and had nothing of research about it. But I could draw on my experience, such as it was, in April of 1975, most of a year after Nixon's resignation and just days before the fall of Saigon. I can imagine Jix listening to much I had to say that afternoon and thinking, "Just where does this guy think he's coming from?" Nevertheless he assented, and a couple of years later—he was chair by then—he assented as well—it may even have been his idea—to my taking over *The Iowa Review.*

---

1. This essay originally appeared in David Hamilton, *A Certain Arc: Essays of Finding My Way,* Ice Cube Press, 2019. It is reprinted with permission.

I'd been given no assignment for my talk. But I knew the position at hand was to teach writing, so I described my experience as a teacher and writer. And I spoke at length of the writing course I took during my first year at Amherst College, which then was still an all-men's college and very much aware of being a customary next step—though it was hardly that for me—after Deerfield, Exeter, or Choate.

"List six principles by which you live," we were asked our first day, and we all did, surprised though some of us were, that we could summon or even pretend to so many. The next day we learned that all but one of us had declared himself "an individualist." Well, then, was the single fellow who hadn't thought of that our only original thinker? What does it mean to be an individual, anyway? Write an essay about that. It was clear right away that we could only speak for ourselves and that it would be a good idea to consider closely just what you thought a self, specifically your self, was.

So, later, do you believe in ghosts? Of course not, we chorused, each of us in a page or two of prose. Who do you think we are, superstitious fools? Then we received several reports of encounters with the supernatural: apparitions, hallucinations, presences, even ghosts. Well, do you believe in ghosts now? And we all bent to qualify our first position. The next step was to observe that most of us had changed our minds and to ask what it means to do that. What happens when you change your mind? How does that occur? Do you change all or just some of it?

But the assignments, the writing prompts, were considerably more cunning than I have suggested. Here are the first three:

> 1. A great American poet is quoted in a recent book as having denounced college teaching that "frisks Freshmen of their principles." Think about the problem seriously for a time and then set down a list of a half dozen of your principles (one or two thoughtful sentences for each), and explain in a paragraph your interest in retaining them. (Note: keep a legible copy of your principles.)
>
> 2. When examined, this metaphor of "frisking" has its interest, has it not. Rightly or wrongly you are being taken into custody, accused perhaps, your principles are your weapons, you may or may not choose to produce them with a show of violence, they provide a defense, etc. Or you are at the racetrack and your wallet is picked. Consider for a moment your principles as weapons of self defense (and of aggression), and write a page telling why in a civilized community of laws and books you need to be able to defend yourself. Who is your enemy? With what does he threaten you?
>
> 3. Leaf through the college catalogue with your principles in mind. Find a course that looks as though it might have the effect

of despoiling you of a principle. Quote the principle involved and the course description; then write a page—it will be imaginative writing, of course—telling how you think this effect might be obtained. Short of avoiding the course, how would you go about defending yourself?

Not only did that course keep me off balance, it seemed always to strive for the ineffable and to demand we write of matters we had not considered. Note that parenthetical clause about imaginative writing; almost off-handedly, we were being asked to invent. Furthermore, the assignments reward close reading that few of us were capable of. Who, I wonder, and it certainly was not I, challenged right off that first metaphor, "frisk," which came as you may know, from Robert Frost? I'm sure the few who did, were there any, were well rewarded by the instructor's taking a close interest in what they said. And what to make, too, of the assumed adversarial relation? We may not have warred with our instructors, each one shepherding about twenty of us through these assignments, but we were soon on guard against their next probing question. Scholarship was beside the point. These were personal questions that challenged us to answer as ourselves. I doubt that plagiarism ever occurred to any of us. That course made me live for an entire school year as an earnest commentator on my own experience, that is, as a writer. It has had the most lasting influence on me of any course whatsoever.

We did not learn formal structures of argument, or even of paragraphing. We had no handbook. We learned to invent, with caution, reflection, and qualification, while reassessing our commitment to whatever we thought. Or maybe I could say, to what we thought we thought, as we found all our clichés challenged. Hadn't we rendered "individualist" a cliché right off the bat? Soon we discovered that metaphor devoid of literal meaning is suspect. As in changing one's mind. Is that like changing your shirt? Changing a tire? Or is it more like changing a habit?

I have heard that the aim of that course was for us to compose our intellectual autobiographies by way of about eighty short compositions sequenced through a school year, three a week the first semester, two the second. Each year gave birth to a new sequence composed by our instructors. "Now I've got you out in the open where I can get at you," an instructor wrote on a paper soon passed around among that writer's friends, which prompted among those friends questions such as, were we the writer, would we want to be got at, and was that like being frisked? Meanwhile, dittoed excerpts from our writings were our reading, a fresh set each day, taken from the papers just handed back, and we walked the tightrope always of hoping to be quoted and wary of what our instructor, and classmates, would find fault with if we were.

Surely both Jix and Carl Klaus took an interest in that part of my talk since I was reporting on a format they had come to value. They too were composing writing sequences. My college course, though I didn't know it at the time, had been a model for their work. Carl told me much later that he and Jix shared their sequences, leaving them typed in the other's mail slot, as if they were exchanging poems.

Meanwhile another factor was at play. The Iowa Institute on Writing, for directors of first-year courses all across the nation, was being planned and would come to fruition four years later. Jix would lead a seminar on rhetorical theory, Carl one on assignment sequences in composition courses, and that left me, possibly, to lead one on writing across the curriculum of the liberal arts. We didn't have the phrasing yet, but it arose soon after, and our Institute had something to do with that. I was being vetted for that position, and my first-year course made an impression on both Carl and Jix.

In fact they found its influence a little shocking as, having come through my talk all right and finding myself at Iowa, I plunged ahead in the only way I knew: making things up as I went along, constructing my own "momentary stays against confusion," as Frost defined his poems, with no help from a handbook.

So, for the next three years, I experimented with a course I called Writing Science. Not Writing in the Sciences, but Writing Science itself. Right off I discovered that students bringing in work from chemistry, physics, psychology, or whatever other discipline had a hard time reading each other. Each writer was too far into his or her own specialization, and it doesn't take many steps in before you have shut the door behind you. In search of work then that we could share, I came upon a text called *Seeing and Writing*, by Walker Gibson, who had been an instructor at Amherst. He had moved on, but he had taken its first principle with him: challenge writers to invent before you worry about shaping their inventions.

My favorite example from his book was "Reading the Wind," which required building an anemometer and describing the wind it reveals to you. Now, assuming you are willing to try, you can come up with hundreds of possibilities without running out to the nearest airport and copying theirs. Moreover, you can revise and improve your anemometer and share your work with collaborators who may help improve it further, which is a lot like the work of science. Open a bundle of newspapers on the sidewalk and describe how they blow away. Dangle a paper cup full of colored water over a white sheet pegged to the ground; punch a hole in the cup and describe the pattern the water makes on the sheet. Set a series of bottles of water in a row, filled to different levels, and write the music you hear the wind play over them. And in each case, try to define the wind you discover. Is the wind writing its face on the white sheet the same as when it is whistling over bottles?

I came to call this not science but a serious parody of science and worked out possibilities for adjacent disciplines. Go out on a winter night and describe movement you find in the stars. Attend a regional girls basketball tournament—it was still six-girl, half-court basketball—and write an ethnography of what you observe. Will the game or the rival gatherings of fans be your subject? Go to an exhibition of unfamiliar art—African masks and pots was one opportunity—and sketch several classifications. These assignments carried over to our Institute. In one planning session, I was describing them to Jix and Carl. They were a little taken aback. In spite of their commitment to invention-first sequences, they still seemed to hope I had a helpful handbook of rules in me somewhere, a dependable structure, or series of modulated structures, that would smooth the way for writing in the sciences, the social sciences, and humanities. But I had no such thing, and now they were stuck with me. Finally, I think it was Carl who turned to me and said, "Oh, I get it. You're working from the inside out." I had never put it like that to myself, but I quickly said, "Yes," and tried to live up to claims an old course had laid on me. Jix, with his calm, Olympian tolerance, just smiled.

Now I can add what I didn't know enough to say that first afternoon in Iowa since I had not yet been surprised by it. All semester long, in that faraway first year in college, not a single passage was chosen from my work as an example, good or bad, for my fellow students. Our last essay was to serve as our exam. It was to be a couple of pages longer and, for the first time, addressed no particular question. I was on my own.

I wrote of work one summer during high school when I signed on to pour cement atop a series of grain elevators rising over the rooftops and shade trees of our midwestern, county seat town. Once the pouring started, crews were needed around the clock, and I joined the night crew, from eleven to seven. Meditative, soul-searching time, especially at seventeen, even if one does not think to say so. We rose to work by standing on the open rim of the big cement bucket, rising between the running cables that lifted it to the working deck. We kept our hands close to the cables for an illusory sense of safety. You couldn't cling to them, but their presence offered a frame within which you stood upright and balanced. The bucket rim was about as wide as a piece of railroad track. We stood a little sideways on it and so were hoisted several stories off ground. Rising upward, we savored our daring and exposure. If I slipped, I'd try to fall into the cement, not to the earth. This was long before OSHA. Once on top, where flimsy board railings served more as warnings than true restraints from falling off, we stood level with our well-lit courthouse dome. There we sorted and placed steel reinforcing rods and pushed wheelbarrows of cement along plank runways over mesh-covered forms to wherever a new load was needed. Once my barrow lurched so that I stumbled toward a rail, and a co-worker caught my arm and steadied me. I won't say I would have plunged through the flimsy plank railing and fallen, but I might have. I remember seeing the ground beneath me for half a second before I caught myself, as he caught me, and I remember the smile we exchanged as he steadied me, and I regained my footing.

A classmate already known to have served time in the state reform school was also on the job. One night he stood below, patting his windbreaker pocket, asking men if they wanted to see what he had. He said he had a gun. Eventually he rose up top on the bucket rim. But he never got to work. The foreman wanted to see the gun and then wanted to take it. Marion wouldn't permit that, so the foreman dismissed him on the spot. It's a persistent image, Marion standing with a few men atop an adjacent tower, their voices accenting the shadowy, summer night, not angry but insistent. Then Marion turning and descending on the bucket's rim. He looked small enough once below, his shoulders hunched, striding off into the night. He didn't come back to school that fall and never returned to us.

I've long since lost that essay, but my instructor found in it, from me, for the first and only time, a note of my being out in the open, unfrisked, perhaps, and venturing exposure. A long swatch of it was the lone example he offered our class on our last day. A classmate who had been in that same section surprised me by reminding me of my essay at our fiftieth reunion. Now a physician, he remembered detail, after fifty-four years, and so reminded me. He remembered because he felt he had learned something: as he put it, writing could be indirect and be the better for it. He said that moment confirmed his scientific bent, just as my mediocrity in a required calculus-physics course tipped me in the opposite direction, which led almost twenty years later to Iowa.

Where, over a good many years, I gradually discovered something like a principle of writers and writing. Many writers, most perhaps, when tasked with writing as a task, begin looking for an exit almost as soon as they start. "How can I get out of here?" is their guiding question. Others, fewer, writers you don't really have to teach although you may be able to coach, take to the page wondering what they can do with it, how they can make that page, and the next one, open up. If you could give the first group of writers the advantage of the second, our problems of teaching Judy and Johnny to write would be solved. The assignment sequence I struggled with and those we invented later attack that problem. Insofar as they manage to engage the student as a person, that person, almost a writer, begins to sense within the self ideas and feelings as yet undiscovered. It's as if one is surprised by finding a forgotten item in a pocket that it would be best to take out and look at before that pocket gets picked. Holding it, looking at it more closely, and rubbing it up a bit leads to invention, while invention summons an inventor.

Taking this a step further, I would suggest that invention stems from seeing intently. Quick leaps to what you think is there, without looking closely, almost always land on clichés. I am reminded of several writing texts from years ago. They liked to posit four kinds of writing: description, explanation, narration, and argument. Furthermore they organized those kinds as a hierarchy with description on the bottom, argument on top. Right off I scoffed at the suggestion that argument should outrank all the great narratives—whichever ones you care to name. But I realized too that the context was our preparation of first-year students for future academic work, most of which would in fact privilege argument. It probably took me another decade, maybe two, to go further and focus on description as much more than just work to be got over quickly before the serious stuff. Fresh description is what counts. Writers who make that discovery work from new ground where they can be "got at." Perhaps frisked. But that's where a writer's adventure begins.

All of this took us a long way, and I had the privilege of teaching writing for years with Carl and Jix, and a host of colleagues who became friends: Paul Diehl,

Susan Lohafer, Carol de St. Victor, Fred Woodard, John Harper, Brooks Landon, Patricia Foster, Jeff Porter, Robin Hemley, and John D'Agata. First came the Institute of 1979–1981, then the Nonfiction Writing Program that started shortly before and has gone much further. Collectively, we went a long way in our efforts but not all the way. We never solved the problem of making a good writer of someone for whom writing remains a task, or for whom—and it's usually the same writer—description relies on recitation of what is mostly known. The sequences Jix and Carl devised, like those that fixed my old college course in the memories of a generation of Amherst students, were one way of addressing the problem: invention first. That our Nonfiction M.F.A. Program has leaned more and more toward invention means that its applicants, and then participants, come to us having discovered motives for writing that they can describe in detail. Thus they seduce us into sharing their interests. In effect, the page is already their pasture, and playground: they have made sequences of their own writing already. Usually it's hard to keep up.

Chapter 5. Among the Ruins of Bethsaida: Reflections on Thirty Years of Teaching Creative Nonfiction

John T. Price
University of Nebraska at Omaha

Yesterday, like almost every day after teaching, I walked by the ruins of Bethsaida. Or rather, a few artifacts in a small, glassed-in hallway display and adjacent exhibit room.[1]

For many years, the University of Nebraska at Omaha, where I direct the English department's Creative Nonfiction Writing Program, oversaw the archaeological recovery of that ancient city in what is now the Golan Heights of Israel. Dominating the exhibit is the stele (or arched stone marker) depicting the "moon god," a bull-faced deity with horns the shape of a crescent moon. The stele was originally located at the "inner gateway" to the walled city and dates back to when Bethsaida, founded in the tenth century BCE, served as the capital of the kingdom of Geshur. This Moon God, as the informational sign explains, was among the most important in Mesopotamia and reigned over darkness and simultaneously "created light, the sun, and the world."

Bethsaida was destroyed in 732 BCE by the king of Assyria, and subsequently fell under the jurisdiction of many different rulers and civilizations, many different gods. Jesus is said to have performed mighty works there, including healing a blind man and walking on water and feeding five thousand with only five loaves and two fish. It was the home of at least three of his disciples, and the place where he called on them to become fishers of men.

A few centuries later, floods and tectonic activity caused the Sea of Galilee to retreat south. The once vibrant city dried up, and in another few centuries, its location became so completely forgotten it was believed by some to be a figment of story and imagination. Until it was rediscovered beneath the sand and rock in 1987 by a scholar here at the University of Nebraska at Omaha, Rami Arav. For years, Professor Arav enlisted UNO faculty and students to help at the dig site, and the exhibit includes a few of their journals and scrapbooks.

I was not among those faculty who visited Bethsaida, but yesterday I carried with me, as if in one of the cracked offering vessels at the foot of the Moon God, a sentence from a student essay I'd just read that made me reconsider the distance. It was written by a woman who had been physically abused by her

---

1. This essay originally appeared in *All Is Leaf: Essays and Transformations*, © John T. Price, and used with the permission of University of Iowa Press.

husband, and the line was: "After months of wandering in the rubble, I knew I needed to rebuild."

You'd think after thirty years of teaching what is now broadly called "creative nonfiction," I'd be more prepared for a line like that, which, divorced from the essay or from the life, is pretty ordinary. But such a divorce is no longer possible for me, if it ever was. That is partly a consequence of the history of my own education as a writer and teacher, which I hold dear, and which I sometimes fear will, like Bethsaida, be lost if I do not in some way commemorate it.

As many others have observed, creative nonfiction is a relatively new term applied to a very old form, which might loosely be defined as fact-based nonfiction that uses creative writing techniques. The label has been retroactively applied to such diverse historical forms as personal essays, memoirs, travel writing, nature writing, narrative nonfiction, lyric essays, speculative nonfiction, prehistoric cave drawings (the first graphic memoirs?), and multiple other sub-genres my students encounter every day, in print or online, but don't think twice about.

Literary taxonomies certainly have their usefulness, but I tell my students that they should also think of literary forms, as with living creatures, in terms of how they behave and interact and reproduce—for art of all sorts does indeed reproduce and evolve over generations and centuries.

What do these forms have to teach us about certain ways of being in the world?

When it comes to creative nonfiction—or literary nonfiction, as some prefer to call it—my answer has a lot to do with the habitat in which I first encountered it. I count myself among the initial generations of university students, in the 1980s and 1990s, to be trained specifically to write and teach creative nonfiction. Not as a sideshow to our primary careers as novelists or poets or scholars or journalists or celebrities, but as our primary calling and craft, for which we earned advanced degrees and then occupied newly created teaching positions in creative nonfiction (the name that first achieved popularity during that time).

At the University of Iowa, when I first arrived as a freshman in 1984, the famous Writers' Workshop did not offer nonfiction courses—not unusual in creative writing programs at the time. That was left to a group of visionary faculty in the English department, led by Carl H. Klaus, most of whom were scholars in literature and rhetoric. They shared, however, a passion for artfully crafted nonfiction and a growing desire to elevate it from an introductory exercise in composition classrooms, where it had been stranded since the 1960s, to its rightful place among the great literary forms. And to offer students a chance to study, practice and teach that art.

I was one of those students. As an undergraduate from a smallish Iowa town, I arrived on campus intending to study the sciences and go on to medical school, which made my grandmother very happy. I was also a big fan of the television medical drama *St. Elsewhere*, and wanted to be just like Denzel Washington—still do. And I wanted to heal people and be rich. While fulfilling those pesky general education humanities classes, however, I encountered, without knowing it, several creative nonfiction writers who also happened to be scientists: Primo Levi (chemist), Rachel Carson (marine biologist), and Loren Eiseley (anthropologist).

Somehow, reading these people didn't feel like a required assignment. It felt more essential, like breathing.

The first opportunity I had to write creative nonfiction myself, outside of that introductory composition assignment, was in an Advanced Writing course taught by Professor Paul Diehl in the summer of 1987—less than a year away from graduation and (I assumed) medical school, where I planned to become a pediatrician. The previous semester, Professor Diehl's literature class on lyric structures in poetry had transformed my relationship to language, which, as an extreme though functioning introvert, had mostly been a source of fear and embarrassment. Professor Diehl apparently detected the small needle of potential in this student's unexceptional haystack, and invited me to join his summer class, which was a slight violation of the rules, since it was a graduate course. Here was an important, early example of the kind of teacher who is willing to risk dishonoring academic "rigor" that they might better honor the talents of their students.

That said, the graduate students in this class were all brilliant, dedicated nonfiction writers, and I sensed the first day that I was way out of my depth. During the next several weeks, however, I did my best to compose an essay about my ongoing job as a nursing assistant for children with developmental disabilities, some of them terminally ill. I had originally taken this job to boost my resume for medical school, but over the years, my experiences with these children had transformed me in profound ways I only first articulated on those pages. The essay was read and discussed—my first experience with serious workshopping—and the responses, in addition to improving the prose, invited me to more closely examine the personal reasons behind that work.

This is another of the many possible definitions of creative nonfiction: using memory and language to trace our ethical lives back to their sources. To cross the distance between the *then* and the *now*, uncovering meaning to share.

That process, with that particular essay, led me to revisit the stillbirth of my brother in 1974 and the feelings I had been carrying inside me, largely unacknowledged, since I was seven years old. With each child I worked with in that hospital, and all those imagined future pediatric patients, I wondered if, in part, I was making up for some personal failing I thought had led to my brother's death. I hadn't been good enough, and never would be.

Maybe it was time to let that go.

While I don't consider creative nonfiction writing to be therapy—there are other degrees for that—its cathartic, personally transformative dimensions should never be dismissed. I'm a living example. In the end, that class taught me a lot about the more technical aspects of good writing, which are valuable in any profession, as English departments frequently trumpet on their websites. But what it also taught me was less easily measured: that the practice of medicine is not the only healing art. A fragment of the human story, previously hidden, revealed and shaped through artful writing by the one who actually lived it, for those who had not, might also claim that ability. For both reader *and* writer.

Soon after, to my grandmother's bitter disappointment, I dropped pre-med and applied to the graduate program in English at Iowa. At the time, their degree in nonfiction writing was called the Master of Arts with an Emphasis in Expository Writing, or M.A.W. Not an ideal acronym, but I have since learned to appreciate how creative nonfiction programs in their infancy often have to learn to live and grow, like hermit crabs, inside the calcified shells of more traditional academic structures. Until they are free to create structures of their own.

And that's exactly what happened. Over the next decade, the program would transform into one of the first stand-alone M.F.A. programs in nonfiction writing in the country, and I would be among its first graduates. We students learned much by watching our mentors, in the guise of both shepherds and warriors, strive to elevate the program to equal status among advanced degrees offered by our university, advocating for precious (and often jealously guarded) resources and faculty lines. It was a cause aided by the excellent teaching in the program, which resulted in excellent student writing and, later, excellent books.

Harder to measure, however, are the ways their teaching improved the quality of our lives, calling us to set forth and become our own kinds of fishers.

Which brings me to another professor of mine at Iowa, Richard Lloyd-Jones. A Victorianist by training, his primary professional interests were in rhetoric, composition, and the teaching of writing, for which he had earned national recognition and awards. I knew none of that when I signed up for his class in the fall of 1990, titled Rhetorical Theory, Analysis, and Application. I was 24 and, unfortunately, this would be the only course I would take with him, since he was nearing retirement.

On the first day of class, he invited us to call him Jix (a surprising intimacy during that era), and all I can say of my initial impression is that he instantly put me at ease. Perhaps it was the bearded, grandfatherly appearance or the pixie-ish smile that rarely wavered, even as he seemed to struggle to breathe. I would later find out he was operating with only part of a lung, due to a teenage bout with bronchiectasis. Every sentence seemed to cost him—but what sentences! They were brilliant and eloquent, yes, but I would also soon learn to appreciate their informing kindness and curiosity and good humor.

There was laughter in that theory classroom, which is no small accomplishment.

The text we used was *The Rhetorical Tradition: Readings from Classical Times to the Present*, a huge tome with thin, semi-transparent pages that made reading them feel like riding a canoe on the surface of an ocean, constantly aware of the depths beneath the oars. Those were some tough waters for me—Aristotle, Locke, Cereta, Nietzsche, Bakhtin, Foucault, Cixous—but it helped to have such a knowledgeable and patient guide. I knew that during the next class, Jix would inevitably bring these luminaries back to earth with his go-to question: "*So why does any of this matter?*" During our often digressive discussions, that was always the orienting issue for him: the application, the relevancy. And most of all, the ways we might use these ideas to become more intentional and helpful as writers, teachers, and moral actors in the world. Everything else was secondary to that quest.

This included, it seemed, his grading policy, which was never mentioned (that I can recall) and would have felt almost blasphemous in a class dedicated to the majesty and ethical power of language. I wrote my final paper on the rhetorician Kenneth Burke and received my first and only A+ in a graduate course. I can't recall why I was initially drawn to Burke, perhaps because the introduction in our book claimed he was "vigorously attacked by both literary critics and rhetoricians for muddling literature and nonliterature, poetic and rhetoric, language and life."

Much like our professor did every day in class.

I didn't appreciate it then, but that course was good preparation for the challenges facing me and other creative nonfiction writers and teachers in the years ahead, many of whom would be vigorously attacked for their own muddling of language and life. In the mid-1990s, even as *The New York Times Magazine* declared it "The Age of the Literary Memoir" and my fellow students were signing lucrative book contracts, there was sometimes an awe-inspiring backlash in newspapers and magazines against "the fourth genre." This includes a still-infamous piece in *Vanity Fair* by Michael Shnayerson, titled "Women Behaving Badly," which implied that popular memoirs by several featured women, some of whom focused on abuse, might be the result of unresolved psychological problems and/or a petty desire to take advantage of a hot memoir market.

Public criticism was also directed at teachers and institutions that offered courses in creative nonfiction, still relatively rare at the time. In 1997, on his show "Politically Incorrect," Bill Maher and his guests skewered college professors teaching memoir writing to students who, they claimed, had experienced little worth writing about. "An exercise in licking the mirror," they deemed it.

Even one of the candidates for the English department's first official creative nonfiction hire claimed, during his visit with students, that he preferred to get personal writing "out of the way" early in the semester then move to more "serious," research-intensive forms such as the cultural criticism he wrote—because, you know, it's all nonfiction. He said this without hesitation or apology to a group of people, ranging from their twenties to their fifties, who were seeking guidance on how to write effectively about personal experiences with, among other things, clinical depression and physical disability and the death of a parent. In contrast, his most recent area of serious research was Barbara Walters.

It is sometimes hard to explain to students in one of the many creative nonfiction courses currently offered in my department, and elsewhere, what it was like back then to be studying, writing and teaching this form while pursuing our degrees. Equally difficult to explain are the challenges that awaited some of us on the other side of graduation. Getting an academic job was no small thing, and still isn't. But then came the sometimes lonely task of building programs from virtually nothing, with little or no resources; founding and editing journals that published nonfiction; organizing and funding (sometimes out of our own pockets) visiting author series; creating entire catalogs of new curricula; advocating for the genre (and for its writers seeking promotion) among colleagues and administrators who had little knowledge of the field; and working locally, regionally, nationally, and internationally to demonstrate the importance of personal stories as a way into social, cultural, and ecological knowledge and understanding. A way into witness.

Today, what seems normal to many in English and creative writing programs is to some of us from that earlier time a miracle—not unlike the loaves and fishes—but one that was the result of Herculean efforts by people we knew and cared about. Still care about.

Most importantly, in the midst of all that, we were trying to mentor our own students as they sought to craft meaningful, public art out of some of the most intensely private experiences. Over the years, I tried one organized pedagogy or another, but ultimately kept returning to what Jix and some of my other nonfiction teachers taught me: to humble yourself to the text and to its author. To fully immerse in the vision laid out before you on the page and to find within that vision, while acknowledging your own potential biases, the standards and expectations it has created for itself.

Then to do your best—through critical analysis but also informed compassion and improvisation—to help that piece live up to its potential, as you interpret it, to transform both writer *and* reader.

For that to occur, I was taught, the work should hold a deep urgency for the teacher, as it does for the writer—even if the writer cannot yet fully articulate that urgency, as I couldn't in that first essay about being a nursing assistant. The work, and the individual life that informs it, should be invited to enter the core of our being and take hold because, we must tell ourselves, this civilization, this world depends on it. Or at least the person seated at that desk in the third row does.

To be trusted with these personal stories and experiences, year after year, is a tremendous privilege, but on some days it feels like something else altogether.

Far from being a "voyeur" (as another 1990s *Vanity Fair* article called memoir readers), I sometimes think I resemble the shape-shifting alien in Ray Bradbury's *The Martian Chronicles*, himself from a lost civilization, who is transformed into the person most loved or hated by the humans around him, until he vanishes entirely under the weight of their desires. High up among those desires, I have found—and I felt it as a student also—is that the creative nonfiction teacher become the long-awaited ideal reader, the one who might not just offer technical advice, but also become the gateway to validation and perhaps publication. The one who will help ensure that their stories—and the life from which they are born—will not be ignored or dismissed or lost or forgotten.

How can I explain to those students or to anyone that their stories, published or not, are never lost? I carry them with me, always.

Just this week, there came back to me three of those stories, those lives—each written on the cusp of distinctly new eras in the history of a civilization. The first occurred when I was purchasing a pastry at our student center, and it had some powdered sugar on it. I was suddenly reminded of the student in the fall of 2001 who wrote a personal essay about 9/11 and being middle-aged and sacrificing most of her personal life in order to take care of her aging mother. The week following the attacks, with all the reports of powdered anthrax, she opened two boxes of chicken potpies—the only dinner she could afford some nights due to her mother's medical bills and other expenses—to find it full of a white powdery substance. She slumped sobbing to the floor, panicked that she would die in that kitchen, cooking potpies for her mother instead of having a life, and called the first response terrorism unit. They soon showed up in their hazmat suits and removed the suspicious substance, which of course turned out to be flour.

Not very long after reading that piece, I watched a local news report on some of the more "unusual" calls to the terrorism unit, which included the potpie incident, but not the story of the aging mother or the medical bills or the vanished personal life.

The second occurred when I entered the men's bathroom on the third floor. I once again avoided the far stall, because a student of mine from a wealthy family in west Omaha had once written about how, after back surgery, he had become addicted to prescribed painkillers and then heroin—well before the national opiate scourge was described as such by mainstream media. This student wrote about how, in that very stall, he had injected heroin into one of his only remaining viable veins, which was in his penis. For him, it was the moment of complete ruination, when he realized he had "roamed in the rubble too long and needed to rebuild," which he did.

Now I look on that stall much the same as I look on the remains of Bethsaida, with the sense that something at once horrifying and sacred took place there. I won't step inside it.

The third occurred while in the midst of teaching a class, simply noticing a desk in the third row that had once been occupied by a quiet, middle-aged, middle school substitute teacher who wrote about nothing more dramatic than his love of teaching, community theatre, and family. A year or so later he took his own life. And yet I can still see him sitting there, hear the words of the essay he read on the final day of class—a work of art, a voice never to be heard again on this earth.

Is this any less important than the fall of empires?

When I think of personal writing teachers who began their careers around the same time I did (or even earlier), I wonder if their days are spent, like mine, roaming through the fragments of such stories, and the memories and wisdom and emotions they evoke. I wonder if we have become a kind of living archaeological site where, inside us, hidden even from ourselves, are the accumulated stories of all the students we've worked with, all the lives we've entered, however briefly, to witness both misery and miracle. Together, we have mentored thousands of these students as they toiled over their sentences, their scenes, their articulated thoughts and feelings and experiences. I wonder if it is true that the life stories we read become in some way a part of our own, completing the grand exercise of compassion that we are told literature is capable of and which, as some of us believe, is its primary purpose.

If so, then over these last thirty years my life has been expanded thousand-fold, tearing down walls and broadening the boundaries of what I might, in some other vocation, have naively considered an individual self.

Within those expanded boundaries, I have vicariously experienced numerous awkward, funny, inspiring, sometimes disturbing family gatherings. I have attended countless funerals and weddings and births and doctor appointments. I have met and loved and grieved every kind of pet imaginable. I have journeyed to beautiful and frightening places, across oceans and in backyards, in old cars and new, in combines and semi-trucks, on bicycles and motorcycles and airplanes, some of which were dropping bombs. I have made love in too many places, in too many ways, with too many people, to possibly recall. I have been married and divorced and remarried and divorced again. I have been lesbian, gay, bi, trans and ace, and been loved as such, but also, as such, been beaten and ostracized and cursed and condemned to hell. I have remained celibate until the night of my sixtieth birthday. I have been a monk who studied wild turkeys, found faith and lost it and found it again. I've had visions of Jesus and Mary and Buddha, recited the Quran, seen the ghosts of ancestors standing at the foot of my bed, and worshipped trees and rocks. I've lost a teenage son in a car crash, adopted sons and daughters, been adopted myself and found my biological parents. I've given birth and had abortions, and been someone who wished they'd never been born. I've been paralyzed and suffered malaria, Lyme disease, breast cancer, cervical cancer—every kind of cancer—a variety of STDs, the full spectrum of mental illness, Crohn's and celiac disease and diabetes-induced blindness, and achieved a full body of tattoos. I've lost my job, worked three jobs, night and day jobs, labor and desk jobs, and still been hungry and full of dreams. I have felt the rage and betrayal and violence of racism. I've been sexually abused by strangers and family members and priests and coaches and employers and neighbors and friends. I have been incarcerated and been set free.

I have died and not gone into the light.

So it continues. With every personal story I read—such as this latest abuse story— there is this opening and excavation, the new words, the new life uncovering other experiences I've read about or remembered, other ways of telling and the new ways they make me see and know and feel. Every time, I ask: How can I help this newly encountered temple of prose draw strength from what has come before, and yet distinguish itself, build itself to the sky, temporary though we know it all to be? How can I assist this word architect in creating something that will last and be remembered by more than a few people in a classroom? How might that work of art unlock hidden rooms inside readers, that the vision can make a home there and do its necessary work? How can I—despite my own limitations—make a home for that vision inside me, where I can preserve and honor it—honor them?

To do so means, within myself, to become transformed—to build and be destroyed and rebuild—with each essay or memoir I encounter. Each student.

~~~

Now, if I were back in that graduate rhetorical theory class, this might be the point when Jix gently interrupts and draws me back to the text at hand, perhaps by Kenneth Burke (whose ideas have stuck with me, despite the decades and fuzzy grading policy), reintroducing the question: "Why does any of this matter?"

Being no expert in Burke, but encouraged by our professor to "make him our own," I might draw liberally from the selected readings for that day, beginning with the selection from *A Rhetoric of Motives* (1950), where he asks, "What is involved when we say what people are doing and why they are doing it?"

Burke's answer involves clarifying the "resources of ambiguity" that lead to "transformation" and "alchemical opportunity," all while acknowledging that, unlike in some "theological notions of creations and recreations"—including perhaps the miracles of a Moon God or a Christ—"in reality, we are capable of but partial acts, acts that but partially represent us and that produce but partial transformations."

Nevertheless, such partial representations and symbolic acts—including, he argues, literature and "personal statements about the loveable and the hateful"—cannot be dismissed as "nonsense." When skillfully rendered, they can lead not just to "persuasion" in a reader, but "identification." They are, in themselves, "real words, involving real tactics, having real demonstrable relationships. And as such, a study of their opportunities, necessities, and embarrassments would be central to the study of human motives."

I might then move on to the assigned selection from *Language as Symbolic Action* (1966), specifically Burke's theory of the "terministic screen"—a selected or received "nomenclature" that "necessarily directs the *at*tention into some channels rather than others" and therefore shapes, even determines, our individual and collective "reality."

Clearly the ruins of Bethsaida—or more accurately, the way they have been organized into a grammar within this exhibit, within the "symbolic environment" of a hallway located physically and culturally within a metropolitan Midwestern university, and received and interpreted by a white, cis-gendered, middle-aged, middle-class professor—have become a terministic screen through which I have come to view the "reality" of my actions as a teacher of creative nonfiction writing. This terministic screen has helped me articulate, but also seemingly contain, an individually experienced reality that, like all those which have come before, in countless civilizations, alive and dead, is ultimately partial, inarticulate and uncontainable.

It has likewise done so by directing "*at*tention" away from certain channels and their competing notions of "reality." This includes deflection from what Burke identifies as "the very scientific ideals of an 'impersonal' terminology" which, as in the case of the Hitlerite Empire, "can contribute ironically to such disaster: for it is but a step from treating inanimate nature as mere 'things' to treating animals, and then enemy peoples, as mere things. But they are not mere things, they are persons—and in the systematic denial of what one knows in his heart to be the truth, there is a perverse principle that can generate much anguish."

"Indeed," he continues, "the very 'global' conditions which call for greater identification of all men with one another have at the same time increased the range of human conflict, the incentives to division. It would require sustained rhetorical effort, backed by the imagery of a richly humane and spontaneous poetry, to make us fully sympathetic with people in circumstances greatly different from our own."

Is this why the writing and teaching of creative nonfiction matters?

Is it—or can it be—a richly humane, spontaneously poetic antidote to the worst within and between those of us who belong to what Burke calls "the often-inhuman human species"?

"*Why not?*" Jix might say, with that pixie-ish smile.

~~~

Across the distance between that class and this hallway, between that unfortunately deceased teacher and his temporarily living student—between the then and the now—I might introduce yet another, final terministic screen, a more recent discovery at the Bethsaida dig site, which is not mentioned in the hallway exhibit.

I read about it last year in *UNO Magazine*, a short article under the title "Finding Romeo and Juliet." It included a photo of two entwined skeletons, an archaeological uncovering that was "the first of its kind in the region, and possibly only the third of its kind in the world—two teenagers, buried together in an apparent embrace." Although UNO Professor Rami Arav, the director of excavations, clarifies that they have "no clue who this couple is or why they were buried together"—did they have experiences "worth" writing about?—their skeletal remains were named after the famous romantic couple because they were discovered during the week of Valentine's Day.

As Burke might say, regardless of original motivations, there is now established a "real" relationship between the symbol and the recipient of the symbol, between the bones and the people at the dig site, and now me. A relationship with new (but equally mysterious) motivations that are now open to new (but equally partial) interpretations, one of which might be that those bones have been granted a sympathetic story of intimacy and identification because, in the end, that is what we hope for ourselves and for those whom we love.

To that I would add my own, more selfish hope: that to every discovery of artful, personal witness, the written words of which might be seen as yet another mysterious collection of bones, readers will grant a story of caring between a teacher and a student.

Regardless, Bethsaida may soon face yet another extinction. Professor Arav has retired from UNO, and our faculty and students no longer work at the dig site. By wintertime, I was recently told, the exhibit I have passed for the last five years will be moved to a college out east and some of the artifacts returned to the Ministry of Antiquities in Israel. The physical memory of this ancient city, its fragments and bones, its stories, will be lost to future generations of students and faculty walking these halls. Bethsaida will no longer be called, daily, into their consciousness or conveniently offered up as a terministic screen through which to view and partially understand human experience. Its sacred stele and offering bowls will be placed within another temporary civilization, another walled fortress of learning and sacrifice, another hallway—another symbolic environment—full of its own opportunities, necessities, and embarrassments. Its own stories of misery and miracle, ruin and rebirth.

Meanwhile, the Moon God will quietly vanish from this portion of the world's darkness, like all those before and after, whether they be deities or students or teachers or friends.

But their light, I can assure you, will remain.

Part Two. Teaching Creative Nonfiction: Practices and Values

Chapter 6. A Compositionist Teaches Creative Nonfiction

Bruce Ballenger
BOISE STATE UNIVERSITY

A few years ago, the M.F.A. and undergraduate creative writing programs unexpectedly left my English department, joining theater and several other programs in a new School of the Arts. The decision to leave was negotiated secretly with the president's office and stunned most department members. Among them were the rhetoric and composition faculty—myself included—who had for years staffed the creative nonfiction offerings, including the introductory undergraduate course and the graduate M.F.A. workshop. The graduate course would surely leave with the M.F.A. But what about the undergraduate class? Introduction to Creative Nonfiction was originally conceived by the rhetoric and composition faculty, who also taught—and cherished—the course. Unsurprisingly, the creative writing faculty argued that English 204 was a "creative" writing course, and therefore belonged with them as part of their new undergraduate curriculum. The department's appeal to the dean to keep our course in English had to address the obvious issue of duplication: How would the department's version of Introduction to Creative Nonfiction differ from the one that would be offered by creative writing? In other words, do compositionists teach creative nonfiction differently than creative writers?

This is the question I hope to explore in this essay. It's not simply a disciplinary question for me, but a quite personal one, since I've written and published in both creative nonfiction and composition studies, at times awkwardly straddling the two. It's a conflict I've always felt most keenly when I teach the graduate creative nonfiction workshop, which typically includes a mix of both M.F.A. and M.A. students—one group strongly identifying as experienced creative writers and the other as budding scholars and novice creative writers. As I gaze around the table at these students in the first few days of the course, each nervously eyeing each other, I also see myself, shifting from one foot to the other: Who am I? Creative writer or rhetoric and composition specialist? The answer, of course, is both, but the tension feels real and unsettling, and I've never quite sorted it out, even after all this time. I suspect some of these conflicted feelings come from what Zukas and Malcolm called "pedagogic identity." What's mine? And to what extent is it at odds with my disciplinary allegiances?

In the crudest sense, those interested in the teaching of creative writing frame this identity around what is valued more: the writer or the teacher. While this is arguably a false binary, it does often figure into hiring decisions, as well as the reward system for tenure-track faculty. Teaching positions in creative writing (including lecturer and part-time) typically prioritize applicants' publishing records over their teaching credentials, especially in M.F.A. programs. Kelly Ritter calls it the "star" system, where famous "writers are hired to teach; such teaching however is usually incidental by design" (283). Once hired, tenure-track creative writing faculty are typically promoted because of their literary publications, not articles on pedagogy (Fodrey). In many ways, this all makes sense. But the system does seem to reinforce an identity that favors writer over teacher, elevating expertise in craft over pedagogy. I can offer some local and anecdotal evidence of this: the creative writing pedagogy course in our M.F.A. program was designed by rhetoric and composition faculty and has rarely been taught. When it was, the instructor was almost always from rhetoric and composition.

I've long found this writer-teacher split in pedagogic identity uncomfortable. The foot I lean on most—the one firmly in composition studies—rests on studying and theorizing teaching. But I also have a graduate degree in creative nonfiction, and my training as a compositionist began as a student of Donald Murray, a Pulitzer Prize winner who often felt like an outlier in the field, in part because his credentials were as a practitioner rather than a scholar. Another composition studies luminary who struggled with competing pedagogic identities was, of course, Wendy Bishop, who wrote that "some days I am a writer-who-teaches (WT), and on others I am a teacher-who-writes (TW), but inevitably, always, I am one or the other." She adds, "For me, the first (WT) is represented by the figure of Donald Murray" ("Places" 14).

Naturally, as a young writing teacher I wanted to be like Don, one whose authority came, in part, from his success as a writer. But as the years went on, I also began to recognize the limitations of the WT pedagogy (and Don's). For one thing, my writerly experiences might be peculiar to me and not necessarily helpful to my students, who often come from different backgrounds and social situations, and so my frequent classroom references to "the writer" began to feel uncomfortable. I knew it was often a coded reference to me. In *The Triggering Town*, the poet Richard Hugo's book about craft, he tells his student readers that "you'll never be a poet until you realize that everything I say today and this quarter is wrong. It may be right for me, but it is wrong for you. Every moment, I am, without wanting or trying to, telling you how to write like me. But I hope you learn to write like you" (3). I really admire this, and I've often shared it with my own creative nonfiction students at the beginning of the semester, but I also know that it's disingenuous. As long as we privilege the "master craftsman" as the source of pedagogic authority in the creative writing class, students will try to write like us, no matter what we say.

I think most compositionists who teach creative nonfiction identify as teachers-who-write, not writers-who-teach, either by necessity—they haven't published widely in literary journals—or (and I think this is more often the case) by training. Sensitive to issues of power and authority in the classroom, our training in rhetoric and composition makes us inclined to take a more constructivist approach, seeing ourselves as "facilitators" or "co-constructors of knowledge" (Manery 208), and this has implications in how we teach creative nonfiction, beginning with the dominant pedagogic approach in creative writing: the workshop.

The Compositionist's Creative Nonfiction Workshop and Its Dilemmas

Though there are many critics of the workshop, it remains a fixture in creative writing classrooms, often used with little variation from the original University of Iowa model. Throughout the semester, students generate drafts for "critique" in full-class workshop sessions. They are instructed not to speak during these discussions, allowing the work to speak for itself. The instructor plays a largely facilitative role at first, but at some point, typically offers judgments and suggestions. If he or she adopts the pedagogic identity of "master craftsman," this is a particularly dramatic moment in the workshop, one that can elevate or deflate the student writer's spirits. It is also a moment that commands everyone's attention as the instructor narrows the focus to flag the key problems in the draft. I taught this version of the workshop for many years, bowing, I think, to the expectation that this was the way it must be done. But I always felt conflicted about it, especially after my training as a compositionist. As hard as I tried to facilitate full-class workshops so that they weren't teacher-driven, including minimizing my own comments and trying to summarize for the writer the patterns I was hearing in the student critiques, I often felt vulnerable to the expectation that in the end it was my judgment of the work that mattered. It was in these moments, usually the final five minutes of workshopping a student essay, where I felt compelled to shift into the persona of master craftsman, putting at risk all my efforts to keep the discussion student-centered. In short, this was the moment when I felt most at war with my identity as a compositionist who teaches creative nonfiction.

The struggle here, one that is very familiar to those of us trained in rhetoric and composition, is how to manage the instructor's authority. This is often less of an issue for creative writing teachers who assume the conventional pedagogic identity of master craftsman; in that case, the authority to judge artistic merit of student work is unambiguous. However, it's much more complicated for the compositionist. Ben Ristow frames the problem like this: "The workshop leader functions as the ballast in classroom instruction, and this power brings forward the pivotal question: How do instructors maneuver their authority in a workshop without impinging on the artistic practice of the writer?" Ristow suggests that "creative writing teachers should imagine themselves as a fluid character, an almost amphibious figure that moves between roles as publishing writer, constructive mentor, workshop facilitator, and more" (95). Drawing on the sophistic tradition, he argues that the workshop should be founded on the principle that more than one idea about a draft can simultaneously be true, and discussion should be organized around the inconsistencies and contradictions in the workshop participants' readings of the draft. In this "neosophistic" workshop, the instructor's role is to point out these contradictions and facilitate a conversation about them, expanding the writer's choices for revision rather than narrowing them down (97).

What this requires is the willingness to listen intently to what students are saying in workshop; it also demands a tolerance for ambiguity. Instructors must resist the pull to assert their authority, and students must accept that the guidance they receive from workshop may complicate revision rather than clarify it. Because of its dominance as a pedagogy, any alternative to the traditional workshop like this one requires something that rarely happens in most creative writing classes: an interrogation of the workshop model itself. What are the critiques? How do conventional workshops confer power and authority? How does this affect the making of art? And especially, what are students' and instructors' experiences with it as writers? This is all familiar metacognitive terrain for the compositionist, and so creative nonfiction students in our classes might begin the course by reading and discussing articles like Francois Camoin's "Reconsidering the Workshop: The Workshop and Its Discontents," or Lex Wilford's "Toward a More Open, Democratic Workshop." When I've done this, it's a rich conversation, and helpfully seeds a discussion about how we will agree to conduct the workshop that semester. I can also clarify the role that I hope to play.

These conversations about workshop conventions often lead us to examine the so-called gag rule, in which students presenting drafts must remain silent as the work is discussed. There are sensible reasons for this—it forces student authors to listen carefully to comments, and it mutes their influence on how readers construe the work's meaning. This seems especially appropriate for fiction and poetry, which often feature ambiguous, implicit meanings. But the gag rule seems much less appropriate for nonfiction, which is typically distinguished by a more explicit purpose. One of the great challenges of writing creative nonfiction is trying to clarify one's intentions in the work so that it can be made apparent to readers. While it would certainly be useful for nonfiction writers to test their success at communicating these intentions by remaining silent in workshop, I think it makes little sense to short-circuit this conversation entirely; to do so would be a missed opportunity to talk over possible meanings with workshop members. This is, of course, a discussion of the rhetorical dimensions of the work, and in particular, it examines the rich moment when a writer's tentative purpose comes into contact with a reader's initial understanding of that purpose. The basic script goes something like this:

> Writer: *This is what I think I was trying to say.*
>
> Reader: *This is what I understood you to be saying.*
>
> Writer and Reader: *What might be said that isn't in the draft?*

It is from this conversation that the nonfiction writer will learn the most from a workshop. While the back and forth about whether a scene is working or the voice is appropriate can be illuminating, the real work, particularly in early drafts and personal essays, is hammering out the writer's purpose, and silencing this conversation with the gag rule makes that work harder. I've experimented with several ways to break this silence, including encouraging student authors to introduce their drafts before we discuss them, highlighting the problems they are trying to solve. I've also tried making space for this conversation in the final five minutes, after the work has been discussed. But I almost always allow workshop participants, at some point, to query a work's author, and this often sparks useful conversations that wouldn't happen if the gag rule were in effect.

Alterations like these in the workshop do make it more constructivist, and potentially more student-centered, but I must admit that I am still often disappointed in myself when I lead these workshops. The Iowa tradition, especially the specter of writer-who-teaches, haunts workshops, and despite my best efforts, I often feel that students are disappointed when I don't act like a Famous Author. I do my best to undermine this. I no longer sit at the head of the table. I try to keep my mouth shut and listen. I explicitly clarify the role I will take in workshop. In short, I try to behave like the student-centered teacher I've been trained to be. Then I hear myself taking over, usually in those last five minutes of the workshop: "I agree with what a lot of what you have said, that Emery's draft seems to be about two ideas, neither of which are developed sufficiently. The more significant idea to me is . . ." People nod, and I feel smart. Then a few minutes later I realize that I've surrendered my pedagogic identity again. Of course, it isn't that I'm giving bad advice, though I sometimes do. And I could have been much worse. I never behave like the "charming tyrant," a version of the Famous Author persona who offers pronouncements on the literary worth of the work (e.g., "I feel like I've read this story before") and who is determined to replicate themselves in their students (Cain 35). The problem is that I've been trained not to take over students' writing, and the full-class workshop is often an invitation for me to do exactly that. At some point, I asked myself what now seems like an obvious question: Should the full-class workshop be the center of my creative nonfiction course? And if it weren't, what would I replace it with? One answer seemed obvious: compositionists focus on the writing process.

De-mystifying Process

The conventional creative writing workshop is certainly a kind of process pedagogy. It draws students' attention to the draft as a transitive moment in meaning-making, one that involves the complicating influences of audience and purpose. Revision is obviously central, and classroom instruction does address the process through discussion of craft. In creative nonfiction, for example, we might talk about how to explode significant moments into scenes, how and where to make reflective turns, or where research might help. But the pedagogy of craft works around the edges of process, focusing attention on burnishing the product not engaging in *how* the work is made or remade. I suspect some of this has to do with the view that the creation of art is not only idiosyncratic, but mysterious. Or maybe uninteresting. One of the things that strikes me when I go to readings by celebrated creative writers is how impatient many are with audience questions about process: "Where do you get your ideas for a story?" "How do you get started?" "Do you ever get writer's block?" As a rhetoric and composition specialist, I find these questions fascinating. Some Famous Authors, perhaps finding them tiresome, do not.

My training as a compositionist tells me to use a problem-centered approach to analyze the writing process, and I've always focused much of my attention on invention. For example, students tend to write from scarcity. They struggle to find topics and generate material. They over-commit to an initial idea. When problems arise, they get stuck. Remarkably, invention is an aspect of composing that receives little attention in most creative writing classes, especially at the graduate level where it's assumed that students have figured that all out. A focus on invention—the many ways to use a notebook, strategies for generating and using "bad" writing, and research methods—strikes me as an instructional approach that might most distinguish how I teach creative nonfiction from my colleagues who are creative writers. A few years ago, for example, I restructured my M.F.A. creative nonfiction workshop in two ways. First, I postponed any full-class workshops until mid-semester and replaced them with smaller peer groups, where students shared and discussed "sketches," or relatively brief, often tentative experiments with material. Each student wrote four of these, hoping that two might be developed into drafts. I did not participate in these peer review workshops. The second innovation was to introduce a new set of readings about "writing practice," which became the basis for writing and discussion that focused on generating material, finding subjects, and developing helpful habits. These readings included pieces from the world of composition studies, including Murray's "Write Before Writing," as well as more popular works like Natalie Goldberg's "Writing as Practice" and excerpts from William Stafford's *Writing the Australian Crawl*. We studied how writers use notebooks and journals. We told stories about how our writing methods have evolved, and the changes we hope to experiment with during the semester.

For many of the students, especially those enrolled in the M.F.A., this was the first time since their composition courses that they had engaged in a conversation about how they work, and our focus on invention challenged them to consider not only how to generate material for essays but how to choose the best material, and because I began the course with an introduction to some of the subgenres of creative nonfiction, students could also decide what forms seemed best suited to a particular project. There is little incentive for student writers to experiment like this in the conventional workshop course. Instead, they are captive to workshop deadlines where authors are expected to present full drafts to which they become committed, often prematurely. The process of how writers find and develop this work is largely ignored. The making of art *is* mysterious in some ways, but no more so than how first-year writers try to compose an academic essay, and compositionists are inclined to take an equal interest in both.

What Do Creative Writers Need to Know about Genre?

In my inbox the other day was an email in which a published essayist offered—for a fee—to review manuscripts. In her biography, she noted that "I don't believe in genre. I believe a work stands or it falls regardless of what it's called." This is a common sentiment, especially among creative writers, and it comes, I think, from the laudable conviction that good art doesn't behave and shouldn't be disciplined. Genre, especially if it's seen as little more than taxonomizing, shackles the work to a category and is hopelessly reductive. Besides, what creative writer actually thinks much about genre except in the broadest sense—this is fiction or nonfiction—or more narrowly as a subcategory of work: lyric essay, short story, memoir, and so on? Even then, does it really influence the act of creation? As a result, creative writing courses typically sidestep much explicit consideration of genre, which is viewed as largely irrelevant to the real work of an artist.

As Amy Devitt points out (696), genre study is a common project for the disciplines in English studies, and with the departure of the creative writing program from English at my university, their courses are even less likely to consider genre theory. But what about the creative nonfiction courses that remain in English? Genre has been a major interest of scholars in composition studies since the 1980s, which moved theory well beyond the original Aristotelian categorization of forms to consider genre as a rhetorical concept (Devitt 697–698). This scholarship has inspired classroom pedagogies that often involve rhetorical and critical analyses of genre, and from this a whole range of new pedagogies for writing classrooms, some of them pioneered by Richard Lloyd-Jones, whose influence we explore in this volume. But the key question here is this: What do creative writers, and more specifically, creative nonfiction writers, need to know about genre?

It's impossible not to at least *broadly* talk about genre, beginning with the nearly inescapable conversation in the first few days of class when someone asks, "what the hell is creative nonfiction, anyway?" This is a question that can easily be dealt with by explaining that creative nonfiction involves factual stories—accounts of what really happened—that are often enriched using literary devices like scene, dialogue, and description. An instructor might then inventory some of the sub-genres—lyric essay, memoir, personal essay, literary journalism, and so on. For the compositionist, this is a key moment. Does one go beyond the taxonomy lesson? Is this an opportunity, say, to crack open the discussion about the status of creative nonfiction, especially compared to fiction and poetry, and talk about how genre classifications are, as Daniel Chandler points out, neither "neutral or objective" (1)? What might be the ideological reasons that nonfiction is sometimes viewed as less imaginative, less artistic, or to put a practical spin on it, less worthy of funding in a creative writing program? (When we founded our own M.F.A. program at Boise State, creative nonfiction was an unfunded third track. Almost 25 years later, it remains so.) In a course focused on students' developing and sharing their own work, is this discussion worth the time? I think that it is, and besides it's hard to avoid when the creative nonfiction class inevitably lands on the explosive topic of truth-telling.

Among the essayists writing about the American West that I most admire is Judy Blunt. The title essay of her 2002 collection, *Breaking Clean*, tells the story of her decision to leave her husband and the ranching life in eastern Montana that she was born into and cherished but had made her feel increasingly powerless and lonely, especially as she began to entertain a life well outside of the role of rancher's wife. In between preparing meals for her husband, Jack, and the ranch hands, Blunt began to write. She ordered a typewriter from Sears and wrote "in a cold sweat on long strips of freezer paper that emerged from the keys thick and rich with ink" (8). Towards the end of the first published version of the essay she writes this: "One day Jack's father, furious because lunch for the hay crew was late, took my warm, green typewriter to the shop and killed it with a sledgehammer." Soon after the essay was published, her father-in-law, the alleged sledgehammer-slinger, wrote a letter to the *Philips County News*, the local newspaper, contesting the account. "No such event ever occurred," he wrote. "This is her story as she chooses to tell it." Blunt later conceded that the typewriter incident was invented and intended to be "symbolic" (Harden).

For teachers of creative nonfiction, this story—or one like it—is also a familiar discussion topic, one that arises from the nearly unavoidable question about whether nonfiction writers can "make things up." More recently, the issue of truth-telling in creative nonfiction focuses on the debate between essayist John D'Agata and his fact-checker from *The Believer* magazine, which is reported in *The Lifespan of a Fact*. The two face off over factual discrepancies in D'Agata's narrative essay about the suicide of a Las Vegas teenager, with D'Agata arguing that creative nonfiction writers have artistic license to change some facts if it improves the story. The fact-checker, obviously, had problems with that. Stories like Blunt's and D'Agata's raise relevant practical questions—what factual matters can a writer play with in nonfiction narrative—as well as ethical questions—what obligations do nonfiction writers have to the living (and dead) characters that they write about? For those of us trained in rhetoric and composition, these stories also implicate genre theory in dramatic and interesting ways.

For one thing, the debate over truth-telling in nonfiction highlights the idea that genre has social consequences. No matter how deeply invested writers are in what Bishop called "the myth of free creativity" ("Crossing" 186), they work within a rhetorical ecosystem in which genre is weighted with social expectations. Readers of nonfiction form a set of assumptions about factual reporting, and when these are challenged, the authority of the work—and specifically the ethos of the writer—is at risk. There is no more dramatic example of this than James Frey's public humiliation on national television by Oprah over the fabrications in his memoir, *A Million Little Pieces*. "It is difficult for me to talk to you because I feel really duped," Oprah told Frey. "But more importantly, I feel that you betrayed millions of readers" (Wyatt). Creative nonfiction writers can choose to ignore these social consequences, but they can't escape them, and sometimes they change the work. Judy Blunt, for example, agreed to omit mention of the typewriter smashing incident in subsequent editions of *Breaking Clean*. For many years, I framed classroom conversations about controversies like these as case studies in the ethics of telling true stories. But as I began to understand them as episodes that also illuminate genre theory, I was more explicit about discussing it in those terms.

As writing theorists remind us, genres arise not simply to fulfill an artistic vision but to solve rhetorical problems. One way to understand, say, the personal essay is to analyze the work that it can do for writers and how it's used by readers. This leads to a discussion about motive and purpose, one that I think is not only a natural move when analyzing rhetorical situation, but essential when working with nonfiction prose. While some critics like Jane Tompkins argued that the purpose of literary art is to "do nothing" (qtd. in Bishop, "Suddenly Sexy" 261), I think that creative nonfiction does work in the world, and it's useful for writers to know what that can be.

A Case Study in Genre Theory: The Personal Essay

One way to explore this is to examine the historical contexts for a genre's rise and evolution, and for the personal essay one might begin with Montaigne. Trained in the scholastic tradition, Montaigne, like many of his literate 16th century contemporaries, was a writer who typically composed in Latin and heavily relied on formal rhetorical structures and proofs for organizing his prose. At some point, he found these conventions utterly inadequate as a mode of expressing his personal experience of a world upended by the butchery of the French religious civil wars and the mass death of the plague. To write about this, Montaigne needed a language that was closer to the reality of his experiences, and vernacular French proved far more expressive than Latin. The argumentative proofs of classical rhetoric also proved inadequate as a lens for making sense of his turbulent, uncertain times, and so Montaigne adopted a digressive, looping structure, one that allowed him to seek to coordinate his experiences rather than subordinate them to some preconceived claim. He gave us what he called the essay—"an attempt" at understanding—and his motive was not to prove, but to find out.

What does a creative nonfiction writer gain by knowing all of this? For one thing, it's helpful to see the work as part of a historical tradition, and this long view not only helps writers to place their own work in that tradition but to see the kinds of problems a genre is invented to address. For example, why write an essay instead of a memoir? Beginning with Montaigne, writers turn to the essay when faced with personal uncertainty, when they want to want to think something through. While both personal essay and memoir, like most stories, are often organized around a significant event, the essay's concerns are often narrower, and even prosaic. One might write an essay about thumbs, for example. Because of its relative brevity, an essay's narrative is limited, especially compared to memoir, and sometimes essays rely more heavily on exposition than story because essays are designed to be vehicles of thought. All of this becomes clearer—and more compelling, I think—when viewed as genre history, especially when the record also shows how, when faced with new audiences and new modes of expression, a genre evolves and changes.

In the 18th century, the essay became shorter, and more focused on character studies, in part because the emerging middle class in England, anxious to learn more about the morals and manners of the upper class, began to read essays in periodicals while sipping coffee in cafes. The periodical essay was often a cup long. More recently, the essay has morphed into the blog, which not only found new audiences but democratized the form. The speed and relative lack of polish of the blog created a new medium for essayists to explore the meaning of recent events in especially tentative ways. Some of this genre history can be dramatized for creative nonfiction students by bookending readings in a course. Recently, I've taken to teaching several Montaigne essays alongside contemporary ones, an exercise that sparks lively discussions about the patterns in the genre that endure—and those that don't. It's an exercise that also lays bare the ideological orientations of the genre, one that historically relied on male authority but later made room for women's voices. But how, we wonder? And soon we're talking about the rhetorical power—and risks—of personal disclosure, and how men and women find different ways of dealing with it in the personal essay genre. In other words, we theorize.

Obviously, theory has long dominated literary study, but creative writing courses largely avoid it, and I think I'm arguing here for the relevance of theory in a course focused on the creation of literature. An understanding of how genres are used, how they evolve, and their ideological and rhetorical orientations seems like useful knowledge to creative nonfiction writers. If nothing else, genre theory helps writers to recognize that recurring patterns in the work aren't accidental nor are they necessarily mysterious. The study of craft—which will always be a central concern in any creative writing course—also becomes a study of genre. For instance, the balance between showing and telling in a work—a question of craft that consumes a lot of the creative nonfiction courses I teach—could be viewed as arbitrary or idiosyncratic. "I'm really into story," a student might say, "and I don't much care for telling readers everything that they should figure out on their own." This is a student who might be naturally drawn to lyric essays, many of which rely more heavily on implicit meaning, but who then struggles when asked to write a more traditional personal essay, a think piece. "I'm just not into that kind of writing," he might decide.

As instructors, we could leave it at that ("let him follow his own muse"), but as compositionists, we see this as an opportunity to have a conversation about genre. A lyric essay and a think piece are doing different kinds of work, and therefore use different conventions. The drama of the personal essay for readers is watching a writer think something through, so exposition—the language of thought—is often more central than narrative. "It's fine that you prefer story-focused nonfiction over think pieces," we might say, "but don't ignore the power of expository prose to help you discover what you think." In other words, pay attention to genre conventions because they do work that might be useful to you.

While creative writing curricula, particularly at the graduate level, try to cultivate single-genre specialists—"I'm a fiction writer" or "I'm a poet"—I think compositionists are more interested in creating flexible writers who can fluidly move between and within genres, making conscious decisions about what genres are appropriate for a particular project or recognizing what the conventions might be and whether they're useful. This flexibility seems especially important in nonfiction, a particularly large tent, with subgenres that range from investigative work to essays that read like prose poems.

I wonder if, in the end, the thing that most distinguishes how a compositionist teaches creative nonfiction from a creative writer is differing positions on artists' agency. If you believe that all writing is rhetorical, it's impossible to see the creation of literary texts as any different, especially if those texts are intended to do some work in the world. If you believe this, then you must also believe that while creation is an imaginative act, and the artist has considerable freedom to invent, it is a freedom that is always constrained in some ways, and that knowledge of these constraints—we usually call this rhetorical knowledge—is extremely useful for writers. It increases their freedom to invent by making the choices clearer. And so when those of us trained in rhetoric and composition teach creative nonfiction, we are likely to see the artists in our charge as writers quite like those in our advanced composition and argument courses. They are still trying to work out writing processes to generate and shape material. Some are entering a discourse community with which they have little experience, and they are trying to find the authority to speak their truths. The traditional workshop model, for all its strengths, isn't enough to teach what these students need to know.

The English department got to keep its undergraduate courses in creative nonfiction, and the creative writing program created their own workshop-focused versions. This is good for all sorts of reasons. It short-circuited any potential animosity between creative writing faculty and compositionists, assigning pedagogical value to both approaches to teaching the subject. The classes provide students with different ways of understanding how to write (and read) creative nonfiction. The crisis over whether the courses would stay or go also gave our writing faculty an opportunity to better articulate the claim that the rhetoric and composition discipline has over the teaching and study of creative nonfiction. Richard Lloyd-Jones, writing about the future of the profession, suggested that "what we can expect to have is what we value enough to fight for and what we can get others to value as we do" (202). Many of us trained in composition are deeply committed to the teaching and study of creative nonfiction. We need to say so, and to keep imagining all that we can bring.

Works Cited

Bishop, Wendy. "Places to Stand: The Reflective Writer-Teacher-Writer in Composition." *College Composition and Communication,* vol. 51, no. 1, Sept. 1999, pp. 9–31.

———. "Suddenly Sexy: Creative Nonfiction Rear-ends Composition." *College English,* vol. 65, no. 3, Jan. 2003, pp. 257–275.

———. "Crossing the Lines: On Creative Composition and Composing Creative Writing." *Colors of a Different Horse: Rethinking Creative Writing Theory and Pedagogy,* edited by Wendy Bishop and Hans Ostrom, NCTE, 1994, pp. 181–197.

Blunt, Judy. *Breaking Clean.* Vintage, 2002.

Cain, Mary Ann. "Revisiting Charming Tyrants and Faceless Facilitators: The Lore of Teaching Identities in Creative Writing." *Can Creative Writing Really Be Taught?: Resisting Lore in Creative Writing,* edited by Stephanie Vanderslice and Rebecca Manery, Bloomsbury, 2017, pp. 35–43.

Camoin, Francois. "The Workshop and its Discontents." *Colors of a Different Horse: Rethinking Creative Writing Theory and Pedagogy,* edited by Wendy Bishop and Hans Ostrom, NCTE, 1994, pp. 3–7.

Chandler, Daniel. "An Introduction to Genre Theory." *Media and Communication Studies,* Jan. 1997. ResearchGate, www.researchgate.net/publication/242253420 _An_Introduction_to_Genre_Theory.

D'Agata, John and Jim Fingal. *The Lifespan of a Fact.* Norton, 2012.

Devitt, Amy J. "Integrating Rhetorical and Literary Theories of Genre." *College English,* vol. 62, no. 6, July 2000, pp. 696–718.

Fordrey, Crystal N. "Teaching CNF Writing to College Students: A Snapshot of CNF Pedagogical Scholarship." *Assay: A Journal of Nonfiction Studies,* vol. 2.1, fall 2015, www.assayjournal.com/crystal-n-fodrey-teaching-cnf-writing-to-college -students-a-snapshot-of-cnf-pedagogical-scholarship-21.html.

Goldberg, Natalie. *Writing Down the Bones.* Shambala, 1986.

Harden, Blaine. "Writers in Place: Suffering and Creativity." *New York Times,* 28 May 2002, www.nytimes.com/2002/05/28/books/writers-in-place-suffering-and -creativity.html.

Hugo, Richard. *The Triggering Town: Lectures and Essays on Poetry and Writing.* Norton, 1992.

Lloyd-Jones, Richard. "What We May Become." *College Composition and Communication,* vol. 33, no. 2, May 1982, pp. 202–207.

Malcolm, Janice and Miriam Zukas. "Constructing Pedagogic Identities: Versions of the Education in AE and HE." *Kansas State Adult Education Research Conference: 2000 Conference Proceedings,* New Prairie Press, 2000, newprairiepress.org /aerc/2000/papers/49.

Manery, Rebecca. "Revisiting the Pedagogy and Theory Corral: Creative Writing Pedagogy Teachers' Conceptions of Pedagogic Identity." *New Writing: International Journal for the Practice and Theory of Creative Writing,* vol. 12, no. 2, 2015, pp. 205–215, dx.doi.org/10.1080/14790726.2015.1040030.

Murray, Donald. "Write Before Writing." *The Essential Don Murray: Lessons from America's Greatest Writing Teacher.* Heineman, 2009, pp. 28–38.

Ristow, Ben. "Performances in Contradiction: Facilitating a Neosophistic Creative Writing Workshop." *New Writing: International Journal for the Practice and Theory of Creative Writing,* vol. 11, no. 1, 2014, pp. 92–99, doi.org/10.1080/14790726.2013.871040.

Ritter, Kelly. "Ethos Interrupted: Diffusing 'Star' Pedagogy in Creative Writing Programs." *College English,* vol. 69, no. 3, Jan. 2007, pp. 283–292.

Stafford, *Writing the Australian Crawl: Views on the Writer's Vocation.* U of Michigan P, 1978.

Wilford, Lex. "Toward a More Open, Democratic Workshop." *Poets and Writers,* vol. 26, no. 2, March/April 1998.

Wyatt, Edward. "Author Is Kicked Out of Oprah Winfrey's Book Club." *New York Times,* 27 Jan. 2006, http://www.nytimes.com/2006/01/27/books/27oprah.html.

Chapter 7. A Harmony of Variables

Robert Root
CENTRAL MICHIGAN UNIVERSITY AND ASHLAND UNIVERSITY

Early in *Research in Written Composition*, Richard Braddock, Richard Lloyd-Jones, and Lowell Schoer discuss variables that affect the rating of compositions. They begin with the Writer Variable:

> One of the fundamental measures in research into the teaching of composition is, of course, the general evaluation of actual writing. Often referred to as measures of writing ability, composition examinations are always measures of writing performance; that is, when one evaluates an example of a student's writing, he cannot be sure that the student is fully using his ability, is writing as well as he can. Something may be causing the student to write below his capacity: a case of the sniffles, a gasoline lawnmower outside the examination room, or some distracting personal concern. If a student's writing performance is consistently low, one may say that he has demonstrated poor ability, but often one cannot say positively that he has poor ability; perhaps the student has latent writing powers which can be evoked by the right instruction, the appropriate topic, or a genuine need for effective writing in the student's own life. (6)

They argue that although "the writer variable cannot be controlled, certainly allowances must be made for it," and recommend evaluating a student's writing more than once to determine the student's ability on the basis of the better of two or more compositions.

The second variable the authors explore is the Assignment Variable, to which they allot four aspects: *"the topic, the mode of discourse, the time afforded for writing, and the examination situation."* In regard to pre- and post-tests, they write, "In planning composition examinations for students from a wide range of backgrounds, it seems especially necessary to consider the student's variations in intellectual maturity, knowledge, and socioeconomic background." They note that "investigators should be mindful of a possible motivational factor in the topic assigned," and argue, "Surely there must be some stimulating factor in a topic and, if possible, in the writing situations too, if the writing they trigger is to have any significance for research" (8). Referring to modes of discourse ("narration, description, exposition, argument, or criticism"), they suggest that "variations in modes of discourse may have more effect than variations in topic on the quality of writing" (8).

The other two aspects in the Assignment Variable (time allotted for writing and examination situation) and two further variables, the Rater Variable and the Colleague Variable, specifically address the complications of determining student writing ability through set composition examinations, and essentially the rest of the book considers the ways in which research in written composition is conducted, both in general and through close examination of extensive reports on such research. The bibliography runs over 500 entries long and covers a panoply of published and unpublished research projects. It's definitely a landmark study of composition practices.

The questions that Braddock, Lloyd-Jones, and Schoer raise in *Research in Written Composition* about the evaluation of student writing performance in testing situations undergird any number of subsequent studies of student writing and guides to composing, works that cover a wider range of writing assignments and occasions than essay examinations. Such texts as *Teaching the Universe of Discourse* by James Moffett (1968), *A Writer Teaches Writing: A Practical Method of Teaching Composition* by Donald Murray (1968), *Telling Writing* by Ken Macrorie (1970), *The Composing Processes of Twelfth Graders* by Janet Emig (1971), *Writing Without Teachers* by Peter Elbow (1973), *The Development of Writing Abilities (11–18)* by James Britton et al. (1975), and *Errors and Expectations: A Guide for the Teacher of Basic Writing* by Mina Shaughnessy (1977) expanded and solidified ideas broached in *Research in Written Composition*. Cumulatively they precipitated what we termed at the time "a paradigm shift" in the teaching of composition; they moved the field away from the "current-traditional" product-centered approach, which focused on quality of end-products, to a process-centered approach, which focused on ways student texts come into being and strategies that would make those texts more accomplished. Essentially, attention in composition/rhetoric/discourse theory turned toward stages of the composing process—pre-writing, drafting, revising, editing and proofing. A host of ideas and strategies surfaced that offered students more motivational ways into the topic and discourse modes of the assignment variable and more promising ways to use the inevitable vagaries of the composing process to enhance and culminate expression. It was an exciting time to be thinking and writing about composition.

~~~

Reading *Research in Written Composition* now, more than half a century after it was first published and more than forty years after I first was exposed to it, I found its relevance still to be current in regard to "the general evaluation of actual writing" in its broadest applications. For example, as I read, both old arguments with faculty colleagues and recent conversations with fellow creative nonfiction teachers started reverberating in my brain; all confirmed Braddock, Lloyd-Jones, and Schoer's sense of "the tendency of a rater to vary in his own standards of evaluation" and "the tendency of several raters to vary from each other in their evaluations" (10–11). But I prefer to dwell on the ideas inherent in their first two variables, the Writer Variable and the Assignment Variable (especially the topic and mode aspects), since they seem to me to get to the center of learning and teaching both composition and creative nonfiction. They also make me aware of how much they apply to the challenges of my writing this very article.

Take, for instance, the aspects of the Assignment Variable, particularly the "possible motivational factor in the topic assigned." Proposing to edit a collection of essays on nonfiction and pedagogy in honor of Richard (Jix) Lloyd-Jones which would "explore conceptual and practical matters in teaching nonfiction as opposed to teaching composition, rhetoric, argument, academic discourse, technical communication, or other foci for writing," Laura Julier and Doug Hesse asked a number of writing teachers, "What would you like to see addressed in such a collection? What are the questions that carry some immediacy or urgency or persistence when you think about yourselves as teachers of nonfiction? What would *you* like to write about in regards to any of the above?" Note the possibilities in the Assignment Variable, those three questions that each of the writers queried might respond to in a different way; note as well that the motivational factor inevitably depends on the Writer Variable—specifically, who the writer is affects what topic the writer is drawn to. In my case, the name "Jix" and the phrase "conceptual and practical matters in teaching nonfiction as opposed to teaching composition [or] rhetoric" together set synapses firing all over my brain. Suddenly I'm flashing across time, surfacing almost simultaneously in a profusion of classrooms where I am here a student, here a teacher, here my students are undergraduates, here M.A. candidates, or I am in a welter of library carrels and departmental offices and private studies laboring at manuscripts of students as well as on manuscripts of my own.

I even flash back to a colleague's comment at a CCCCs (Conference on College Composition and Communication) commending my flexibility for, as he put it, "shifting from composition to creative nonfiction." It was supposed to be a compliment, but I remember my surprise at the remark and later realized that I didn't feel as if I'd "shifted" all that much—I was simply doing what I learned at Iowa, from teachers like Carl Klaus, Paul Diehl, David Hamilton, and Jix.

My own career in composition and creative nonfiction was something I more or less backed into. I was a grad student at the University of Iowa in the first half of the 1970s, a former high school English teacher and a Writers Workshop dropout in fiction. After completing a pretty standard M.A., I continued into the doctoral program, happily teaching core literature courses as a teaching assistant, eventually completing a dissertation on Restoration comedy, and belatedly developing an interest in composition theory. When my new doctorate got me none of the three jobs in 18th century British literature available that hiring season, Jix and Carl Klaus both recommended my staying on for a post-doctoral year in composition and discourse theory, in courses that would eventually evolve into Iowa's graduate degree program in nonfiction. The exciting thing about those courses, taught principally by Jix, Klaus, Diehl, and Hamilton, was how expansive they were, simultaneously theoretical, pedagogical, and adamantly literary. Montaigne, Addison and Steele, Lamb and Hazlitt, long-time staple figures in rhetoric readers, and Orwell, Woolf, and E. B. White, popular authors in contemporary composition anthologies, all turned out to be composition practitioners whose work confirmed the wisdom of the writing teachers who had launched the process-centered writing curriculum. Their heirs seemed to be the current practitioners of the New Journalism and the literary essay: Joan Didion, Tom Wolff, Annie Dillard, John McPhee and others. When creative nonfiction later became established as an actual literary genre, it was evident that its most prominent authors had been practicing it as an anonymous form for some time and that composition teachers had been teaching it as models for the composing process approach to writing.

Eventually, as the genre became more established and more popular, it found adherents and practitioners in three distinct groups: in creative writing, especially fiction (most prominently in the "nonfiction novel" of writers like Truman Capote and Norman Mailer), in journalism (particularly as "literary journalism" or "new journalism"), and in composition/rhetoric (most simply as "personal essay" or "familiar essay" or "memoir," though nevermore as "belles lettres"). The variety in those access points suggests something about the nature of the Rater Variables that often surface in both pedagogy and literary criticism. It also helps explain the need for studies in nonfiction to find a distinct and separate role within English departments rather than to be a reluctant adjunct to a creative writing or rhetorical studies program. At national conferences, nonfiction panels at CCCC were listed under "creative writing" sessions and at AWP (Association of Writers and Writing Programs) under "pedagogy," in both cases separate from the "mainstream" sessions in the field. When graduate courses in nonfiction were approved at the university where I eventually taught, they were included in a new Master of Arts in composition and communication, the program title an indication of its origins.

By that time, I had been director of composition and was still a long-standing member of the Composition Committee; now I was also the principal professor of creative nonfiction. An alteration in focus, perhaps, but not essentially a shift, especially when I could see my nonfiction students struggling with the same elements of the composing process, the same variables in composing, that my composition students struggled with—the same ones I struggled with in my various writing projects. The Writer Variable, the Assignment Variable—they applied to the writing in the composition course and the writing in the nonfiction course in the same way, which meant that as a teacher I had to be attentive to their effects on my student writers in either course and find ways to mitigate their impact on the composing processes the students went through.

~~~

When I was an undergraduate, my student teaching mentor advised me to remember that after you meticulously generate a perfect set of lesson plans, you inevitably discover that the wrong set of students have filled the classroom. It was his way of reminding me to learn *who* my students were and design my lessons to teach *them*. It was a valuable reminder.

Required college composition courses serve the broadest range of students, relatively few of whom have come to college to be writers and all of whom vary, as Braddock, Lloyd-Jones, and Schoer remind us, "in intellectual maturity, knowledge, and socioeconomic background." Their motivation in taking the course is largely external, to meet a requirement imposed by the university. One of the most persistent challenges they face is identifying "a possible motivational factor," "some stimulating factor," that will prompt their writing. The composing process approach to teaching writing essentially individualizes the experience of writing and encourages a deeper commitment to it. It takes advantage of the Writer Variable and the Assignment Variable; it acknowledges that the writing has to come out of the writer.

Creative nonfiction courses have a somewhat narrower range of students, usually English majors, and may be elective rather than required courses, but the same variables affect the writing performances of the students. Some students may be principally creative writers in other genres, some mainly literary academics, and, depending on the course or the program, non-English majors may also enroll. Student backgrounds and motivations will vary widely, and the kinds of writing projects that arise will be determined by the interests and intentions of the students. Some of the students will even be pursuing topics that opened up for them in their freshman composition courses years before; certainly those composition classes are likely to have been the only venues in which they may have written anything resembling creative nonfiction—personal essays, memoirs, narratives of place or period, personal cultural criticism. Creative nonfiction students are likely to have had more experience as writers than composition students have had, but they face the same kind of challenges of discovering what to write about and how to write about it, the challenges that only the composing process can help them meet and overcome.

Trying to fit ideas or content into a prefabricated mold is more difficult and less often true to the material than trying to find a shape that accommodates the material. As with any composing, student writing can be derailed by lack of topic knowledge, lack of genre knowledge, lack of perspective or critical distance or rhetorical awareness. It can also be stalled by a failure to trust the process: composition students often hope the first draft will simultaneously be the final draft; creative nonfiction writers, with more confidence in their own prose, may be less inclined to fully explore the hints and confusions of early drafts. In either case the reluctance to commit to the process impacts the performance.

What seems consistent here is the need to be aware of the Writer Variable— what the student brings to the writing, what she needs to get from the writing— and the Assignment Variable—what topic the student needs to confront, what mode would most effectively serve that confrontation. Braddock, Lloyd-Jones, and Schoer tell us, "perhaps the student has latent writing powers which can be evoked by the right instruction, the appropriate topic, or a genuine need for effective writing in the student's own life." What is likely to bring creative nonfiction students to the creative nonfiction course is the hope of being able to find the appropriate topic and to meet the genuine need for effective writing in their own lives.

After all, creative nonfiction, unlike other literary genres, is not exclusively made up of texts by former English majors. The range of literary nonfiction is broad and mutable, from lyric essays that flirt with prose poems to personal cultural criticism that wobbles on the border with academic and journalistic texts. As a consequence, those who write creative nonfiction are likely to stretch the boundaries of the Writer Variable more broadly than those who write in other genres do; they are likely to be as varied in their interests and careers as the student population in a typical freshman composition course. And if you expand the Writer Variable to such a degree, the Assignment Variable automatically becomes more expansive to match the appropriate topics and needs for effective writing of those writers.

James Britton and the London Schools Project described the "functions of discourse" as "expressive, transactional, and poetic," essentially suggesting a Motive Variable or Function Variable. The functions of discourse model—other writers have presented similar sets of aims or motives—has the advantage of suggesting why a writer might initiate a composition and also recognizes that, unlike the Assignment Variable per se, the impulse for writing comes out of the needs and intentions of the writer. It also acknowledges the motives underlying all writing composed in courses in composition and nonfiction alike.

If we consider what Braddock, Lloyd-Jones, and Schoer term the Assignment Variable in light of writing courses rather than composition examinations, we recognize at once what any writing teacher knows—that those variables arise from the purpose and subject of the course and within the course are met by the variables in the students and their responses to the assignments. Teachers' design of course work and assignments and their expectations for student writing depend upon the level of the course, its potential position in a chain of courses or its programmatic situation—the Instructional Variable, if you will—all the elements that generate the context for the composing the students do. The courses may be variable—various from one another, as the courses that Jix and his colleagues taught in my post-doctoral discourse theory program were—but all teaching of expressive, transactional, and poetic writing, and all mastery of those functions, depends on a harmony of variables, within the performance of the student writer and within the awareness of the writing teacher. For writing students, the transition from composition to nonfiction isn't so much a shift as it is a necessary progression, a more intense and more motivated application of the strategies inherent in the composing process, in those variables that Jix and his colleagues got us all thinking about decades ago.

Works Cited

Braddock, Richard, Richard Lloyd-Jones, and Lowell Schoer. *Research in Written Composition*. National Council of Teachers of English, 1963.
Britton, James, et al. *The Development of Writing Abilities, 11–18*. MacMillan, 1975.
Elbow, Peter. *Writing Without Teachers*. Oxford UP, 1973.
Emig, Janet. *The Composing Processes of Twelfth-Graders*. National Council of Teachers of English, 1971.
Macrorie, Ken. *Telling Writing*. Hayden Book Company, 1970.
Moffett, James. *Teaching the Universe of Discourse*. Houghton Mifflin, 1968.
Murray, Donald M. *A Writer Teaches Writing: A Practical Method of Teaching Composition*. Houghton Mifflin, 1968.
Shaughnessy, Mina P. *Errors and Expectations: A Guide for the Teacher of Basic Writing*. Oxford UP, 1977.

Chapter 8. Making Matters

Nancy DeJoy
Michigan State University

> It was not always heaven in those days. Small communities can be narrow and tyrannical. We who now salute you belong to a much larger community, those of the generation after World War II. Let me for a few moments engage the questions of who we have been, who we are, and who we might become.
>
> – Richard Lloyd-Jones, "Who We Are, Who We Should Become," 487

I was born in the late 1950s and grew up the fifth of eight children, turned 11 in 1969, graduated from high school in 1976. Like many other white eastern North Americans whose parents grew up in the city and moved to the suburbs, my defining experiences were about moving from one class to another. Economic class, a corporate brat, yes, but also from one school classroom to another. From one side of Rochester, NY, to another, from there to suburban Chicago, and back again to the suburban east side of Rochester. Inside these moves were others from public to private schools or vice versa, until by 1976 I had attended five grade schools and two high schools. I have often wondered how the more general cultural shifts in aspirations in middle-class suburbs for second- and third-generation white U.S. citizens, especially after WWII, has affected the idea that Richard Lloyd-Jones took as a theme throughout his work: that language makes things. Clearly, valorization of "English only" reverberates in making immigrant life a function of a more general historical trend, one in which middle-class life was unilingual, being multilingual a marker either of lower citizen status or, less often, of wealth that provided trips abroad and Ivy League educations. What it has meant to understand reading and writing as relational open spaces within this history has been more than a personal journey, although understanding the personal in varied contexts has defined my academic journey as a first-year writing teacher and administrator in many ways. What does it mean to understand self as maker within the contexts of curriculum design and others' lives? This was the question Lloyd-Jones posed for us early on, and one we would do well to ask again now. What process is it that we put in motion?

The need for reflection and the making of meaningful lives is a constant source of anxiety in the lives of many of the students and teachers I have worked with over the past thirty years. It frequently manifests itself as an inability to see one's self as making, being able to make, or sometimes even having made, a life of joy and gratitude, a sustaining existence. Sometimes, students articulate their anxiety in phrases that walk into our writing classrooms with histories of their own.

"I'm not a (good) writer" could mean anything from "I got bad grades in English in high school" to "I am afraid to say what I really need to say," to "I embody the scars of an educational system in which no one cared about me." We know these phrases, too: "I don't have anything to say," "I can never figure out what the readings mean," "I'm not really that interested in anything, can you just give me a topic?" Sometimes teachers articulate this anxiety as resistance to the ways of reading that grading seems to demand, ways that bump up against their own histories as readers, writers, and literate human beings in uncomfortable ways. The gulf between reading and grading can be so big that in workshops that shift the ground from grading students to reading student writing, people experience some distress. The papers aren't meant to be read that way, they'll say, or it will take too much time. There is a parallel here with shifting the ground from explication to nonfiction: explication can be put on a scale of "correct" interpretation in ways creative nonfiction can't. When readers respond to texts solely as graders, it puts reading in relation to criteria that precede the act of reading itself. It limits the operationalization of those criteria, interrupting their relationship to the texts that have been made. This doesn't mean that everyone gets the same grade, or even a passing grade, but it does enable me to explain their grade in relation to the criteria as they emerge through reading and not just through some laying on of the criteria hands. I am still amazed to hear that teachers read a paper for the first time and grade it as they go. I know there are time issues here; I experienced them while teaching 4/4 and 3/3 and at the same time directing writing programs. What I found most effective was to read through the whole stack first as if they were chapters in a collection. This gave me a good idea of the subject matter I was working with as well as how to set the terms for evaluation in relation to the assessment criteria that had been shared or developed with the students when the assignment was set. It also allowed me to clarify which were most ready for that collection, which were at the revise-and-resubmit stage, which were rejections, which were conundrums, and why. It occurs to me now that this is why my assignments have become, over time, more and more like calls for chapters. Phrases such as "just tell me what you want" and others like that may be ways of saying that students know how their work is going to be read in the end, so let's stop pretending and get to it. How many of us teach writing even as we struggle with our own literacy histories, writing blocks, and rejections from readers whose responses indicate criteria different from those we expected them to use? The relationship between reading and writing, and the fissure between them in most of our lives, cannot be ignored, as they return us to relationships between those who write and those who read in writing classrooms.

For me, these issues collided early on with the common practice of putting students in groups to do peer response. As someone who had gone to so many different schools and who knew what it was like to walk into classrooms not knowing my peers or their histories, I understood the limitations of responding to others from nowhere, or within only a very limited and mostly unconscious and unexamined set of assumptions (gender, for example). Even with the peer response guide sheet we were given and required to use as graduate teaching assistants, I grew anxious on peer response days. I would tamp down the feeling that I was recreating a situation that favored surface responses, unexamined assumptions about the relationships between readers and writers, and criteria that limited those relationships. Ultimately, I felt I was undoing any chance for getting past the mere laying on of the hands of criteria in the constitution of our lives as literate human beings. It brought back memories of something I still have trouble naming clearly, a vague sense that I was doing what was expected of me, settling for what was "good enough," but not really accomplishing much.

The fuzzy desire for deeper connections to place, to others, to myself had led me down many paths by this point in my life, and I sat in great discomfort whenever situations made me feel the absence of those connections, but I had no way to do more than experience it. This wasn't about an inability; it was about pedagogical norms that offered no other options, replicating the experience of beginning from nowhere. I was more comfortable than most designing experiences for 14- to 16-week blocks of time. In fact, one of the advantages of the way I grew up was that at a fairly young age I knew what it meant to organize life around fairly small chunks of time. We all bring hidden histories to any opportunity for response, especially in higher education classes where one semester ends and another often begins as if the previous one never happened. I decided that I had to find a way to get reading back into my writing classes and back into curricula, and as much as possible into the lives of the teachers that I was responsible for training. I had to do so in ways that opened up some of these conversations while keeping writing at the center of teaching and learning. I had to rebel against two major disciplinary assumptions that eclipsed Lloyd-Jones's ideal of offering to writers ways to "define themselves as crafters, to govern their own materials, and to relate to the rest of the human world" ("Poesis" 46): that first-year writing classrooms were not places where reading should be a making activity (because literary explication had limited reading for so long) and that the literacy histories embodied in those spaces were merely individual personal narratives.

These assumptions became more than a theoretical issue, and addressing them posed questions for me about the heart and soul of my work as a teacher and as a practitioner who was hired to make things. How had the history of devaluing reading to remove literary explication from the center of the first-year writing classroom in first-wave process model theories reinstituted another form of explication at the center of that movement? How was the over-valuation of theory and the absenting of creative nonfiction driving this machine? What discursive tendencies were being reinstitutionalized here? How did these practices replicate structural devaluing of first-year writing programs over time and across radical pedagogical changes? If we weren't teaching writing, what were we doing?

The questions emphasized my status as an outsider in ways both clear and muddy. On the one hand, I knew that class, gender, and a history of not doing well in school were factors in keeping me out of line with the poststructuralist theories defining subjectivity with which I took issue. I had come to the field from stints in factories and bars and from reading Audre Lorde, Gloria Steinem, and Ivan Illich, books I had procured from the free book rack at the library near where I lived, a place where I dodged in and out of somewhat dangerous alleys and streets to get to other places between shifts. At that time, after flunking out of college twice, I had given up on school. I was struggling to understand my past and what it might be like to conjure a future that wasn't one of living from day to day or paycheck to paycheck (almost making it each week) or even year to year. The loss of hope loomed larger and larger every month. On the other hand, I was in one of the premier rhetoric and composition programs in the field. I had arrived at a time when first-year writing was starting to become the "low" end of the field from the inside, and I had chosen to focus there. But more about that later.

Like many next-generation college students (first generation, but with older siblings who went to college and parents who went back later in life, Dad in his 50s and Mom in her 70s), much of life was mediated by a vague belief that there might, just possibly, be more going on than the surface of our stories revealed. As the reading I was doing before I went back to undergraduate school had made its way into my consciousness and my poetry, I began to think that my educational failures might be connected to something other than a lack of ability. Ivan Illich, Audre Lorde, Jonathan Kozol, Mike Rose, Sherman Alexie: I read these tales of education as one of the characters in the stories, not as ideological tracts or as a critic. It was sometimes painful to read them in graduate seminars and listen to people talk about the characters as if they were mere discursive figures, lives rendered in acceptable or unacceptable ways by a writer who was or was not creating representations through acceptable lenses.

Before graduate school, there had been a successful graduation from undergraduate school, no high honors but a pretty clear introduction to the conflicts of academic life in English studies. It began one morning in the early summer of 1986 when I woke up and took the bus to Nazareth College of Rochester. The admissions office was quiet. The receptionist told me that no one was around to help me. I began to cry. As I sobbed and asked for help, Jonatha Elliott stuck her head around the corner and said she would talk with me. My memory of much of the conversation is vague, but I do remember telling her that I needed to go back to school, that something woke me up and sent me there. She said, "OK, that shouldn't be a problem." Which was fine until I said I had flunked out twice, at which point she said, "OK, now we have a problem." As it turned out I would have to take two classes and get grades of B or better to matriculate and qualify for financial aid. I signed up for Rhetoric I, a class that would fulfill the first half of a general education writing requirement and started a few days later in the first summer session.

I have no memory of how I actually paid for the course. Installments probably. But I do remember working at the bar until well after closing and going home to either get a few hours' sleep or finish the assignments as they came due. The prof, Dr. Deborah Dooley, met with me throughout the course, holding paper conferences that acknowledged both the importance of how I dealt with subjects and the need for more organized papers with greater clarity of purpose. My most distinct memory from that first course is a conference about the first paper, in which she told me that obviously I had a lot to say and didn't have to try to say it all in three pages. Then she sent me off with the assignment to choose any one sentence from that paper and to write three pages about that. The only reading we were assigned was the first half of Edward Corbett's *Classical Rhetoric for the Modern Student* (the second half was for Rhetoric II). In our individual conferences Dr. Dooley and I discussed the readings I had been doing while not in school, and she suggested some others I might be interested in. Serious issues of being and becoming, of choice as an available alternative to reenacting what Dr. Dooley called the "old tapes" we carry around in our heads, arose as a consequence of our study of rhetoric and the conversations it inspired. By the end of the semester I had my grade of B or better, and with the encouragement of Dr. Dooley, I signed up for her second summer session course to study women's narratives.

I knew when I went full time in the fall—and fully maxed out my student loans each year until graduation—that I would be a writing major. I was lucky, though, because writing majors had to do the full core requirement of the literature part of the English major, and so even though I was an older returning student, I was introduced—mostly through experience—to what was already becoming and would continue for years to be the major tension of the modern process-model movement ideology of the field of first-year writing: the relationship between reading and writing. My undergraduate degree required all writing concentration majors to complete the full literature core requirements, but the literature majors were not required to take any of the core writing requirements. My writing-major peers used to gripe about this; I thought that we were the lucky ones. I also had the good fortune of being introduced to lots more creative nonfiction in women's studies courses. But the disciplinary tensions that dis-integrated literacy studies haunted my graduate school career.

During my M.A. program I chose a second field in literature instead of theory (not a highly valued choice in the program), selecting a focus on modern women's writing that included fiction and nonfiction, and found paths for overlapping that course of study with my work in rhetoric and composition. When I stayed to continue work toward the Ph.D., I added courses in the theory track to meet expectations that had become unspoken requirements. We read some feminism, mostly to criticize it using male poststructuralist theoretical frames. I did find Julia Kristeva's *Revolution in Poetic Language*; it reminded me of Lorde and Steinem and became a touchstone for my dissertation. But it also became much more than that: it became a way to understand the effects of the historical absence of the poetic, and the absence of creative nonfiction, in my graduate studies and in the process model movement I had been oriented toward. It became a way to think through the consequences of that absence, rather than merely experiencing it, and it extended even further to the pain and joys of reclaiming the poetic as writer and as reader for myself.

It became a way to understand the effects of that absence in my life, too, and it made central again the question of the relationship between reading and writing to composition studies and to those studying in the field. Like Lloyd-Jones, I watched as the problems of first-year writing—economic, ethical, ideological—became not opportunities for change and inclusion, but grounds for devaluing the field and those who teach and learn under that requirement, sometimes as a hopelessly unethical endeavor and sometimes, as one colleague put it to me, as a course that shouldn't be necessary—i.e., people who need the course shouldn't be admitted to higher education. These things resonated very personally for me—someone who by luck had ended up in rhetoric just by dint of being a continuing education student and tracked into an alternative way of fulfilling the first-year writing requirement, but who was, nonetheless, underprepared. Someone who had flunked out of college twice and who was committed to more open access, second chances, and approaches that acknowledged the complications and histories that could inhibit success for many students (moving from school to school, for example, or being labeled "not college material," or experiencing financial challenges or benign neglect, or having big boobs at a young age and being sexualized by peers and many adults).

The relationship between reading and writing became a central issue of inclusion not only for me, but for whether students would see themselves as vital and integral to our endeavors. Course anthologies and writing textbooks that included readings became more inclusive of work by multilingual writers, writers from historically underrepresented populations, and writers who presented challenges to mainstream histories of the west. But expectations for student writing shifted less quickly as the question of how to put those readings in relation to writing assignments without reinstitutionalizing explication, exhortation, or exaltation as the end of writing instruction went unasked. How, for example, could we position inclusivity as an invitation to enhanced literacies? How could we avoid positioning diverse voices as objects to be analyzed, argued about, accepted or rejected, and rather engage with them, expanding our own practices as writers and readers? Listening to students, some of whom were genuinely relieved to be reading texts they could identify with and some of whom were stressed out by those texts, I realized that in either case the unspoken source of the relief and stress was, at least in part, because the texts engaged unfamiliar invention, arrangement, and revision practices.

And so, I set out to reclaim invention, arrangement, and revision for purposes not related to those set forth in the classical or mainstream models. I repositioned those tools as transactional activities that move us across reading, writing, and researching. I can't emphasize enough how the move away from criticism and critical theory as the frame for making things with language put me at the edges of the profession and brought me and the students I worked with to the edges of the limitations of our literacy educations. Centering theory had created a huge gap between the discourse of honor and the discourse of first-year writing students, a gap not unlike the one created by the earlier honoring of fiction and the restriction of student writing to the much less valued discursive forms of explication. The consequences of my migration away from this theoretical gap and the practices it encourages affect me professionally even today, and not in ways that are always comfortable or make me "good enough" in year-end evaluations, annual reviews, merit pay decisions, and other professional structures.

In the spirit of reconfiguring the relationship between reading and writing, I created a set of questions to guide our reading practices and our discussions of readings, including how we read one another's work. The questions resulted in lists of possible invention, arrangement, and revision strategies students could consider available to themselves as writers and as researchers. It opened discussions about who has access to which resources, whose experiences are considered valid sources of knowledge-making, and whose less so or not at all, whose voices are considered valid in the arrangement of evaluative practices, and many other intellectual, emotional, and ethical questions that exposed the decision-making processes central to our lives as literate human beings. Virginia Woolf's and Audre Lorde's essays, poetry, and fiction were constantly echoing here. I have discussed these questions in other places, but will give a quick overview here to set the context for the remainder of this essay. Originally, there was a set of six questions:

> What did the writer(s) have to do to create the text?
>
> What does the text hope to create in the world outside of itself?
>
> What's being put in relationship with what?
>
> How are those things being put in relationship with one another?
>
> What is/are the writers trying to change?
>
> What specific strategies are used to inspire that change?
>
> (There may be some overlap here with invention strategies.)

I had, in fact, been using versions of these question to guide my own (re)reading of feminist texts, including Krista Ratcliffe's *Anglo-American Feminist Challenges to the Rhetorical Tradition*, Virginia Woolf's *A Room of One's Own*, Mary Daly's *Beyond God the Father* and *Wickedary*, Adrienne Rich's *On Lies, Secrets and Silence*, Audre Lorde's *Sister Outsider*, Gloria Steinem's "I Was a Playboy Bunny" and her later essays "The Masculinization of Wealth" and "Revaluing Economics" from *Moving Beyond Words: Age, Rage, Sex, Power, Money, Muscles: Breaking Boundaries of Gender*, and Kim Chernin's *Reinventing Eve*. Eventually that process would inspire me to try a hybrid approach to articulating the effects of the absence of feminist rhetorical and creative nonfiction traditions on my own life as a teacher of writing ("I Was a Process Model Baby"). I had, in fact, been using those questions to begin to build a writing life that would, for many years and many reasons, take me out of the mainstream professional publishing game of rhetoric and composition, a venue that wasn't very inviting or accepting anyway. As I worked to create inclusive, transactional relationships between reading and writing as a writing teacher and as a writer, then, I experienced what it was like to do so for creative purposes not central to the field, not the least of which has been the creation of enriched and enriching literacy life practices. The invention, arrangement, and revision questions were meant to be more provocative, to position readers in ways that were unexpected. I had little interest in limiting students to explication—accurate or not—of the content of the essays we read or in some "agree or disagree" flattening out of "the" main point, or in their assumptions and/or judgment about the author. I also had to clarify—and still do—that we were not concerned with where the writer(s) sat or what writing implement was used, or even with their intentions, but with what the text inspired us to see as the "Transformation of Silence into Language and Action" (Lorde), and how we might use that transformation to give us ideas about enriching our own lives as writers. (For a longer discussion and examples of the kinds of invention, arrangement, and revision practices that emerged from our work see *Process This: Undergraduate Writing In Composition Studies*.)

Like any first-year writing curriculum pedagogy, this one had its structure and had to be positioned in relation to more general education expectations, but it also allowed for a clearer and more inclusive central purpose: enriching the literacy lives of diverse students in ways that enhance their academic and varied personal lives and relationships to language and in ways that make their writing relevant to a variety of creative processes and writing situations. This was a sort of revolution/revelation about making curricula, especially as it altered assignment frames to invite essays and creative nonfiction that made a difference to the literacy lives of my students and me. I started reading student work the same way that I read the texts we looked at together in class, started responding to the writing and writers in process, reflecting what I saw to start conversations about the relationship between a reader's view and the writer's purpose. And you know what? More of those writers started caring more about the ways that they communicated with and inspired readers than I could have anticipated. They pushed me to help them become better writers. They made books of their work to give as gifts. They asked one another for copies of their essays. They asked me for honest reactions to and evaluations of their essays for purposes other than meeting course requirements. They wanted me to get something out of reading their papers, and they wanted to know if I had read them carefully and had not missed their meanings. Some of these students were reading my work for me too—or the ones that wanted to and had time. Some of them still do, current students and students from the past. The first person to read an early draft of this essay was Amanda Fields, from an undergraduate course I led in 1997–1998. In the past month, I have written to, or with, and read for, or shared my own writing with four students from 20–25 years ago, and even more over the past five or ten years.

This isn't some feel-good story about the hero teacher—although we should be much more careful than we are about criticizing those stories and positioning success as some sort of failure for teachers. It is a story about how a certain approach to curriculum building, pedagogical practice, and open-heartedness affects writing classes and the teachers and students who inhabit them. It is, in fact, a story about how those students sustained me as a writer and as a literate human being when no part of my professional life could—or even seemed to care if it did or not. It is a story about students being successful and how I agreed to embody that success instead of doing something else to their texts. It's not a story about how I must have missed something or the students were just "doing what I wanted" and how there is no way to change or get out of some traditional power dynamic in a required gen-ed course. It's a story about change and all the struggles that change can embody when the goal is something other than replication/explication of the way things already are.

It was no coincidence that at this time I had started doing community literacy work with Project READ in Decatur, Illinois, where I lived. I implemented a service-learning component into the course, tutoring GED (and sometimes other) students. At the time what held most of the GED students back was the writing section. The first-year writing students were brilliant; they noticed the problem right away. The workbook did not tell any of the secrets, so they created a guide: thesis sentence at the end of the first paragraph, consider two sides of the issue in paragraph two, cite a source, preferably a statistic (this could be made up if credible) in paragraph three, assert strongly how this all leads to the favoring of one side over the other, conclude by noting why it is important to take that side. Voila! Everyone started passing that section of the GED. And the first-year writing students gained a tangible picture of the limitations we were up against in creating more enhanced literacy lives. We all knew that we couldn't leave the GED students in this limited relationship to literacy, so after practicing for the test, we would write other things together, such as responses to letters the GED students' kids had brought home and requests for assistance to power companies and revisions of statements from medical professionals that made them understandable.

The silence of my academic writing life bumped up against the ways that I was figuring out how to inspire students to write and how they were inspiring me to live. The creative nonfiction I was using in class collided with my history of writing across genres—personal narrative, poetry, professional writing—in ways that made the absence of writing these genres emerge as a hole in my life. I simply couldn't think about or through some things without them. That's why early on I started writing every class assignment myself. I was in the process of recovering what it meant not to hide from or feel shame about writing as a reflection of the relationships between self and world. And it shifted the way that all of this work became the making of relationships.

In fact, creative nonfiction as a genre, diverse as it is, always opens space for this kind of reflection and action in relation to how language creates—and sometimes restricts—the making of relationships between and among self and other people, animals, nature, things, and ideas. This kind of reflection is vital in academic contexts given the pressure to define oneself, whether student or teacher, more and more narrowly in relation to academic criteria and expectations for what it means to be literate.

While I had been resisting putting these limits on my students by insisting on using creative nonfiction, my own literacy life was, in fact, becoming more and more frantic and split. My narrow relationship to the academic world was defined as a discordant rhythm of "accept me, accept me, accept me" and "I don't accept the limits you use to define me." This was no adolescent rebellion; it was a genuine crisis of identity. When I went up for tenure, the department chair wouldn't sign my letter because he thought it a travesty that someone would use the story of failing in school so publicly; the fact that I was there at all was, he thought, a sign of all that was wrong with higher education in the contemporary world. He couldn't stop the process, because I had clearly exceeded the criteria for promotion, but he did get away without writing the letter required of him to stand against the case, choosing to make my life miserable instead. I simply couldn't tell my story within this narrative rhythm. But the curriculum making and pedagogical work I was doing was getting me out of this bind.

This struggle took most of my energy for many years and created a gulf between how I experienced the world and how the world experienced me. Anyone who knew me during this long stretch of time will tell you that I was fiercely and sometimes aggressively committed to the use of creative nonfiction in first-year writing pedagogies, in writing theory courses, and indeed throughout any major that dared to call itself a professional, or creative, or integrated writing major. I was often critical of other approaches in unproductive ways. The kinder version of this story is that I was consumed by my work— and I was. I had defined my work as enriching the opportunities for others to have writing experiences that were transformative. I had been living one of those transformations for years even as I was silenced by some of the things that transformation had brought. And I knew these things extended beyond the semester or one-year time frames that define a life in school. My syllabi, assignments, evaluation tools, and overt reflections on literacy as an untapped human capacity over my time in higher education will attest to that commitment. In 2004 I published *Process This* with Michael Spooner at Utah State University Press, an experience that taught me that a good human being who was also a good editor is one of the truly special gifts for any writer.

As a woman whose life had been saved, quite literally, by the inclusion of creative nonfiction in her writing and women's studies courses, I couldn't give it up as a classroom practice. I made the deeply buried, unconscious, disciplinary mistake of thinking that positioning it as reading was somehow enough, as long as the writing spaces were opening for students. There were public fissures, like the essay "I Was a Process Model Baby," but they were few and far between. Most of my writing was kept private, especially the poetry that was sustaining me. The first time I went public with paper-published poetry was when I was invited by a former student who was the featured poet one month in Contemporary American Voices, an honor that allowed him to pick a few poets' work to include in the volume. It wasn't until fairly recently that I realized this was a disciplinary sand trap, one deeply embedded in my graduate training, where even though we were supposed to aspire to the kinds of disciplinary prose held up as publishable in our courses, in our teaching we were to invoke another kind of writing altogether. I had found a way to have a life of connection, but it wasn't as comfortable as I had expected such a life to be when I was growing up.

These either/or ways of thinking attached to my self-image as an academic, even as I resisted pedagogies that trapped students in literacy limitations, and even as I engaged creative energy to make alternative curricula. As it became more and more impossible to find a professional path on which to explore these attachments, I became less interested in participating in those conversations. Again, it wouldn't be until years later that I realized how much of my frustration was connected to the fact that I was serious about process, and specifically about opening spaces for processes of expanded notions of self/other and self/world relationships in academic environments that substituted activity for process.

I had been asking "A process of what?" (in response to the assertion that writing is a process) since the late 1980s. When I analyzed the invention strategies at work in Audre Lorde's essays or in the chapters in Gloria Steinem's *Moving Beyond Words*, I could see that experience, as well as certain ways of rendering memory and reflecting on the self in context, were vital to the process of writing the self—as opposed to the process of creating a textual ethos so common in process-model pedagogies of the time. Creating the writing self instead of an ethos. In fact, I could see that while a reader could never know the truth of a writer's process, texts could be read as generative of expanded repertoires of invention, arrangement, and revision. This wasn't textual analysis of any kind I had seen before. So, I made the questions above to honor the fact that reading as a writer is different from other kinds of reading, especially in writing classes. That sounds simple, but buried within one sentence is a lifetime of creative struggle to move classroom practices from consumption (of texts) to participation, and from adaptation (to expectations for student writing as a genre unto itself) to contribution. Ultimately, this is about reconfiguring the relationship between reading and writing, about reading student papers from the perspective of being not merely audience addressed, but a reader.[1]

---

1. For a discussion of the ways we are all positioned as audience addressed and the ways that that positioning affects how we come to know ourselves, one another, and the world, see Matthew B. Crawford's *The World Beyond Your Head: On Becoming an Individual In an Age of Distraction*.

This flew in the face of my training, but also in the face of a world in which every space, from cafeteria trays to grocery store carts, from television screens to social media feeds, consistently positions everyone as audience addressed. The luxury of not being addressed has become increasingly rare and expensive. The first textbook I had to use as a T.A. had students think about audience by asking questions about age, gender, class, etc. I wouldn't do it because I was asking myself what you could really know by identifying your audience in these ways. At one point a mentor accused me of not understanding the concept of audience, mistaking my rejection of that configuration for some cognitive failure. I didn't want to be that kind of audience—the textbook kind—for my students' work or our classroom encounters, and creative nonfiction seemed to offer a different way of being the reader who had to grade while continuing the move away from explication as the main genre for student writing. It took a long time to understand how this happened and to fully understand the intellectual and affective impacts of doing this work in the writing classroom. Creating a pedagogical frame for reading that did something else was merely the start of a much longer and increasingly deep commitment that would eventually lead me into conversations about the field more generally—and into conflicts at the institutions at which I worked.

All of these factors came into play as I transitioned from graduate school and the use of prescribed curricula to having the responsibility of framing first-year writing programs to honor the diverse literacy histories, passions, and real needs of students and teachers. Given the realities of many adjunct positions and the lives of people who teach first-year writing from those appointments, creative nonfiction also became a way to design and get implemented policies and procedures that improved their working conditions. Pay, choices for class schedules, consistent full-time employment—these were, for me, matters at the heart of program leadership, and I often wrote policy and procedure manuals in the form of narrative practices. I made charts that clarified the role of department chairs, deans, and others in the conditions that defined programs. Later, when I moved to an institution that sent graduate students from various departments to us for T.A. appointments, the relationship between their program demands and requirements and the training and materials they needed to understand in order to be successful also became important. For them, and for many adjunct and early career faculty teaching in first-year writing programs, the writing class is often also the place where professional development happens. Success meant people had the opportunities they needed to get better jobs. For undergraduate students, the reason for first-year writing requirement is often vague, and the literacy histories they bring to the classroom are often not strongly connected to their work in the course.

All of this can become less daunting when you think about the teaching and learning of writing as an opportunity to develop an integrated literacy life, one that can be richer and hold more opportunities for understanding self and others and constructing conscious relationships to the worlds (disciplinary and others) you choose to inhabit—or not. Creative nonfiction opens these conversations about language in ways that can be justified in relation to the general goals of required first-year writing courses in the US. Why? Because the genre is self-conscious about being a made thing. And because it lends itself to the kind of reading that can position readers as writers-makers rather than as explicators of other people's texts. This shift—which is monumental—is still in process in writing studies, and depending on where you are, is somewhere between not-yet-started and just-begun and in-recession.

The shift toward participation and contribution (and away from consumption and adaptation to process model guides in textbooks, for example) meant creating curricular frames that students and teachers could individualize, while still experiencing what it was like to do so as part of a larger group of literate people whose relationships to one another could seem random and disconnected. This could be true in one section of the course, and certainly across multiple course sections, especially in a program that sees over 7,000 students per year. Combine that with the fact that you have multiple people teaching—from graduate students to very experienced fixed-term and tenure-stream faculty—whose relationships to one another are organized in equally random and disconnected ways, and you begin to see why the relationship between the pieces of a curriculum had to create spaces for identifying how literacy might create bridges between and among all the people in any given section and across sections. Looking at personal histories to identify how something we loved from that history included skills, knowledge, and attitudes that could enhance our literacy, then, opened the door for the kind of bridging required by the structure and logistics of the program itself. Teachers in workshops and students would select something they loved—playing an instrument, cheerleading, skate boarding or other sports, drawing, quilting, thrifting, collecting vinyl, etc.—and they would explore how loving that thing involved them in certain ways of knowing, in activities, in ways of being in the world and in relationships, and the attitudes that made them successful. As these things are explored, different versions of certain practices like patience, dedication, persistence, attention to detail, rejecting others' low judgments of our performance, trying a new way, for example, would emerge. Differences too would emerge between those passions that could be pursued alone and those that required group or team participation. Students and teachers would then ask: How can the skills, knowledge, attitudes, and practices that make up my relationship with what I love enhance my literacy life? And, specifically, how can they make me a more successful reader, writer, and researcher during my time in this course, as I figure out who I am and who I want to be in this new context, and during my time as an undergraduate student?

The course begins then by exploring what we love, how loving it affects the skills, knowledge, attitudes, and practices we cultivate, and how those can be transferred to other areas of our lives. It also creates a way to begin understanding ourselves in relation to the literacy expectations affecting our immediate futures, relationships that we could ground in what we bring with us and how that might contribute to our own and each other's successes. The writing assignment asks students to choose an audience who would benefit from the insights they gain doing the reading and invention exercises (including invention, arrangement, and revision analyses, class discussion, teacher presentations about grading, etc.) and to do so in a way that might lead to delivery of the paper, either orally or in writing, to an individual or group. What made us see that this work can be done and delivered was, in part, the short pieces of nonfiction that we read: a river guide who uses her knowledge of cooking to create great tours, a crew coxswain who learned leadership skills, a Harvard dean of education who transfers staid theory into five questions for a meaningful life. We read examples of bridge-building, analyze how they were done, and what things may have led to their creation, what purposes they might serve, what relationships they create and how. We ask how they were made and imagine how they got there. This expands our own repertoires of invention, arrangement, and revision strategies as we create lists of these at the start of the semester and add to it every time we come across approaches new to us.

Reading in this way is also a practice that helps us develop the skills, knowledge, and attitudes it takes to do this kind of work ourselves: to read as writers. It embeds reflection into the process at every stage, unlike curricula and pedagogies that must include these things as ancillary or add-ons, separate from the development of meaningful products. Such disconnection is the residue of the long-standing over-valuation of explication in the composition classroom, just another version of read (in this case your own work) and explicate (in this case reflect on your own product). Positioning creative nonfiction as the product flies in the face of that tradition, partly because it repositions our relationships to literacy reflectively, in ways that are enacted rather than deferred.

Each subsequent assignment frame pulls from the last and into the next, creating what I hoped would be an experience of continuity so seldom available in classrooms. The second assignment asks for another way of looking at something familiar, this time something more transparent in our everyday lives, to imagine what it means. Often this involves taking something we usually experience the surface of and slowing down to try to understand not only our own encounter with it, but also why that encounter occurs. To open up these questions, we read together the lyrics of popular songs selected by the students. Students share why they selected those lyrics, including any events they might associate with them. This is often the first time they have seen the lyrics on paper and considered them without the music. We ask how we might come to understand what the lyrics mean. There are the words themselves, of course, and sometimes we need help knowing what the references are (especially true for me if the songs use words or contemporary references I don't know). There are the events mentioned in the songs—a breakup, a riot, the loss of a parent—and questions about the autobiographical, historical, and other factors that may create a relationship between the singer, songwriter, and events. There are the cultural issues or issues of identity that may explain why one singer uses words that would resonate differently if spoken by someone else in another context. There are patterns of referring to people across the songs—women, African Americans, heartbreakers, liars, mothers, teachers, for instance—and we ask what they can tell us about why such patterns are popular.

One goal is to slow down and move beyond the experience of listening to the song, to explore what it means to like it. This pulls on one thread from the previous assignment, looking at something we love from new perspectives, doing so in a way that poses new questions about where meaning comes from—historical contexts, autobiographical events and experiences, social justice issues, identity, to name a few—to prepare us for a major research project. The list of what we might consider as we try to make meaning is extensive. We can discuss which routes seem best for looking at popular culture artifacts and why, and create a way to have those questions guide us in future situations where research may be necessary, as we create a frame for coming to understand. We can then practice creating individual approaches that fit our own focus, selecting artifacts that will support our process, and identifying resources and paths of access to those resources. The guiding questions for writing sound like this: How did you come to know the words of the songs so well? What do you know about the songs, their meanings, and why you love(d) them that you didn't know before? How did you create a frame for that understanding? What is the importance or relevance of what you have discovered? Who would care? What purpose could coming to these insights serve? What else would you like to explore in this way? The questions take us far past explicating the song lyrics without devaluing the importance of knowing them well, a practice to support student success during the major research project for the course.

I have to pause a moment here to clarify that the effort on my part to create continuity does not mean that the classroom is a calm and happy place. To different degrees, most students are intrigued, inspired, annoyed, and downright angry at the ways the course fails to meet their expectations. They miss explication as the default for their relationship to literacy. Early on they ask, in many ways, including generating pages of explication with paragraphs of reflection at the end, for permission to explicate and then reflect, to keep the two separate, and they promise to say what they think I want to hear in their reflections: "I learned so much, I'll never think about X in the same way again." In some ways they are keeping their end of the writing class bargain, and I'm the one breaking the deal. I hold this discomfort the way that I held not fitting in to school from early years through graduate study. I know that the bargain is a trap, that it limits our relationships to our own literacies and to the possibility of creating a life story rather than just living one. What good is a life if you don't know why you are living it the way you are, what it means, and how knowing what it means might help you live it more fully or differently? It limits what we ask about the futures we plan, and therefore limits how we can walk toward those futures.

For first-year writing students, walking toward their academic futures is often related to choosing a major. And this is where we turn next: to explorations of the literacy practices of a discipline or field of study selected by each student. It doesn't have to be something they are sure to pursue; it doesn't have to be the thing they came to study. The shift to thinking about one's future in a specific field is informed by our work making bridges and discovering what things mean. By this time, explication has also been positioned as a particular and not necessarily effective way to create relationships to literacy in most situations. As students identify the disciplines/fields they want to explore, I strive to find a piece of creative nonfiction about each. Richard Seltzer's "The Knife," Horace Miner's "Body Rituals Among the Nacirema," Richard Rodriguez's "A Public Language," selections from Mike Rose's *The Mind at Work*, Lex Runciman's "Fun?", Lewis Thomas's "On Societies as Organisms," selections from Rachel Carson's *Silent Spring*, selections from *The Creative Economy*, and an assortment of contemporary pieces about every area of study, from culinary arts to kinesiology. They are out there.

These pieces open up a space because they are often written by practitioners—some new, some experienced—and are written for more general audiences with purposes deeply connected to the writer's need to deal with some aspect of a profession. How does one position oneself as a learner whose goal is to do more than explicate the already known? This gap makes the questions about invention, arrangement, and revision meaningful to our process. They help us begin to understand what it means to learn from our research in a new way. For example, the readings often indicate some of the reading, writing, and researching activities the author engaged in and/or identifies as key to the field under discussion. In Rachel Carson's *Silent Spring*, the introduction makes clear that years of research and consulting primary resources about the changes in specific health environments and the animals of those environments are key invention strategies. Observation and primary research, then, emerge as potentially important literacy activities for environmentalists. When we step into more scholarly writing in academic publications, we know what to look for and how to read in ways that help us respond as people with our own reasons for reading.

The process begins with the knowledge that the audience will be peers who are interested in pursuing that field. A sense of audience isn't always the best way to frame a writing assignment, but in this case it reminds us to keep asking how and why the information might be relevant and to take notes from the readings in relation to those questions rather than merely summarizing the sources we consult. It also helps us formulate questions for the interviews that are included on the list of sources, moving us to include not only questions of interest to us, but also to consider what will be helpful to ask in interviews and other primary research activities. I explain some of the ways that students have presented what they learned in past semesters: the student interested in film studies who wrote his paper as the week in the life of a producer, the education major who created lesson plans and narrated the classroom and emotional life of a sixth-grade teacher, the nursing major who illustrated the differences between the literacy challenges faced by emergency room nurses and nurses working in a walk-in clinic, the computer science major who wanted to be the expert user-tester for gaming programs rather than the programmer, the hospitality management major who wanted to work at a ski lodge. These conversations move us further away from consulting secondary and primary sources merely as texts to be summarized and explicated.

I do not hand out sample papers. I often invite past students to my classes at the start of a new semester to answer questions and reassure students that what may seem crazy actually does help. They often tell stories of how they have used specific things from this course in other classes and places in their lives, as well as what has been less useful. This focuses me on what works and starts the class with some awareness that there is value to the discomfort we might experience along the way. Repressing these narratives or making them the object of critique became trendy at some point in our profession, and it did a great disservice to the variety of ways those of us who teach and learn together in writing classrooms understand our own and one another's relationships to literacy, and how those relationships affect our interactions.

Conversations about teacher evaluation will expose how claims that the teacher has all of the power as grader or instructor in any classroom are surface level. I remember the first time I used Herman Marcuse's *One Dimensional Man* in an undergraduate course. It inspired multiple journal entries about the ways that positioning people below or above some strata on a hierarchy was a false distinction, that while it seemed to favor people "higher up" structurally, that was only true if the system in question assumed certain values (e.g., capitalism). As a writer I found the repression of narratives about the successes regarding curricula, teaching, and learning in the first-year writing classroom to be paralyzing. As one older student put it in my research for *Process This*, it was like asking a piano student to begin with scales at the start of each new semester. In that older model, my understanding of what students bring to the class was constructed before they got there, and their understanding of me and of the possibilities for learning were similarly constructed before they arrived, the whole thing just a game of making everything fit or not fit those expectations. It blocked any pathway except, perhaps, repetition. It limited identities and repressed or punished difference. It especially and purposefully favored identification of and identification with—the major apparatuses of explication—as the preferred routes to literacy.

For those of us who had not done well in school, who had figured out why, and who didn't want to replicate those conditions, the idea that we couldn't do anything to make things better was just another way to position us as failures. I dare say it worked pretty well. Look around you. How many admitted to grad school were unsuccessful undergraduates? How many who teach didn't like school? How many of the women who retire without being full professors have chosen a path to avoid being judged again by the same people who devalued their stories about their work in the first place? How many of us might have chosen not to have been made into characters in some story in which we had no agency and in which our choice was not an opportunity for institutional reevaluation? How many of the people who want us to go up for promotion convinced us long ago that we would never be judged as successful by them or those they helped put in power? Look around you before you answer these questions. Do something other than explicate or merely experience what you see in a pre-constructed frame. Take the kind of approach to understanding process that sets aside explication so that you can ask questions. You have to get it out of the way to ask any questions that don't just confirm your assumptions. Those of us who learned this as a survival technique or as a way to open up spaces for our stories know the joy of this struggle. But we often experience it in academia as something to hide, something to protect. As Audre Lord wrote, "your silence will not protect you." We know that pretending explication isn't at the center unless you yourself take it out is a limited and limiting approach to writing studies today. Your explication will not reveal anything; it will merely replicate what is already known, positioning knowledge as power, rather than as a way to offer more open invitations to lives enhanced by the literacies we might develop outside of those limitations.

There are other assignments in the course: a remix and a final paper that is an opportunity to use new invention, arrangement, and revision processes to internalize some understanding about life as a literate human being. They extend and expand the ways we think about and practice other, often unfamiliar, forms of literacy and that reposition us as having possibilities for lives of participation and contribution.

When I read and reread Lloyd-Jone's work, especially "Poesis: Making Papers" (1997), I see in it just such an invitation, one to which the profession has RSVP'd many times. Thank you, it has said, but we'll stick with MLA and APA and maybe a dash of Chicago style. We'll put examples of what look like persuasive or "take-a-stand" essays, shore up the argument culture, and call synthesis higher-order thinking. Students must be oriented to other people's work, must read it not to make something else, but to mimic a student version of it as closely as possible. As a poet who repressed her relationship to that form of language for many years, I know what the repression of one form of literacy does to a life. As a rhetoric and writing scholar, I have seen firsthand what the repression of creative nonfiction in favor of explication has done to our profession. A broad range of writers inhabit our first-year writing courses, and our job is not to make them all one (kind of) writer. The idea that these are mutually exclusive endeavors hurts us all. It is an institutional split that became a professional practice.

Take a look at the final two paragraphs of Lloyd-Jones's essay "Poesis" (which is reprinted at the end of this volume), in which he writes, "I prefer to classify us as poets, primeval makers, enabling the culture to know itself and connect its people into a productive wholeness." If writing really is to be a process of something meaningful, we would do well to remember the work of Richard Lloyd-Jones as we create the curricula, institutional practices, and policies that configure the lives of writing teachers and students, especially those in first-year writing classes, and as we create responses to the question "A process of what?"

Works Cited

Alexie, Sherman. "Indian Education." *The Lone Ranger and Tonto Fistfight in Heaven*. Atlantic Monthly Press, 1993, pp. 171–180.
Carson, Rachel. *Silent Spring*. Houghton Mifflin, 1962.
Chernin, Kim. *Reinventing Eve: Modern Woman in Search of Herself*. Harper Collins, 1987.
Crawford, Matthew B. *The World Beyond Your Head: On Becoming an Individual in an Age of Distraction*. Farrar, Straus and Giroux, 2015.
Corbett, Edward. *Classical Rhetoric for the Modern Student*. 2nd edition. Oxford UP, 1971.
Daly, Mary. *Websters' First New Intergalactic Wickedary of the English Language*. Beacon Press, 1987.
———. *Beyond God the Father*. Beacon Press, 1973.
DeJoy, Nancy. "Being and Not Being"; "Spike Heels"; "Age and Change." *Contemporary American Voices: A Journal of Poetry*. contemporaryamericanvoices.word press.com/2012/07/, accessed 27 Jan. 2022.
———. "I Was a Process Model Baby." *Post Process Theory: Beyond the Writing Process Paradigm*, edited by Thomas Kent. Southern Illinois UP, 2009, pp. 163–178.
———. *Process This: Undergraduate Writing in Composition Studies*. Utah State UP, 2004.
Illich, Ivan. *Deschooling Society*. Calder and Boyles, 1971.
Kozol, Jonathan. *Illiterate America*. Doubleday, 1986.
Kristeva, Julia. *Revolution in Poetic Language*. Columbia UP, 1984.
Lloyd-Jones, Richard. "Poesis: Making Papers." *Writing on the Edge*, vol. 8, no. 2, spring/summer 1997, pp. 40–46.
———. "Who We Were, Who We Should Become." *College Composition and Communication*, vol. 43, no. 4, Dec. 1992, pp. 486–496.
Lorde, Audre. *Sister Outsider*. Crossing Press, 1984.
Marcuse, Herbert. *One Dimensional Man*. Beacon Press, 1964.
Miner, Horace. "Body Rituals Among the Nacirema." *American Anthropologist*, vol. 58, no. 3, 1956, pp. 503–507.
Radcliffe, Kris. *Anglo American Feminist Challenges to the Rhetorical Traditions: Virginia Woolf, Mary Daly, Adrienne Rich*. Southern Illinois UP, 1996.
Rich Adrienne. *On Lies, Secrets, and Silence: Selected Prose 1966–1978*. Norton, 1979.
Rodriguez, Richard. "A Public Language." *Life Writing*, edited by Winifred Bryon Horner. Prentice Hall, 1997, pp. 192–199.
Rose, Mike. "I Just Wanna Be Average." *Lives on the Boundary*. Penguin, 1989, pp. 11–38.
Rose, Mike. *The Mind at Work*. Penguin, 2004.
Runciman, Lex. "Fun?" *College English*, vol. 53, no. 2, 1991, pp. 156–152.

Selzer, Richard. "The Knife." *Mortal Lessons: Notes on the Art of Surgery.* Simon and Schuster, 1976, pp. 92–102.

Steinem, Gloria. "I Was a Playboy Bunny." *Outrageous Acts and Everyday Rebellions.* Henry Holt, 1983, pp. 33–78.

Steinem, Gloria. "The Masculinization of Wealth." *Moving Beyond Words: Age, Rage, Power, Money, Muscles: Breaking the Boundaries of Gender.* Bloomsbury, 1995, pp. 175–198.

———. "Reevaluating Economics." *Moving Beyond Words*, pp. 199–248.

Thomas, Lewis. "On Societies as Organisms." *Lives of a Cell: Notes of a Biology Watcher.* Bantam, 1974, pp. 11–16.

Woolf, Virginia. *A Room of One's Own.* Houghton Mifflin, 1929.

Chapter 9. On Failure: Notes Toward a Pedagogy of Risk

Jocelyn Bartkevicius
University of Central Florida

I

Writing is built upon failure, dozens or hundreds of flawed openings, paragraphs, images. Full drafts of essays, scholarly papers, books.

For most anyone who has tried to make a career as a writer, this isn't news. Libraries are filled with failure, special collections with rough drafts by famous or local writers. For years, scholars have built careers on such cast-off writing. In one such library, completing research for my dissertation in an intimate study that featured Charles Dickens's writing desk and large paintings of the benefactors, I studied Virginia Woolf's notebooks and drafts, early versions of some of her most brilliant novels and essays.

They were profoundly flawed. Riddled with clichés, flat images, failed attempts at narrative. Woolf had crossed out vigorously, rewritten passages in the margins. Far from being the natural genius I'd assumed she was, writing stream of consciousness in a sustained session of inspiration, she was a hard worker who toiled away at draft after draft, throwing away sentences and chapters, tossing notebooks aside. Even for iconic writers, working full time their whole lives, failure, I discovered, inevitably came first. Failure came first and returned with every new project. It wasn't the peculiar fate of the novice. Failure was imminent in artful writing.

I sat at a polished table, copying Woolf's flawed sentences and revisions into my notebooks. I felt like a medieval scribe. I discovered her interest in inaccuracy, because in it imagination and discovery lay. I witnessed the evolution of her essay on the painter Roger Fry, how she'd wanted to sketch him with the same license for interpretation that Fry had as he painted a sitting subject. From her failures emerged beauty and truth.

Years later, I would tell this story in every writing class I taught.

I was encouraged by Woolf's failings. By then, I'd had a taste of failed drafts of my own, piles of terrible openings of personal essays and stories, only two of which eventually were salvageable enough to see publication. Reams of printed drafts with cross-outs stacked in a plastic storage bin in the corner of my small apartment. I'd saved the drafts in the hope that an image or line could be salvaged in another writing session, but mostly, failure had left me discouraged, feeling like a perpetual beginner. Stuck.

But after I'd seen the extent of Woolf's recurring bad writing, and the resurrected drafts, my faith in my own writing returned. I'd never be Virginia Woolf or Charles Dickens, but my bad drafts suddenly struck me as part of the natural life cycle of any essay or story.

The problem I faced is one many students of writing still face: in college and graduate classrooms that required faculty to assign letter grades, there was little room for failure. Some sympathetic professors graded holistically, and a writing student could earn an A for a body of sustained drafts if some of them panned out by the end of the semester. Others applied a kind of law of averages, assigning letter grades to each draft, under which system one failure could lower your overall grade point average. In one stunning instance, during the first week of a graduate writing class, the professor assigned a topic for our writing—something about the necessity of animals, a prompt that at the time left me uninspired, and wrote a letter grade in thick sharpie at the top of the first page—in my case a C+, the lowest grade I ever received in nearly twenty years of being a student. He then directed us to exchange our graded essay with the person sitting next to us, so that we could listen to an "objective" explanation of why the teacher's grade was our just deserts.

If writing began with failure, but I didn't want to fail my courses, it seemed that writing would have to wait for holidays and summers, for after graduation when I could write failed drafts that no grade-wielding professor could see.

And then I signed up for a graduate seminar, Theories of Style, taught by Richard Lloyd-Jones at the University of Iowa. His seminar would inform my teaching for years.

II

I'd never taken one of his classes before, and his reputation was huge. He'd been chair of the College Council of Composition and Communication (CCCC) and the National Council of Teachers of English (NCTE), associations central to the field of teaching writing. These were the organizations that held annual conferences where we strove to deliver papers, and studying with the man who'd chaired them was exhilarating. But intimidating. I entered the seminar expecting little room for any failed draft. Every paper, I figured, would need to meet the standards of CCCC and NCTE.

But that wasn't Jix's style. On the first day, he told us to call him Jix, a nickname that matched his informal classroom style and embrace of writing as a way of grappling with ideas. Writing that semester was a means of exploration and discovery. We emphasized thinking on paper, not finished products cast in stone. This approach struck me as all the more remarkable in that the course was not, officially, a writing course, but a theory course. And yet Jix's approach was writing-centered. We would not so much theorize about theory as enact it in our writing. It was one of the only courses in my doctoral program that related directly to my chief area of interest: writing.

Some educators assume that such a combination of informality, openness, and exploration is "education lite." Not under Jix's watch. We began with a formidable reading list. We read highly theoretical works: Walter Ong, Wayne Booth, Plato, William H. Gass, E.H. Gombrich, and others, along with an anthology, *The Concept of Style*, edited by Berel Lang that included some theoretical essays about the nature of style and the "styleme," as well as essays on style in the visual arts, "narrative codes" political and theoretical writing, and poetry. We read writer-centered books, among them, Denise Levertov's *The Poet in the World*, E.M. Forster's *Aspects of the Novel*, and Henry James's *The Art of the Novel*. We studied classical rhetoric. We read theory by the then-trendy and new Stanley Fish. We read the quirky book *The Five Clocks: A Linguistic Excursion into the Five Styles of English Usage* by Martin Joos, already out of print near the end of the 20th century. Instead of writing term papers, we interrogated our reading in detailed reading notebooks.

Because Jix considered writing central to making discoveries, even in an academic course, he rewarded risk. Failure was welcome, as long as we explored, in writing, what had gone wrong and what we could learn from where the writing had taken us. In writing assignments in which we enacted what we were reading about—such as irony and epistolary form—whether or not we were excellent ironists or epistolary writers was beside the point. We followed each sketch with an analysis of how writing interacted with our reading and whether or not we found anything salvageable in the sketch.

Over two decades have passed since I took Theories of Style with Jix. The memories that stuck with me involve exploring style from the macro level (an artist's choice of subject as an aspect of style) to the micro (punctuation, sentence length, types of sentences). Most of all, I remembered—or thought I remembered—that we employed imitation: a study of style by not only analyzing it, but entering it. Or letting it enter our own writing. Such exercises were in part about understanding a writer's style by getting the feel of it, and in part about understanding our own style by forcing ourselves out of writing in it.

Such studies reminded me of how much more I learned about English grammar by studying French (where our learning was steeped in practice, in writing and speaking) than in elementary- or high-school grammar courses, where we had to memorize rules.

Years later, setting out to write about Jix and the pedagogy of risk I use in my own teaching, I reviewed the notebooks and writing I preserved from that class. Memory, as every writer of nonfiction knows, is never as detailed as a transcript or film. And one of the first things I discovered in those old notebooks from the class was a conversation between me and Jix about memory, in particular, what aspects of the assigned reading stuck with me days or weeks after taking copious notes in the journal he assigned. I hadn't even remembered all of the books, essays, and articles that we'd read.

More significant, I'd forgotten that, on the first day, he asked us to prepare a hypothesis for our own reading, a program for our own interest in theories of style. Each of us in the seminar might choose to be theoretical. Or pragmatic. Or metaphorical. Perhaps we'd want to conduct a case study. Our writing would not be the polished papers I expected, but rather ways of "testing out" the theoretical readings. He wanted us to let the reading tempt us to see language differently. He wanted us to be brave enough to write in ways we wouldn't ordinarily write. Jix had, in essence, allowed each student to customize his or her approach to the semester.

My previously unexamined memory of the class led me to the mistaken belief that every graduate student in it wrote a sequence of failed drafts followed by critical analyses of their failure, style-centered self-critiques. Reading through my notebooks from the semester, I discover that, with Jix's permission, my own hypothesis, writing-centered, failure-centered, led me down that path.

He created the ultimate seminar, one in which each of us could, with his direction, customize our relationship to the texts, interpret open-ended assignments, and engage in an individual dialogue with Jix even as we collaborated as a group in class discussions. Thus, my experience in and memory of the class will inevitably be different from others who participated that same semester.

I filled two 80-page perfect-bound composition notebooks with notes on my reading, page by page details pinning down key ideas and phrases, with margins filled with ideas for teaching and notes for revising or beginning various essays.

As I'd remembered, Jix encouraged us to apply our reading to the writing of canonical writers, to practice elements of style we read in assignments such as irony, epistolary essay, and demonstration of the self, and, finally, to write a sustained analysis of the style of a piece of our own writing, using every aspect of style we'd studied during the semester, macro, micro, and in-between. On the other hand, I couldn't find a single exercise in imitation, which I'd thought was the heart of the class. I've realized that a later seminar or independent study I took with Jix involved exercises in imitation.

For me, the notebooks became the heart of the class. They began as a dutiful students' copious notetaking, but ultimately became a conversation with Jix, who reviewed them every few weeks and put in margin comments of his own: "Society is normative," for instance. In response to an aside about falling in love with Joos's take on writing: "You do keep thorough notes; I've never been able to manage it. I too am very fond of the book, partly because a scale based on social intimacy seems so important." Or, when I questioned several passages in Ong's *Orality and Literacy*, he sometimes asked new questions along with me, other times agreed with my point, or offered a differing interpretation of Ong.

The notebook became a portrait of a growing intellectual exchange. As Jix responded first to my observations, then to the questions I dared ask of these theoreticians, I began asking Jix questions directly. The one that most reveals the clash of my world view and academic and writerly goals with the pressures of a Ph.D. program that had recently embraced critical theory was this: I listed the British and American novelists and poets whose criticism I loved, and asked whether, if I study and write about them, if I apply their view of texts to my studies, would I be considered not just old-fashioned, but—as I put it in the journal—"even worse, a new critic or formalist"? Jix's wry answer: "Only if one must publish."

He encouraged my growing interest in the lyric essay, my use of quotations from the reading to bolster an argument and definition for making a place in teaching and writing for essays with that approach. Instead of resisting my interest in Taoist approaches—which I occasionally pitted against a theoretical position that struck me as overly dependent on finished products rather than processes—his margin notes made pertinent observations, sometimes referencing Heraclitis ("You can't step into the same river twice") and once, my favorite margin comment of his, obliquely, William Butler Yeats, with his simple: "dancer/dance."

III

Teaching, like writing, involves rough drafts (little failures) and revisions. And a splash of imitation as the teacher seeks her own voice. Jix had been a great mentor. However, I was no more going to become Richard Lloyd-Jones in the classroom than I was going to become Virginia Woolf on the page. Nevertheless, I wanted to find a way to give my students Jix-style opportunities to use writing as a way of thinking openly and honestly (without fear of failure) about their reading. And I wanted them to be able to explore their original writing—whether essay, memoir, fiction, or poetry—without the pressure to produce a polished product on their first try. I wanted to shift the emphasis from finished product to the processes of exploration and discovery. I wanted them to explore the dancer and the dance, the motion of the river.

Often, my students start out suspicious of this approach. Until I studied with Jix, I was much like those students of mine, distrustful. Too many teachers had approached writing as the building of a perfect object, not the messy process of discovering our own voices. Charles Schultz captured that kind of student response in a 1975 comic strip featuring Charlie Brown's little sister Sally, who raises her hand and asks the teacher, "Do you want us to write what we think, or what we think you want us to write?" I used to stand outside the office door where that comic strip was taped, and where I first encountered it: Iowa's Department of Rhetoric, where Jix's colleague Cleo Martin introduced writing as thinking and exploration to generations of college first-year students and graduate teaching assistants.

My students in Central Florida by and large come from a tradition of classrooms focused on writing what they think the teacher wants them to write. With students who are conscious of getting good grades and a system that requires letter grades for all courses, it's a challenge, even if a teacher builds in opportunities for failure, to convince students to take those opportunities. To convince them that they are not traps. Or tricks. At the undergraduate level, I've found that low-stakes sketch assignments—graded pass/fail—used repeatedly at strategic points in the semester allow many of the students to accept the invitation to risk failure. After all, they know they will receive credit no matter how the draft pans out. In two levels of workshop-style courses in literary nonfiction, we intertwine craft studies with sketches for several weeks before the due date of a more sustained and polished (and graded) draft. The sketches are short (two to five pages) explorations in response to somewhat open-ended invitation. These pass-fail sketches count for a full 20 percent of their final grade.

Currently, in the senior-level nonfiction writing class, in which students can be expected to have completed one semester of reading and writing nonfiction, we begin these pass/fail sketches with an imitation, a study of craft. They start by reading around in a volume of *The Best American Essays*, and on the basis of reading the titles and first paragraphs of every essay, selecting one they most want to read and one they would really rather not read. They follow up with an analysis of how and why one opening worked (for them) and the other didn't, and the ways in which the rest of the essay lived up to their expectations or failed to do so. They write about structure, setting, concrete details, and the like, and using terms mapped out in Vivian Gornick's *The Situation and the Story*, they analyze how the writer has created a self-implicating narrator and transformed the situation (what happened) into a story (an exploration or discovery). The students are also asked to do the more challenging intellectual work of exploring the difference between their personal taste and the qualities that make an essay well-crafted, even if it is not to their liking. They write about what qualities they think led to the essay's getting accepted for publication twice, first by the editors of the original journal, then by the editors of *BAE*.

Their first sketch is an imitation of the essay they selected as the one they most wanted to read. Students are free to interpret imitation in any way they would like, whether topic or opening strategy or some aspect of voice or structure.

The remaining two or three sketches in this series might involve a sketch about their first memory, a sentence structure-driven sketch (e.g., writing one long sentence or nothing but short, simple sentences and selecting a topic that "matches" that style), and a tough-topic sketch (something they've long been hesitant or even afraid to write about). As open and inviting of failure as these sketches are, they are not entirely throw-away exercises. The first graded workshop essay is generally an expansion of one of the sketches, revised after getting feedback from a small group of peers (as well as from me). Students are not forced to use any of the sketch material. If they deem all of them complete failures, they are welcome to start from scratch. Knowing that they have free reign with the sketch material adds another layer of assurance to students that these are not trick pass/fail assignments. They are invited to fail in each individual sketch as well as in the full collection of sketches.

Near the end of the semester, after they've written longer essays and conducted large-class workshop discussions, students return to writing low-stakes sketches before their final project, in most cases a major revision. These sketches invite students to explore writing flash nonfiction, using braided segmented structures, or writing in points of view other than first-person singular. Those later sketches, like the first imitation sketch, blossom out of reading and studies of craft. Before writing a flash sketch, for example, students read the two brief essays that open Jo Ann Beard's *The Boys of My Youth* (the preface, and "In the Current") or some new essays from online journals such as *Brevity*, *Hippocampus*, or *Sweet: A Literary Confection*. Before writing in a braided form, they read Beard's "Cousins" and "Coyotes" (also from *The Boys of My Youth*). Before exploring a point of view beyond "I," they read short essays from the above online journals that are written in first-person plural (such as Jaquira Diaz's "Beach City" in *Brevity*) or a variety of second-person approaches, from simple second (such as Peter Ives's "Night Attack," in *Hippocampus*) to how-to (such as Billy Howell's "How to Leave Your Mother" from *The Florida Review*) to the epistolary form (such as M. Sausun's "Root," also in *Brevity*).

Before writing their final project for the course, a revision, my undergraduate writing students are asked to apply at least one of these experiments to the essay they plan to revise, whether rewriting the first page in another point of view or layering in a second, related narrative to form a braid. They know in advance that they will not be forced to use any of the material in this experiment—unless they want to. In this way, they experience, at least in a fleeting fashion, how revision can be discovery—even play. It's not always "fixing" up a draft. Your writing is not broken, I tell them. It's in progress.

With low-stakes assignments, students are less likely to become overwhelmed by the anxiety of trying to write what they think the teacher wants them to write in order to get a good grade. Low-stakes assignments invite students to be open to the possibility that they might dislike their draft—that it might be a failure—but that they can learn from that failure. There are a variety of ways to make sure that students understand—and trust—that any given writing assignment is not going to put their overall grade in danger. The method I tried first was to make all sketch assignments entirely pass/fail. No rubric. Turn in writing and you pass. This approach, I discovered, worked best for self-motivated students, who responded by writing with a real attempt to make discoveries. Already committed to devoting time to their writing, they were grateful to put aside concerns about how the product would be judged. But some harried, overworked, or less-than-motivated students dashed off quick drafts ten minutes before class, motivated, ironically, to aim for a failed draft since they'd earn credit no matter how quickly or poorly they wrote. Failure without trying didn't strike me as productive failure.

Over time, I've developed a rubric that has encouraged most of the students to see these sketch assignments as requiring a genuine attempt to make some discoveries, take risks, and try out new aspects of craft, while also rewarding them for doing so if the result is a messy draft that they don't like. Most recently, I've designed the course so that 20 percent of the grade consists of such sketches, and instead of pass/fail, they are scored on a rubric that grants five percent for including all aspects of the sketch indicated in the guidelines, five percent for careful proofreading and editing so that the sketch is error- and typo-free, and ten percent for a sketch that is fully developed, uses concrete detail and/or reflection, and shows attention to craft. Students who take the sketch assignments seriously and use them to make discoveries and risk failure inevitably earn the full 20 points.

Committed and motivated students tend to earn full points on all such assignments. Inevitably, however, the few students who dash something off on the way to class are of course prone to make clumsy errors. Worse, they are also unlikely to leave enough time to take risks with content and style or to engage in a substantive way with other aspects of craft. Those who are more grade-motivated tend to get serious after their first low score on what should be a fun assignment. After a while, students at all levels of skill and commitment write more effective workshop essays after these sketch exercises. They begin the full essay assignment as most professional writers do, with a few drafts to explore and expand.

At the graduate level, in our M.F.A. program in creative writing, where students are more motivated, all exploratory sketches are scored on a pass/fail basis. Like most M.F.A. programs, we offer workshop classes that focus on students' original work in their chief genre, supplemented by classes that focus on reading to explore craft and the historic or contemporary scene in their genre of choice. In some M.F.A. programs, writers have the benefit of an entirely pass/fail program, where workshop courses are focused on written commentary and discussion of their original work. In the M.F.A. program where I teach, letter grades are required. After years of trying out various rubrics where I could score graduate students' original writing for originality and craft, I've turned to an approach that aspires to the kind of freedom for exploration and failure that a grade-free course might offer. With the old rubric system, students writing revisions were rewarded more than those making discoveries. To allow for more generative writing, I began scoring all early drafts on a pass/fail basis. Under this system, the writers can work hard on an experimental essay that pushes their skill level, have it fail, but still succeed in the class. If a student tells me an essay is generative, then workshop discussion focuses on exploring the story, undercurrents, discoveries, and possibilities. Such essays are still in progress, in flux. If a student tells me an essay is a revision, we discuss it in a more rigorous way as a product.

To accommodate my university's emphasis on letter grades, and to hold students' feet to the fire in terms of dedicating themselves to reading each other's work seriously, I give letter grades on their written and spoken commentary to each other. Under this system, the dedicated students always earn those coveted A grades. The students who are likely not long for the program can still end up with the low B or C that signals their lack of commitment to the community of writers.

In the craft-centered courses that emphasize reading, I try my best to emulate Jix's approach and to use open-ended writing as a way of thinking. Students can opt to use open-ended notebook entries to reflect on (and question) the reading or to write short reviews focused on an aspect of craft that they find central to the book or essay under discussion. Or they can study one or more aspects of craft central to their own writing. Students who choose this option might, for example, examine ways various writers structure a memoir, or how to create an engaging and complicated narrator, or how to use irony or research. After the reflection, they write an imitation based on any aspect of style they are intrigued by in the writer's work or wish to practice for their own writing. The craft studies receive a letter grade. The imitations are pass/fail and add up to count as a percentage of the final grade.

Graduate students tell me these are some of the most inspiring assignments they've encountered—although, inevitably, they are skeptical at first, assuming that as a professor I am more likely to trick them into writing the way I want them to write rather than embrace their glorious experiments and failures. For a surprising number of graduate students, it is one or more of the imitations—not the manuscripts they write for workshop—that end up as the inspiration for and basis of their thesis projects.

Their risks and failures, they report, lead to the kinds of discoveries that contribute to their becoming the writers they entered graduate school hoping to be. I find it striking that even with the permission to fail in their workshop classes, they so often learn more about their own writing from the imitation exercises. I suspect that, as Jix knew when he designed his seminar on theories of style, sometimes it is when writers are at play, distracted from—or looking only in their peripheral vision at—becoming the kinds of writers they were willing themselves to be that they discover their voices. As I look back at the margins of the reading notebooks I wrote in Jix's class, I see paragraphs of discoveries about essays in progress and old failed drafts. Some of those essays became the heart of my work as a writer.

With Jix's teaching as a touchstone, I found that risk and failure can be built into even the most stringently letter grade-centered program. And within such classes, students at all levels can experience the way little failures, surprisingly, are integral to nuanced thinking and writing that genuinely matters.

Chapter 10. Personal Essays as a Path to Effective Transactional Writing, or No, You Haven't Always Wanted to Be a Doctor

Rachel Faldet
LUTHER COLLEGE

I am in a Scandinavian apartment with a five-day-old infant, his transitioning-into-no-longer-the-star brother, a slew of plastic trucks, a potty chair, air-drying laundry, an IKEA sheepskin, and a nonfiction book called *Severed Ties and Silenced Voices* about Swedish immigrants in Minnesota. My oldest daughter is married to a Swede, and it is a heat-wave July. My mind is far from English courses and classrooms.

I am negotiating with a toddler whose sense of danger and consequences is limited. Attempts at successful transactions can fail. What I want is maybe what he wants, but he is masterful at changing his mind. No breakfast slice of toast. Yes toast, but only if he puts it in the toaster that he can't reach. When the toast is covered with requested butter and strawberry jam, he doesn't want it. He lives in a bilingual home, and I cannot speak Swedish, his preferred language. Though he understands some English, he responds to me in a mix of accurate Swedish and words or sounds that, at times, even his parents cannot decipher. No wonder toddlers cry or try other rhetorical strategies, like saying "come," extending a hand to hold, and leading the way to a basket of construction site diggers and green tractors, a plush rabbit hiding under pillows, a closed door.

Not everyone gets what they want.

After summer slips away and I am guiding undergraduates (first-year at-risk writers, international students transitioning into the U.S. academic system, writing-emphasis minors, or seniors gunning for coveted healthcare slots), I give assignments that help students gain skills, knowledge, and rhetorical power to use when they try to get what they want. Practice in creative nonfiction—truth in content, artistry on the sentence level, and research—helps people on the cusp of adulthood become successful transactional writers. But to achieve this, my classroom companions and I must engage our hearts, minds, and hands in a risk-taking, yet lovely, bargain.

~~~

It's the early 1980s. In the University of Iowa Writing Lab in the English-Philosophy Building, I travel between four students each hour. Part of a team of grad students working shifts throughout the weekdays, my goal is to help at-risk writers gain fluency and confidence, ability to move beyond generalities, and understanding that their voices are valuable. We young teachers care about our assigned students who sit at carrels and tables; near the door are bins for portfolios of their growing body of semester's work. Some of us completed Teaching in the Writing Lab, taught by Lou Kelly, the Writing Lab director. Others are learning how best to listen to what students are saying and grasping the theory behind the practice of asking writers to talk on paper about what they know from life experiences. Our students commit to attending lab at designated times. This isn't a random drop-in, fix-it, good-bye operation.

Throughout the semester U of I lab students use pens and pencils to respond on lined paper to Lou's sequence of mimeographed invitations to write. Lab students (anxious or relieved, miffed some authority sentenced them to the lab, thrilled their "bad" writer label is evaporating) write on site: no hours-long or weeks-long procrastination. Students write what comes to their mind and receive individual encouragement and feedback often in the form of "tell me more" comments.

Specifics have power.

Lou is famous for wearing Birkenstock sandals. She integrates language acquisition research of James Britton, whom in her Louisiana accent she cozily calls "Jemma," into lab pedagogy. Lou's notion is that successful writing instruction starts with expressive writing for the self and branches into writing for a wider audience—just as babies make self-soothing noises, toddlers insert words about their family and daily activities into an off-tune *Twinkle, Twinkle, Little Star*, and elementary school children verbalize in paragraphs with folks outside their family. Britton calls these branches of communication transactional and poetic.

In his essay "Writing to Learn and Learning to Write," Britton says, "Transactional language is language that gets things done, language as a means. Poetic language is a construct, not a means but an end in itself" (107). Britton promotes the notion that when "you read a piece of transactional language . . . you take what you want from it and leave the rest . . . With transactional language, what goes on is *piecemeal* contextualization" (107). Poetic language, for Britton, is "language as art—poetic in the original Greek sense, something made, a verbal object" (106). He claims that "the further you move along this scale [from expressive] towards the poetic, the greater the attention paid to forms, to the organization of form" (107). The writer in the poetic realm wants the reader to engage in "contextualization *as a whole*" (107).

In the lab, where Lou's pedagogy is in sync with Britton's, no struggling writer immediately leaps into demoralizing thesis-driven analytical essays about literature. Academic writing instruction has been slim for our students: small-towners whose schooling is dictated by boards that hate to spend money, athletes from neighborhoods far from Iowa City passed from class to class despite limited communication skills because they score big for their high schools, graduate students from diverse continents who are hampered by limited written English fluency or sense of organization. These writers have potential. Lou advocates a building-block approach. Learning to effectively craft essays about what you know transfers into more effectively crafting essays about new knowledge. Being a stronger writer means being an active reader. Being a stronger writer means embracing a messy process. In *From Dialogue to Discourse*, Lou writes,

> you learned to talk by living in a family of talkers. And you learned to use words in meaningful contexts, you learned to accomplish things with words, by using what you had already learned in personal encounters with your family—as a group and as individuals in that group. These experiences prepared you to cope, with varying degrees of success, with the people and the situations you encountered in the world you discovered beyond your family . . . That is learning through living. And I think composition and speech courses at all educational levels should be an extension of that living-learning process. (5)

In my twenties, I am intrigued by the idiolect, dialect, and standard English mixed in my students' writing. I wonder how many surface errors I should or should not correct, whether commanding students to write about personal experiences is prying, or if content is more important than sentence-level refinements. I am startled by Lou's practice of wearing sandals in bone-chilling winter.

~~~

This newborn in Sweden, his umbilical cord's bloody remnant drying until it falls away, operates on reflex, arms and legs flaying seemingly at frantic whim. Involuntary facial movements practice smiles, grimaces, and pursed lips as if blowing smoke rings. Crying alerts his parents who try to interpret. His whimpers sound, according to his toddler-brother, like a puppy. Newborns use helplessness to influence people who could feed them, diaper them, and ask health professionals for survival tips on their behalf.

~~~

I am thrilled to be a writing lab teacher during grad school, negotiating rhetorical challenges and figuring out how to produce a worthwhile transaction for each person. As I do with other students on their first day in the lab, I ask Steve (a pseudonym) to write the first in Lou's series of "invitations" based on personal experience. He chooses a table in front of a window, his back to the room. After twenty minutes he puts down his pen, stares. I walk to his table, sit next to him. When I inquire if I may read what he wrote, Steve silently pushes his paper my direction. In printing that grows larger with each word, he writes, "I hate writeing. I hate this. I hate this. I feel like a pieace of shit. I feel like a iliterite fool because I can't even spell a word like pieace."

Reading Steve's words, I am embarrassed to be a writing teacher. Steve, a first-year college student, was humiliated by his high school teachers. Being sent to the lab by his U of I rhetoric teacher is new humiliation. Momentarily, I am uneasy, tongue-tied. Then I say I'm sorry he'd been made to feel that way. I ask him to tell me more about his feelings and experiences. Eyes focusing on the window to the outside world, Steve reveals a bit more, not much. Realizing his profound anger and embarrassment, I say he doesn't need to stay for the entire hour. As Steve leaves, I wonder if he'll ever come back.

I almost vow never to mention the word "error" to any student, and only to require them to work on content. Steve's teachers had focused on surface errors, cementing his notion that working on writing is a punishment to be dished out as long as he is in college. Each semester another hellish spelling lesson. In *Errors and Expectations*, Mina Shaughnessy writes,

> By the time he reaches college, the BW [basic writing] student both resents and resists his vulnerability as a writer. He is aware that he leaves a trail of errors behind him when he writes. He can usually think of little else while he is writing. But he doesn't know what he can do about it. Writing puts him on a line and he doesn't want to be there. (7)

Steve feels "on the line." Two days later when his lab hour arrives, he doesn't show up. But the next week he returns and writes nearly a page. When I ask Steve why he came back, he says, "Because you didn't tell me what I did wrong."

~~~

"I'm sorry," I say to my grandson, "but I don't understand everything you are saying to me. I only understand English, but you know two languages, English and Swedish. You are lucky." His third birthday is soon. His bilingual parents—his translators—are in the hospital, the baby just born, so repetition of single words at increasing volume doesn't help me understand. The toddler, my husband, and I are playing in a Swedish park, where a city librarian has created a temporary mini-library on a blanket spread under a group of trees. Bilingual, she chats with us three, invites the toddler to pick out a book, sit down, and listen while she reads aloud in Swedish. He has so much to say to this stranger. My husband and I stand back. I say, "He's probably thinking, 'Finally someone understands me.'"

After a few stories, we lure him to us with the promise of swinging.

~~~

During the early 1980s, Susan Lohafer, in her Advanced Expository Writing, asks our class to write about something that irritates us, using three paragraphs: A, B, and C. Each paragraph should be about the same topic, but audience and purpose varied. We grad students go home to typewriters and correction fluid; a few days after turning in our assignment, we receive her handwritten comments.

I talk about my husband. He and I are in different grad programs, have different schedules. During supper, he is often chained to NPR's *All Things Considered* listening to Susan Stamberg and Noah Adams, not talking with me. Midway into paragraph A, I write,

> Every night it is the same. The addict walks in between 4 and 5 . . . I get a quick hello and then voices from Israel, from Capitol Hill, of BBC correspondents in Iran, of Big Ten economic department chairpersons from France and from Missoula speak to him. Reports about President Reagan and nuclear arms pull words from his mouth like "that idiot" and "what do they think they're doing?" He adds, "I can't believe it. Geez," as if he and the reporter were having an intimate conversation in a restaurant.

My teacher writes, "humorous, believable, telling."

In paragraph B, I plead to newspaper advice columnist Dear Abby to ask her readers to "flood NPR's headquarters with letters requesting that this husband-snatching program be taken off the air" and sign it "Silenced at Supper."

My teacher writes, "clever choice of format! Well done—especially the implicit parody of the Dear Abby genre itself."

Paragraph C follows a requested format of "inverted stance."

My teacher writes, "I guess I really wasn't convinced."

~~~

In 1989, I begin my career as a part-time teacher at a small liberal arts college located in northeast Iowa. Some semesters, part-time should be called full-time. I routinely hand out assignments on Stardust, a creamy-white paper flecked with small colors, or paper of solid purple, blue, or green. Sometimes I give pencils as gifts. On day one, before students depart, they write in response to a set of self-as-writer questions; their words help me see their accomplishments and concerns. Interacting with first-year students in Introduction to College English, I incorporate an adaptation of Susan's assignment. This Irritant One and Irritant Two sequence ignites young writers returning to classes after fall break. They're back to doing their own laundry and living in a dorm. Fledglings are surprised when I ask them to switch audiences, challenge them to request action, not merely complain. It's nonfiction practice in successful transaction.

Irritant One: An Informal Exercise in Persuasion & Audience

As a way to work with persuasion, write about something that bothers you—something that irritates you, makes you wish it were different. It doesn't matter how big or small your irritant seems to others; what matters is that it troubles you. It might be something as small as your work-study hours. It might be as big as a college policy. Maybe it's connected to a person back home or a government action. Maybe it's a particular point of view someone holds. It should not be something about yourself, or me, or anyone in our class. It should, though, be something that a particular person or group of people has power to change.

What exactly is it? What happened? Be specific. Why does it bother you?

Your readers are your classmates, so select a topic you feel comfortable having all of us know about. If you write about a person at school, don't use their real name. Write at least two, but no more than three, double-spaced pages.

Irritant Two: A Persuasive Exercise in Changing the Audience

Now that you've written to us, a group who probably can't fix what bothers you, write about the same topic, but to a particular person—or group of people—who could fix your irritant. Include an explicit thesis—stating what you want done and why—in the first paragraph. Type this in letter format—as if you are really writing to that person or group. Length should be short and concise—the single-spaced letter must fit on one page.

If you wrote about your work-study hours, for instance, write to your supervisor. Tuition? Write to the Board of Regents who set the fees. An unfair governmental policy? Write to one of your country's leaders. An action many people do? Write a letter to a newspaper. The topic is the same, you are the same writer, but the audience changed. Use material from Irritant One—but shaped/trimmed/reworked for the new reader.

In class, fifteen or so students sit in our customary circle to read each other's Irritant One pieces. They laugh and smile, show empathy, comment aloud when compelled, and hope to read everyone's complaint. My presence as a reader would be an intrusion so I hover at the edge. Near the hour's end, I hand out the Irritant Two assignment and ask the students to help each other figure out their new audiences.

Later, after reading Irritant One and Two at home, sitting near a Victorian parlor window with its bubbled and wavy glass, I comment on the tone of voice I hear and point to several especially persuasive areas. No one gets a letter grade, though I make sentence refinements and usually award a check-plus.

By the middle of the semester, these teenagers have improved their fluency and realize that, as Margaret Atwood says in *Negotiating with the Dead: A Writer on Writing*, "the secret is that it isn't the writer who decides whether or not his work is relevant. Instead it's the reader" (122).

~~~

While my daughter naps in her apartment bedroom, her newborn lies wide-awake on his back, on my swaying thighs. The baby and I are on a fading green hand-me-down sofa, the perfect height for the standing toddler to kiss the baby's head. Within moments, the toddler flexes his arm muscles, to show he is similar to Pippi Longstocking, his freckled hero who is not only strong but kind. The toddler's long-sleeved t-shirt features Pippi's likeness and signature stripes. As the boy transitions into a sibling who uses meltdowns to cope, he is entranced by a fictional Swedish girl with upturned pigtails who can lift her horse with one hand. Stories, true and invented, allow us to try on lives, help us see who we are, maybe should be. The infant sibling, though, is not yet a story gatherer or creator, but "programmed to search out faces, although this may just be because the two dark spots that are your eyes are the easiest things for them to focus on" (Alcock 17).

~~~

After 2010, I negotiate for Introduction to U.S. Academic Writing to be added to our college's offerings. I've worked with first-year international students in the Introduction to College Writing classroom and realize most are superb linguists, fluent in numerous languages besides their mother tongue: global citizens. Yet they often haven't written the type of college-level essays expected in a U.S. educational system, have never argued a debatable thesis in prose, have respectfully deferred to the wisdom of elders, have followed a protocol neglecting documentation, have employed flowery phrasing with vague substance. Though verbally fluent and strong readers, some have not composed anything in the English language beyond clusters of sentences. Their strengths and concerns are similar to, but not the same as, native speakers of English, though both groups build on their high school accomplishments.

With support from division colleagues and a faculty vote, the course is approved. It's not an ESL course, nor necessary for all incoming international students to enroll; students invited to take the course are chosen by an administrator familiar with global transcripts. Sections meet twice a week for fall semester; students write about personal experience. A first assignment asks them to talk about one of their talents. The second might be a person or place within a country that represents home, and how interactions with that person or place give them strengths to take with them into this new place. Sometimes it seems like Lou and I are co-teaching, as these are adaptations from her series of writing lab assignments. I ignore surfaces errors and don't give any grades until after midterm. I move the students into thesis-driven writing about literature, after the personal essay format offers a foundation of practice in supporting general ideas with specifics, analyzing audience, and revising pieces they thought were finished.

My classroom companions—we are a community of writers—are swamped with adjusting to a fast-paced academic schedule, work-study shifts in the cafeteria, speaking to teachers, asking for help. They are searching for friends and teachers to trust, time to sleep, chances to call their families on other continents. Writing their thesis-driven analytical essay about a nonfiction book—such as *The Moth* or *The Girl Who Smiled Beads*—is often stress-producing. I measure their essays against a standard grid to determine a sometimes-disappointing letter grade. These students don't know it yet, but at the end of the semester when they hand in their portfolios, they are better able to assess this paper as if they are the reader not the writer, and to articulate its problems and strengths with a cold eye.

To make self-critiquing skills stronger after the thesis-driven essay about literature, students dip into persuasive writing. In letter format, they tackle persuading a real person they know from home to come or not come to study at our college. Their argument combines the person's or outside reader's interests, the writer's experiences in college, quotes and paraphrases from an interview with a friend on campus, an interview with one of their current teachers, and information from the college catalog. It's nonfiction close to their hearts, as I assign the topic during registration for spring semester. Thinking about their chosen college's suitability for another person demands soul-searching about what they themselves are gaining or not gaining. So maybe joining a club to meet more people might be a good idea. Sending the letter-essay to the outside audience is optional.

At the end of the semester, students write answers to a set of self-reflection questions including "which essay do you think is your strongest and why?" The essay often chosen is Cultural Identity Persuasive Essay: Opinion and An Outside Source. The prompt asks for a four to six page, double-spaced, persuasive essay in which they support their opinion with specifics from personal experience of living in the US during recent months, include an explicit or implicit thesis, and incorporate quotes gained by interviewing a friend about whether or not they think of the writer as someone from another country:

> You are living in a country where you didn't grow up, a guest in a culture you went to great efforts to join. Some of you have traveled in the US before this semester; some of you have never been in the US until you arrived for school. Who are you when you are here? Do you strongly identify yourself with your home country? Do people think of you as a country? Are you an outsider, looking in, or an insider? Are you yourself or a version of yourself?

In the semester's sequence of activities, this essay comes after I meet with each student individually about using specifics, and we go over sentence-level issues that give them trouble. They read aloud to me. Before they draft the Cultural Identity essay, we discuss as a class what they dislike about their present academic environment. They say some U.S. students think Africa is a country. Some U.S. students assume they own pet lions, or, if from Brazil, play soccer. There is too much food wasted in the cafeteria as evidenced by leftovers sent to the dish room. The tossed-around label "America" is demeaning, as it signals Latin America, Central America, and South America are inferior or non-existent. Not enough U.S. students want to get to know them.

Some concerns are heart-breaking, but adaptation strategies show strength. They know I am listening.

~~~

Severed Ties and Silenced Voices, the nonfiction book I'm reading in Scandinavia—when I'm not washing dishes or playing a made-up game of *No! Nej!* with the toddler—traces interwoven tragedies of three immigrants who left Sweden during the Great Famine of the 1860s. The bleak trio and their kin are outsiders, users of two languages, Swedish of home and limited English of a place they might not want to call home.

My daughter first tried on life in Sweden nearly a decade ago; a new language and culture has joys and sorrows. Though she speaks Swedish successfully in her job, sometimes to receive what she absolutely needs, such as getting a medical professional to understand health concerns about the children or herself, her husband speaks on her behalf. The sound of her accent can be a blur to native speakers' ears, indicating she is "not really from here."

According to *Your Baby's First Year*, before babies are born, they hear in the womb, though "it is not until 35 weeks [gestation] that they are able to hear the full range of sounds. The intonation and timbre of your voice and that of your partner are already very familiar to your newborn" (17). After birth, babies operate by reflex—startle, grasp, rooting, sucking. They can set off a reflex even by hearing their own crying.

~~~

In the 1980s, the formidable Carl Klaus, in our Expository Writing Workshop, tosses out blunt comments. His strategy is to make us look closely at paper copies of our drafts and base analysis on sentences, paragraphs, and words—and to decide whether the overarching whole of an essay deserves long-term attention. Today it's my turn to be the center of roundtable critique. Readers speak in my essay's defense, but we're edgy. When it's over, I'm unhinged. It is hard to separate myself from a personal essay. Other pieces written for Carl's course I stash in a folder for a few years, reread with cold eyes, and revise for publication in regional literary magazines. Over time, practice and risk-taking mean discovering what's possible to say, and discerning what elements work, don't work, and why. Though crafting a particular essay can be a lengthy process, often in Carl's workshop it's as if I am a pale green luna moth granted a life span of about one week. I'm urgent, driven.

I don't yet know my hoped-for career as writing lab director will remain a daydream, nor that I will morph into a "basic writing" classroom teacher who adds upper division courses such as Creative Writing: Nonfiction or Literary Ventures: Life Stories to her repertoire. But some of my grad student cohorts and I ponder how we would run peer workshops. I form a resolution. I will ask for honesty and helpful kindness, not mean-spiritedness, as readers write comments following a prepared set of questions meant to guide revision. *What are the draft's messages to you? What is especially effective? Why? What do you want to know more about?*

Offer at least three specific suggestions. Underline any hard to follow sentences, but don't make sentence-level corrections. Without re-looking at the draft, what images or scenes stay with you? A quick "this is great" or "this is horrible" is not an option. Each reader will sign their name to take ownership.

~~~

A few weeks into September 2017, my Creative Writing: Nonfiction class reads Paul Kalanithi's beautifully crafted memoir *When Breath Becomes Air*. Before materializing mid-afternoon on Tuesdays and Thursdays, my student Carly Mester and her classmates write responses to prompts that aim to foster close reading. This jump-starts conversations about what the dying-while-living neurosurgeon says and how he relays messages about being a doctor and patient.

In their late teens or barely into their twenties, my student-writers prepare for their futures. Kalanithi died in March 2015, at age 37, closer to their age than mine. During one discussion, the focus pivots to whether a doctor being treated for stage IV lung cancer should perform brain surgery. Carly raises a hand, reveals she recently underwent brain surgery. Paul, she ventures, is smart enough to know when he should stop doing the job he loves. The junior data science major trusts him as narrator and character. By speaking aloud, Carly gives herself permission to wrestle with her unwanted medical story, put some control on the emotional and physical experience of allowing her skull to be opened. Carly shapes words for others to hear. She makes her personal connect to universal, untethers her internal voice from external silence.

Though Carly doesn't know it yet, this semester she'll build a collection of creative nonfiction pieces on the diagnosis and aftermath of a brain tumor. In the nonfiction textbook *Tell It Slant*, Brenda Miller and Suzanne Paola suggest "sometimes, what matters to us most is what has mattered to the body" (7). In an email, Carly tells me she is "not one to talk much about my brain tumor and the consequential unilateral hearing loss stemming from this, apart from the occasional social media post. Because of this, most students and professors in courses I have taken have no knowledge of my disability." She does not "desire special attention." While brainstorming possible topics for assignments, Carly decides writing about her life situation is not a "cop out." It is freeing and frightening.

From September to November 2017, Carly drafts and polishes essays on a "golfball-sized dragon, medically categorized as large" that "was now discovered: full of rage, spitting fire, wanting to burn down my castle." "Slaying My Dragon," Carly's first essay, begins with the dateline August 1, 2016 and a neuro-ophthalmologist saying, "We'll just get an MRI done, just to rule out anything serious." In paragraph two, datelined August 2, 2016, Carly sits "on the chilled concrete steps outside of my workplace, hysterically sobbing over a phone call." The essay quickly abandons a diary format, its sections inconsistent. The tumor is "rare, benign" with imagery evoking kingdoms and battles in an undated paragraph three. Undated paragraph four is a show of strength against "my dragon" and a list of abilities to summon for the "slaying" of the "beast": "guts, resilience, intensity, toughness." The structure switches to a series of paragraphs or sections talking about each of these words, including the information that she has two surgeries, but elaborating on only the second. The last paragraph keeps up the knight versus dragon imagery (though the essay never says "knight") and reveals the September 8, 2016 date of the first surgery.

No wonder this tumor pummels my student's mind: I dished out this Aspect of You memoir assignment close to the first anniversary of her initial brain surgery. The anniversary of the second surgery will be in late December 2016, just after the end of the semester. As a creative nonfiction writer, Carly is trying out format and metaphor to proclaim that she is victorious; she concludes "My dragon has been slayed, not only physically by teams of astounding surgeons from across the country, but mentally by myself as well. Its fire and rage are extinguished, no longer trying to burn down my castle. For I will not let it."

The piece is a fine first attempt, but too empty.

Carly's second essay about her brain tumor is a response to the assignment, Rooted in Place. This requires weaving research about a particular place and personal experience of being in that place. She titles her meditative essay "Abyss of Solitude." Carly's place is the Grand Canyon, the national park she and her family visit five days before her second brain surgery is performed in Phoenix. Carly sections consistently and uses a single asterisk between four sections spanning five pages. At Mather Point on the canyon's south rim, Carly hints at the aftermath of the second surgery: "My soon-to-be-lost unilateral hearing takes in the chirping of the birds, the wind whistling through the rocks. I appreciate the magnificence before me."

I learn she has a twin.

After a section ending with reflections on feeling "nothing but alone" while her family will have each other during her upcoming operation, and that "the loss of control has hit," Carly writes this section of three paragraphs:

> The Hopis are one of the oldest living cultures in documented history, with a past stretching back thousands of years. Referred to as *Öngtupqa* in the Hopi language, the Grand Canyon carries great spiritual significance for the Native American tribe that has long inhabited the region. Upon death, a Hopi is believed to pass westward through the *sipapuni*, or "place of emergence"—a dome of mineral deposits that sits upstream from the union of the Colorado River and the Little Colorado River inside the canyon—on his or her journey into the afterlife.
>
> I mull over the concepts of death and the afterlife with increased frequency as each day closer to surgery approaches. The likelihood of demise under the knife in this procedure is well under

one percent. One percent is not zero. I am given waivers, signing that my knowledge of the risks is clear. At some point, death is inevitable. For a newborn little girl, exuding amazing health since the womb. For an ornery old man, lying in a hospice center. For a nineteen-year-old woman, living life seemingly normal until an attacker is uncovered in her brain. Not many things are certain. Death is.

About 4.5 million people visit the Grand Canyon each year, and an average of 12 people die there annually. The deaths can be attributed to anything from natural causes, medical issues, and suicide to heat, drowning, and traffic crashes. An average of two or three deaths per year are from falls over the rim. Whether control is lost in a person's hands or in higher jurisdiction, death cannot be escaped. The Grand Canyon covers hundreds of miles of Arizona desert, a human is only a speck in this area. The canyon does not have any regard for life, for its inanimate nature does not let it. As living creatures, cherishing life is possible. No matter the circumstances that death may arise, relishing time on Earth is vital.

Carly has eased herself into the slippery genre of creative nonfiction, where answers can be elusive.

The last in Carly's trio of essays connected to her brain surgery is titled "Hear Me Out, " a revision of an earlier piece for an early November due date. This is the star product of her attempts to corral her altered life: specifics developing a narrower focus of hearing loss, more showing than telling, cliché phrasing absent, no dragon slaying or castle burning, a consistent diary pattern, threads of repeating imagery about her mother crying, a fast-paced present tense, streamlined inclusion of facts, developed scenes tied to some of the five senses, more sentence-level artistry. Of December 23, 2016, Carly writes,

> Once again, events unfold just like the first surgery, except this time with my twin brother: check in, pre-op, paper gown, anesthesia, mother crying, reality fades to black, eight hours, ICU, oxygen mask, family appears.
>
> A neurosurgery intern approaches me while I lie motionless in the ICU hospital bed. While he asks standard post-operative questions, I suddenly say, "I'm not sure if I can hear out of my right ear." The intern cups his hand over my ear and speaks. I still cannot decipher with certainty whether my hearing was damaged or not, for my mind is still cloudy and processing things around me at a lower-than-average mental speed. However, I do notice a slight muffling of the surrounding noises. I

look at my family and weep, creating intracranial pressure and pain in my freshly carved skull.

In an email to me, Carly says about her disability and writing, "I am not ashamed of what I have been through and it is a part of me, and you have instilled that mantra in me." In spring semester 2018 Carly threads pieces of these essays about her tumor, two surgeries, hearing loss, and constant ringing in her ears into application material for a Pediatric Brain Tumor Foundation scholarship to help with college expenses. She wins.

~~~

In *Prospect and Retrospect*, Britton writes that for a toddler, "talking to himself about what he is doing helps him in two ways: first, he interprets to himself the situation that confronts him, clarifying and defining it; secondly, he organizes his own activity within that situation. At this stage his monologue is in a strict sense 'a running commentary'" (72). In *Bird by Bird*, Anne Lamott writes, "tell the truth as you understand it" (226). Reflecting on nearing his final undergraduate years at Stanford before training to be a neurosurgeon, Kalanithi writes, "I was less driven by achievement than by trying to understand in earnest: What makes human life meaningful?" (30). Perhaps this familiar question is at the heart of allowing students to expand their rhetorical flexibility through crafting and reading creative nonfiction: these intersecting ways humans capture and examine life stories, shape the personal to have universal significance, wrestle with truths calling our names.

~~~

Taking a break from childcare, my husband and I tread a gravel path at the Baltic Sea's edge in Stockholm—an archipelago city of islands and water. We have just left the galleries of Waldemarsudde, the former home now art museum of Prince Eugen of Sweden, a landscape painter and art collector who lived from 1865–1947. We discuss the paintings of Sigrid Hjertén, a stranger to us until today. People and places, categorized by decades, speak from stark walls. A 1916 self-portrait in a black dress enhanced by a light blue yoke. Red lips sneering on a purple-suited man with a beaky nose. A full-lipped child looking toward the viewer while its parents are in profile. The artist invites me to gaze and judge, consider life, hers or mine, parceled into episodes, before my husband and I board an evening train.

With brush strokes and color, Hjertén, who died in 1948, has made a successful business transaction; I enter the museum gift shop hoping to buy postcards of her work.

~~~

It's spring 2018 in Literary Ventures: Life Stories. When introducing the unit on personal statements with a prescribed number of characters for an online application, I spin a true tale of two scientists: my brother and my sister-in-law. One hires graduate students for wildlife field research in the United States and Canada. The other hires post-docs for experiments in a Midwestern plant pathology lab. One says if he is not reeled in by the end of the first paragraph, he doesn't read the rest. The other reads to the end of each statement. Applicants don't know if their readers (who put hopefuls in a yes, no, or maybe category) will be like my brother or sister-in-law. I urge my students to compose with honest specifics so they come alive in their bid for an internship, job, graduate program, scholarship.

Make someone care.

For inspiration, I read aloud a few examples from past students. My tip sheet urges them to begin a personal statement with a narrative, drop it, and pick it up in the end. I recite its list of familiar phrases and words to avoid: I remember, things, stuff, everyone, it was something that, I am someone who, I was given the opportunity to, out of the blue, and also, I began to realize, I started to panic, I believe, I could hardly contain my excitement, in today's society, I personally think, it made me the person I am today, memories that last a lifetime, I have always wanted to be a doctor.

I lose my filter. *No, you did not want to be a doctor when you were born! Or a physical therapist! Or a summer camp counselor! Or a CPA in Minneapolis! Or work for an NGO! Or even always help people! You were a baby! Delete the word always! And while cutting, reduce the number of times you use I, my, and it. Trim lengthy verb conjugations to past, present, or future. You'll have better results—trust me!*

My charges are surprised I can be bossy.

Our three-week Personal Statement unit includes one-on-one brainstorming conferences (where I pose questions and jot down spoken answers for on-paper-take-away), a peer workshop on a draft-in-progress, a peer workshop on an improved draft, and a finished-for-now living document to change as needed. If a student already submitted a personal statement for graduate school or a job, they write a fresh one. Selecting truths to persuade an audience can be tough. Neither cockiness nor meekness is persuasive. Because it's easy to sound like a resumé list, blending specifics with analysis is challenging. Approaching a personal statement as a personal essay—a portrait, or perhaps essay of ideas with a thesis, supported by life experience specifics and analysis—can be persuasive. Just ask Meredith Arpey, a senior who *always* wanted to be a doctor.

After a class period early in the semester, while other students are clearing out or chatting, Meredith inquires if I will read a personal statement that she already sent to medical schools which rejected or ignored her. I skim silently while she fusses with her backpack. The statement presents Meredith as a generic shadow rather than a capable person. The first paragraph is visually off-putting. A colon after the lead sentence, an indented long quote from a story whose author and title aren't mentioned, a quote within the quote, and a flush left return to the long quote's conclusion. Meredith's eight-line quote from "a father of a fifteen-year-old boy" starts, "It begins with a young boy on the beach amongst thousands of starfish." Meredith tacks on some attributes "a great physician" should possess, such as "weighing risks and benefits," says "death is a natural part of life," and ends the paragraph with "I see traits of a physician in that young boy on the beach, and I see those traits within me." Talking with Meredith, I discover she had summoned the ghost of Loren Eiseley and his much-googled Star Thrower, a story not hers to tell.

Paragraph two further buries Meredith's personality and accomplishments in, for example, a random dance marathon reference and vague sentences, including "pediatricians have a unique opportunity to serve as role models for sick children." Paragraph three begins, "There is one unifying characteristic I have noticed among all the physicians with whom I have interacted and who have become my role models: their ability to connect with and develop relations with their patients, who come from all walks of life." She finishes by connecting "fifteen years of playing club and collegiate soccer" with "environmental science," and generalities applying to teammates playing with a ball and students having a major.

I say, "Meredith, I would not have let you send this personal statement. There isn't anything compelling enough to make a reader care. But you can write a strong piece. Think of this one as practice. Did anybody besides you read this?" To her answer, I say, "Parents are not necessarily the best judges, because they love you."

Meredith accepts this challenge: she wants to win.

After numerous drafts of a start-from-scratch personal statement and conferences where I question her abstract claims and push her to craft true scenes, Meredith presents herself as a multifaceted person who comes alive on the page. Flood waters and mosquitoes bookend her finished statement. In her soul-searching writing process, Meredith realizes she can happily see herself in a public health graduate program, not medical school. After completing a public health program, maybe she will try for medical school; maybe, though, public health is her true calling. Meredith's revised statement begins:

> On Wednesday, August 24, 2016, I awoke to see my favorite place on Luther College's campus under four feet of standing water. It was pre-season of my junior collegiate soccer season, and our team was looking promising; we had only graduated three seniors, and we were excited to get the season underway. Instead, our practice and well-kept game fields looked like a mosquito breeding ground. Our community was more important than any practice, so 150 Luther student athletes flooded Decorah to push water out of strangers' homes, salvaging all we could. This unfortunate event instilled a deep commitment to help communities determine and better understand ways to protect and enhance their public health.

As reader, I am hooked. Paragraph two talks about how "pursuing a degree in environmental science opened my eyes to worldwide risks created by a changing environment." Meredith illustrates that claim with specifics that include "an environmental policy and politics course gave me insight into issues such as China's one-child policy and water quality in Flint, Michigan." Paragraph three discusses her "senior capstone research paper on ways a changing climate will affect the spread of malaria primarily in African countries" and that "malaria control leads to resistance to anti-malarial drugs and poses further environmental and individual health concerns."

The personal statement is about Meredith. Paragraph four reveals she was a summer "intern at the State Hygienic Laboratory at the University of Iowa" where in the sample preparation lab, she "completed ancillary tasks including stocking and cleaning glassware, disposing of drinking water as well as oil and water samples, preparing standard solutions, and chopping and pulverizing foliage samples for testing." Paragraph five shows her compassion for strangers through sponsoring "an impoverished Haitian child, ensuring he eats daily and attends a school where he can receive attention from a nurse" and being "heavily involved in Dance Marathon, an organization that provides emotional and financial support for children battling life-threatening illness at Children's Miracle Network hospitals."

Who knew, until now? Meredith concludes:

> A few weeks after the Decorah flood that drowned our first five home matches of the season, the breeding ground dissipated, leaving a terrible smell, an excess of mosquitoes, and a muddy playing surface. Even though our soccer team dedicated our practice times to serving our community, for the first time in Luther College Women's Soccer history, we made it to the second round of the national tournament. We lost to the eventual national champions, but more importantly, we helped our town recover. Though my competitive playing days are now over, I remain dedicated to and excited for a lifetime of learning, working with others, and serving both the public and the environment, and enthusiastically look forward to the next steps in my education and career.

This young person welcomes me, her reader, into her life experiences and yearning with images of water and mosquitoes. Meredith "pledges," as Miller and Paola say, "to be as honest as possible with the reader and to make this conversation worthwhile" (149). Meredith is accepted at seven out of the eight schools that receive this personal statement in her application.

Meredith is accomplishing what she wants: a life-enhancing transaction.

~~~

Now a seasoned professional with publications and a wealth of spiral-bound blue grade books, I can't shake a sometimes frustrating conundrum. I graduated from the University of Iowa's Master of Expository Writing Program during its trail-blazing infancy, when creative nonfiction was not a much-used phrase. Under the leadership of Richard Lloyd-Jones, my companions Lou, Susan, and Carl intersected with my journey inside the English-Philosophy Building, fostering my desire to become an effective, intellectually curious, and confident teacher and writer. The academic world I encountered after my Iowa City life is hierarchical. Some colleagues question the unfamiliar M.A. degree. Do I fit in their Ph.D. scheme? Years after the innovative program's name is changed to Nonfiction Writing Program (NWP), offering an M.F.A. "terminal" degree, the then-director of the NWP assures me I am grandfathered in and belong to the respected M.F.A. clan.

But who am I and what do I say in a Notes on Contributors entry? According to *Your Baby's First Year*, "Newborns are very sensitive to smell and your unique body smell is an important part of how they learn to recognize you" (17). For sure, I *never* wanted to be a doctor.

~~~

The end of August 2018. I toss around the notion that maybe this academic year is my swansong. Teaching writing is labor intensive. Maybe this is the last of the hundreds of students, thousands of papers, and hours of creating or revising sequences of meaningful nonfiction activities to help students gain confidence on the page, preparing them for the successful transactions they want in college and beyond.

I flirt with revisiting a languishing memoir a decade in the making, compiling my newspaper essays about British royal watching in which I'm a quirky character, drafting a personal essay about a Victorian-era Dollar Princess from the Midwest who married an impoverished English lord. I conjure my University of Iowa teachers as I walk from my house to day one of classes. On my way home, fresh batches of Self as Writer responses in my satiny-beige backpack, I fall into rhythm. On-the-cusp-of-adulthood souls, some frightened and some eager, willing to learn, are entrusted to me for a short time. It is an honor to be their guide as we engage in our risk-taking, yet lovely, bargain.

Within hours, my husband and I will leave for the United States. A ripened bouquet of pink roses and airy leaves sent by my daughter's Swedish co-workers, and zinnias picked from a community garden plot are on the kitchen table alongside a roll of paper towels and last night's plastic bib decorated with a smiling purple elephant riding a scooter. Pushing three miniature cars and trucks on the tabletop, the toddler is singing in his version of Swedish about his personal world to the tune of *Twinkle, Twinkle, Little Star.* His song names his family, including the baby, and wee-oh, wee-oh sounds of an ambulance's siren, a vehicle crash. He says the word "crash" in English. I understand the concept as this is his morning pattern, his ritual while lying in bed, faintly awake, or after he pads into another room, holding his plush rabbit.

This has been my life for over three weeks, this gentle quietness my child's child and I share before the others in the household, including the newborn, awaken. *Severed Ties and Silenced Voices* is back on a bookshelf. The toddler straddles two languages and has no firm concept of time, yet internalizes that we are connected through transactions and love.

And sometimes through toast smeared with strawberry jam.

Works Cited

Alcock, Anastasia, with Beth Graham and Lulu Baker. *Your Baby's First Year*. Quadrille, 2015.

Arpey, Meredith. Essays. Luther College, Decorah, IA, spring semester 2018.

Atwood, Margaret. *Negotiating with the Dead: A Writer on Writing*. Anchor, 2002.

Britton, James. *Prospect and Retrospect: Selected Essays of James Britton*, edited by Gordon M. Pradl. Boynton Cook, 1982.

Kalanithi, Paul. *When Breath Becomes Air*. Random House, 2016.

Kelly, Lou. *From Dialogue to Discourse: An Open Approach*. Scott, Foresman, 1972.

Lamott, Anne. *Bird by Bird: Some Instructions on Writing and Life*. Anchor, 1995.

McKnight, Roger. *Severed Ties and Silenced Voices: Separation and Social Adaptation in Two Swedish Immigrant Families*. Nordic Studies Press, 2008.

Mester, Carly. Essays. Luther College, Decorah, IA, fall semester, 2017.

Miller, Brenda and Suzanne Paola. *Tell It Slant: Creating, Refining, and Publishing Creative Nonfiction*. 2nd edition, McGraw Hill, 2012.

Shaughnessy, Mina P. *Errors and Expectations: A Guide for the Teacher of Basic Writing*. Oxford UP, 1977.

Chapter 11. Redefining Preparation: The Need for Creative Nonfiction in High School

Nicole B. Wallack
COLUMBIA UNIVERSITY

> How does the writer of personal narrative pull from his or her own boring, agitated self the truth speaker who will tell the story that needs to be told?
>
> – Vivian Gornick

> Trying to work toward emotional, spiritual, familial, intellectual, professional, political and the big ETC. of truths is not just a part of, but is the process of writing, of composing nonfiction.
>
> – Wendy Bishop

> If we theorize creativity as a highly sophisticated and valuable form of cognition, it must also, then, by definition, be regarded as a necessary and indispensable part of any curriculum in a writing classroom.
>
> – Patrick Sullivan

We need more occasions to tell the truth, nowadays, both in school and outside of it. The methods and forms of creative nonfiction are premised on the idea that attending to real life—first-hand experiences, observations, memories, encounters with texts, and other phenomena—can lead a writer to pose hard questions, do research, and move beyond what makes them comfortable or safe, intellectually or otherwise. Creative nonfiction, regardless of subgenre, depends on the writer being willing, able, and welcome to be present on the page, as well as intentional about the experiences they craft for their readers. Writers of creative nonfiction are often self-aware and sometimes self-conscious. In the best cases, these qualities can inform surprising ideas in essays, create thick descriptions in travel accounts, reveal our stances as connected critics, and prompt frank, nuanced reflections in memoirs.

As readers of creative nonfiction, we may be introduced to phenomena that are outside our ken, but even if the subject matter is familiar in some way, writers of what Ronald Weber has called the "literatures of fact" newly navigate territories of all kinds for their readers—often simultaneously. For example, E. B. White, James Baldwin, Joan Didion, Ian Frazier, Colson Whitehead, Eula Biss, Rebecca Solnit, and Phillip Lopate render New York so that their versions remap our visions of a city many of us know well. They show us a knowable world, enlivened by their distinctive presence and distilled through the fine-grade alembic of their prose. With all of this showing and telling to do, who better to try their hand at creative nonfiction than teenagers in high school? After all, high school is a time when you reckon with what your presence in the world means and how to ask questions about that real world whose answers matter to you, for one.

A high school student's daily experience of writing begins—at this moment in the 21st century—on their phones. They text, they post, they respond, react, link. They don't edit much as they seek readers, some known, some not, in genres they value for their speed and ubiquity. Imperfections are expected, because this writing occurs as part of their lives outside of school, often for people they know (or believe, or hope) exist. Once the student arrives at school, the phone may have to be relinquished or hidden; sometimes they can use it, but only for purposes authorized by a teacher or administrator, who may or may not put their own phones away. Without a phone, the student might write in a notebook, by hand, or on a tablet or laptop, which may have been provided by their school district, if they live in an area where tax revenue or a philanthropic donor funds them. This writing they do is real, too, in its own way. But it's different. Teachers and perhaps other students will read their homework, their quizzes, their in-class exercises. Students may value and seek out these readers, but they mostly do not have a hand in shaping the *purposes* or the forms for the writing. So, the writing may be high-stakes, but not feel as real as what they choose to write for themselves.

As in other subjects, English and language arts teachers assign writing to inculcate skills and prepare students for formal assessments and, perhaps, for college. However, the bulk of these assignments are designed to reflect knowledge students have already acquired. Less common are writing assignments that foster students' capacities as seekers of new knowledge. We teachers, students, citizens need more actively to identify genres and practices that invite us to tell the truths of our lives so that we can examine them, share them, trouble them, and revise them. In the 21st century, high school students and teachers need to read and write creative nonfiction.

When we do not teach creative nonfiction genres in high school, we miss an opportunity to foster negative capability. The term comes from the Romantic poet John Keats and is used to identify the power of some poets to tolerate "being in uncertainties, Mysteries, doubts, without any irritable reaching after fact & reason" (109). A robust, diverse, and sustained creative nonfiction curriculum in high school can fulfill in under-appreciated ways the goals of literacy standards documents such as the Common Core State Standards, and exceed them. At the same time, a creative nonfiction curriculum can create greater coherence among subject areas, provide meaningful ways to teach what the composition scholar Patrick Sullivan asks us to rethink as "critical *and* creative thinking," improve knowledge and skills transfer, and perhaps most important of all, help teachers and schools to devise high school writing curricula that produce assignments that are worth reading and worth writing. As American students and teachers know all too well, high school is an environment no more sheltered from the world around it than any other place in our public lives. We show that we value high school as a real time and real place when we teach writing that students will know is meaningful for them *as* high school students, not just as people who are waiting for their "real lives" to begin in college or at work.

Then again, there are reasons—some better than others—why high school teachers and administrators might be reluctant to make creative nonfiction writing a centerpiece of English Language Arts curricula. Here are three common concerns:

- Creative nonfiction writing is for more accomplished people—artists and others who have already demonstrated that they know the "basics" of school writing, whatever they might be.
- Creative nonfiction encourages writers to indulge their narcissism.
- Creative nonfiction does not teach writerly skills that will transfer to college or the workplace.
- It's not possible, really, to grade a piece of creative writing.

But I suspect it is equally likely that we are afraid . . . of students' possible revelations of trauma, or confessions of things that we might not be able or willing to hear about their experiences and perception of themselves and their world. Of being confronted directly with their politics-in-formation. Of their ignorance, vanity, mean-spiritedness, and biases. Of first thoughts that masquerade as choices or beliefs or commitments. Of the possible responses of their peers. Of blurring the line between judging their work and their worth as a person. Of assessing a writing genre that most of us have not written ourselves.

Teachers of writing face all of these issues regardless of whether or not we ask students to read and write memoirs, essays, op-eds, travel writing, open letters, and speeches. All seasoned teachers know that we cannot prevent troublesome material from showing up in the first place. If we really want students to be nimble thinkers, then we need to teach them the genres of writing that we have available to us in which to realize and test their thinking.

No teacher denies that it is hard to read through a stack of student work. Yes, it's the volume—it takes a particular kind of stamina to stay with the 138th student paper in a pile of 150 of them; what truly makes it difficult to sustain our attention is when we sense that the writing is missing the *presence* of the student in it—all of their terrifically odd, striving, difficult, eager, questioning, touchy personhood. When they don't have a place for their presence, or when they believe (because we teach them) that they should show up on the page in their school work only on special occasions, then we are forfeiting an opportunity to teach them how these seemingly unlovely qualities can give them the motivation to write and a method to articulate the exigence of what they write for others.

Students in public high schools whose literacy curriculums align with the Common Core State Standards (CCSS) are assured that they will build their skills for "college and career-readiness" by practicing various well-known school genres: the literary analysis in English class, the procedural lab report in science, the summary and analysis in social studies. According to the CCSS, these writing assignments will produce three kinds of "texts": "narrative," "argument," and "informational" (CCSS 18). Of course, these are simply abstract skills, not genres at all. However, in the odd taxonomic organization of the CCSS, it appears as if each of these kinds of texts requires its own curricular focus. It is no wonder that even expert high school teachers and administrators might make the choice to keep assignments focused on one literacy skill at a time. So, a student might write arguments and textual interpretations in an English class (perhaps as they practice for an AP language and composition exam), and write informational and procedural texts in science or social studies. But what about narratives? Well, perhaps there will be room for the student to write them when they are practicing their college application essays.

It is, in fact, too easy simply to blame the CCSS for what we are and are not teaching in high school, although there are reasons to explore its impact. A decade after the CCSS were initially adopted, literacy researchers including Arthur Applebee, Judith Langer, and Morgan Polikoff, among others suggest that it is still unclear exactly how school districts have implemented the CCSS, how we can measure their efficacy in terms of student "outcomes," teachers' professional development, or according to any of the measures on the National Assessment of Educational Progress (NAEP).

One thing is clear, however. Despite the CCSS, students do not write very much in high school, and when they do, it is almost entirely to summarize or analyze the ideas of others, usually in the form of an answer to a multiple-choice question or one that requires, as Arthur Applebee puts it, "formulaic on demand writing," even in English class (6). Narrative writing and almost all creative writing, while still sometimes a feature of grammar- and middle-school classes, has largely disappeared from high school English Language Arts curricula, despite the requirement on the CCSS for students to become proficient in writing "narratives" to "develop real or imagined experiences or events using effective technique, well-chosen details, and well-structured event sequences" (18).

This fact should interest David Coleman, one of the architects of the CCSS and president of the College Board. Coleman has argued that the CCSS's emphasis on information and argument "texts" was meant to be a corrective to what he has called the "two most popular kinds of writing [in high school] . . . the exposition of a personal opinion or the presentation of a personal narrative." Moving away from personal writing is warranted, he argues, because "as you grow up in this world, you realize that people don't really give a shit about what you feel or what you think." High school students, like other thinking people, likely would have plenty to say back to Coleman about the rhetorical strategies he employs here, what kinds of evidence he might need to demonstrate its value, and to explore the implications. Here is one of those implications: too many students learn that they write in school to inculcate testable skills, without a role for their personhood or the languages in which they render it visible. Under these circumstances, these students are less likely to trust writing as "a technology of thought" with which to engage the materials they encounter, as I have written elsewhere. When we teachers frame writing primarily as the performance of skills that students will "really" need later on, we blunt its epistemological force and miss a chance to see how writing fosters social visibility and connection among a wide range of what writing studies scholars now understand as threshold concepts—which Linda Adler-Kassner and Elizabeth Wardle first defined in *Naming What We Know: Threshold Concepts in Writing Studies* as "concepts critical for continued learning and participation in an area or within a community of practice" (3). For example, Kathleen Blake Yancey explains in her section the threshold concept that "writers' histories, processes, and identities vary." She notes, "we write as both individuals and as social beings," which are not writerly stances but rather writerly conditions (52). The pedagogical implications of this are significant: "[h]elping writers mature requires helping them write to others while expressing themselves" (52). Threshold concepts tend to register as common sense, even obvious, until one considers what we lose without these understandings informing our classroom practices and curriculums. Students are not likely to write to anyone besides their teacher if the writing itself is understood solely as an exercise. So perhaps it is time to offer an additional threshold concept: writers' contexts need to be valued by those within and beyond them. The degree to which students experience their writing in high school as real reflects a belief in the fact that high school itself is not just a waiting room for college and career—the "real world"—but a time and place that has intrinsic value.

In the same decade that teachers and students of writing in high school have been reckoning with the impact of the CCSS on curriculum and instruction in their schools, which has reduced to almost nothing direct instruction in creative writing across all genres, the number of creative nonfiction programs and courses in colleges and university have seen exponential growth. Although the Association of Writers and Writing Program (AWP) has been in existence since 1967 and has published its journal, *The Writer's Chronicle,* since 1970, the academic field of creative writing studies has begun to emerge more visibly since the turn of the 21st century ("Our History"). According to AWP's most recent figures, as of 2016 there were 1,808 college-level creative writing programs internationally.

The presence of creative writing instruction—and specifically creative nonfiction—has also found its way into professional schools and training outside of the humanities and arts. Rita Charon, an internist and literary scholar, instituted the Master of Science and Narrative Medicine program at Columbia University Medical Center in 2009. Charon has led the effort to recognize the intellectual and emotional value for health practitioners and researchers of writing creative nonfiction in her articles, books, and talks, including *Narrative Medicine: Honoring the Stories of Illness*. Charon writes: "[M]any of us within medicine and within literary studies have realized the critical importance that writing—autobiography, memoir, pathography, fiction, personal essay—has developed within health care" (62) for clinicians, patients, and families. Of course, narratives of health, illness, science, and care have driven creative nonfiction writers from its beginnings, but the more recent turn to its training value for practitioners signals a significant shift in focus.

Creativity itself, as a teaching and learning goal, is finding new proponents both inside and outside of educational contexts. Patrick Sullivan offers a helpful review of the current literature to argue that creativity ought to be a central pedagogical focus for college composition courses. In "The Un-Essay: Making Room for Creativity in the Composition Classroom," he cites the eight "habits of mind" identified in the "Framework for Success in Postsecondary Writing": curiosity, openness, engagement, creativity, persistence, responsibility, flexibility, metacognition (16). Not only is creativity one of the Framework's goals, but, Sullivan notes, "creativity manifests itself in a variety of ways on this list. Curiosity, openness, flexibility, and metacognition can all be grouped together within a suite of dispositional characteristics that feed and nurture creativity" (16). Exploring methods for people outside of school contexts to increase their creativity is the focus of popular books by Daniel Pink, Elizabeth Gilbert, the cartoonist Lynda Barry, the educational researcher Ken Robinson, and the biologist E. O. Wilson.

Sullivan's exploration of creativity ends with a section detailing an assignment that offers an example for what a creative alternative might be for students in a writing course. In the directions for his final assignment, he exhorts his students to find a different form for their work:

I would like you to think about all that we've done in this unit and then construct an "UnEssay" that pulls together your thinking about the fine arts and creativity! But it can't be a traditional essay. It can't be a five-paragraph theme. It has to be something else and it can be whatever you want it to be. Invent a new form! Write the kind of "paper" or essay you've always wanted to write in an English class. Feel free to include pictures, photos, links, and multimedia if you wish. Most importantly: Have some fun with this! (26)

It is clear Sullivan trusts his students to find or invent forms for their ideas. It is likely they would find it liberating to move away from a "traditional essay"—figured here as a five-paragraph theme. At the same time, his invitation suggests that the students have only a single, dominant paradigm in mind for what essays are or could be, and he is not alone in this experience and belief . . . even if it is not entirely accurate.

While Sullivan does not claim explicitly that the five-paragraph essay was imprinted on his students in high school, it is a common complaint among college faculty (Dennihy; Wallack), which has led both to calls for "unteaching" it or "laying it down" (Tremmel) in both high school and college writing courses.

It might not be surprising that what high school English teachers should do with or about this form has been an evergreen concern; articles on the problem have been published steadily in the *English Journal* since its first volume in 1912. In "The Aims of the English Course," William D. Lewis characterizes the "written theme" as multi-faceted horror: a "poison . . . to complete the destruction of a lurking fondness for our glorious literature," "a nightmare to the pupil and a night-grind to the teacher" (12). Where he notes progress in teaching composition, it is in teachers' then-new willingness to "[assign] themes from the daily lives of pupils, only insisting that in their efforts they make us and their fellows see and hear and feel and think with them" (13). Elizabeth Hodgson, writing two years later, notes that students are asked to "conjure together a few ideas from nowhere, addressed to nobody, and aimed at nothing—that is, nothing but credit for one theme duly written" (233). Missing from these themes are both life and purpose. Hodges suggests that writers should "orient" themselves, by deciding prior to writing, "what public to address, upon what subject, and with what purpose" (234).

The enduring current-traditionalist orientation to teaching composition relies on the form's limits to address every writerly "weakness" from poor grammar to leaky logic (Tremmel). Unfortunately, as Michelle Tremmel notes, "rather than form following function, the formula of the five-paragraph theme precedes function—and is often a-rhetorically and inappropriately grafted onto function—in ways that derail composing" ("What" 34). Defending her high school colleagues who teach the form, Melissa Dennihy explains that they "present [the five-paragraph theme] as one starting point for essay writing" (162). It is possible that in high school there are more teachers who are ready to move past a limited vision for what essays and essaying might entail, but this shift will require a clearer sense of the alternatives.

In literacy and writing studies, scholar-teachers who are concerned with how students learn the essay in school, decide to disavow the essay as a genre. Joanne Addison and Shannon McGee ask almost 100 years after Lewis and Hodges "whether or not 'the essay' as a genre is a useful or viable genre upon which to base writing curricula at all levels" (171). The scare quotations are worth considering further. They tell us that a particular variety of essay is suspect; they remind us that the school essay, even beyond five paragraphs, is an unnatural entity, a "mutt genre," as Elizabeth Wardle so memorably described assignments in first-year composition courses. Genres are mutts (a term she credits to Jamie Heiman) when they "do not respond to rhetorical situations requiring communication in order to accomplish a purpose that is meaningful to the author" (777). Mutt genres such as five-paragraph essays or, as Wardle suggests, the ubiquitous "position paper" not only fail students because they are not responsive, they also actively "[conflate] purpose and genre" (777). They also can impede students from transferring their knowledge and skills from one rhetorical, compositional, or creative context to another (777).

The school essay then not only feels inauthentic; it also acts as a placeholder for some other, more real genres. Addison and McGee suggest that we need to "do more to encourage instruction in genres that embrace both the deep learning promoted when writing is an integral part of any course as well as exhibit the multimodal skills now required across the curriculum and into the workplace" and name as alternatives, "literary journalism that is rooted in artfully crafted narrative and critical research-based writing" (171). That is, they propose that starting in high school, students begin to explore the myriad genres and praxes of creative nonfiction.

Since the Civil War, and arguably earlier, in North America anyone with a stake in shaping English education has sought to identify the goals of English classes. Whenever we have gotten stuck and tried to imagine innovations to our curriculums, we turn to creative writing—poetry, drama, and fiction. Only since the beginning of the 21st century have high school teachers of writing started in earnest to "[imagine] a place for creative nonfiction," as Douglas Hesse suggests (in his 2009 article of the same title) we could. Hesse argues that the varied genres of creative nonfiction in high school would "provide students with a better map of the textual world" and "teach reading and writing for life beyond institution" (20). As important is Hesse's understanding that reading creative nonfiction—i.e., works that "let us see 'the real' imaginatively or 'the imaginary' realistically . . . shape our civic, social, and personal lives, our senses of the world and ourselves in it" (21). Writing in these genres "reminds us that, while facts may be waiting for finding, interpretations are waiting for making" by a specific, individual consciousness—the student's writerly presence in the text (21). In creative nonfiction, not only are writers expected to be visible, they are also responsive and responsible to the realities they are depicting for the publics they call into being.

Hesse is not alone in offering both reasons and practices for increasing creative nonfiction's visibility in high school writing classes, particularly in the age of the Common Core. Valuable studies by teacher-researchers have explored the power of creative writing in high school, and yet, these pieces tend to feature or foreground single assignments or units, largely focused on poetry or fiction (see DiMarzio and Dippre; Leigh; Carolyn Miller). Rarer to find in the literature are accounts such as Laurel Taylor's "More Than a Reading Assignment: Using Nonfiction Texts as Mentor Texts." In this essay, Taylor describes a year-long experiment she conducted in her high school class featuring Jonathan Kozol's *Savage Inequalities* as a "mentor text" for her students. Kozol's book models his approach to writing research-based creative nonfiction. She made this choice to "help [her] students move from their current writing style—that of a five paragraph model—into something more appropriate for college writing and beyond" (49). The projects they produced are 25-page papers exploring an injustice that students want their own readers to redress. After two years of refining this project, Taylor has plenty to revise and rethink. She speculates that the students' successes had to do with their sustained focus on Kozol's writerly strategies and the incremental pre-draft and revision exercises she crafted to help them produce their own papers.

It is not entirely surprising that Taylor calls these final pieces of extended writing "papers," the most generically featureless name we can give writing in the humanities. It is worth noting that in the sciences and social sciences, the term "paper" is a meaningful genre category whose forms and purposes are known to their writers, both experts and novices. It is not usual to hear a scientist say that they recently read a "beautiful paper"; here, "beauty" is ascribed not to the prose but to the design of the study. While there are no meaningless genre names, scholars of writing-in-the-disciplines such as Chriss Thaiss and Terry Myers Zawacki have argued that there are no guarantees that the expectations for these genres will carry across disciplines.

What should Taylor have called these extended pieces of writing that looked nothing like the academic essay as Taylor and her high school students knew it? Perhaps the notion of writing "papers" also resonated with what they thought professors teach in college. When teachers do not name papers like these "essays," we miss a chance to make our rigorous and exciting projects for our high school students into the centerpiece of a fully realized creative nonfiction curriculum, a curriculum that depends on teaching genre awareness.

The 21st century has seen a surge of scholarly interest—in the fields of writing studies and English education—in the distinct contribution genre awareness can play at the high school and college levels. In their helpful overview of contemporary views on the subject, *Genre: An Introduction to History, Theory, Research, and Pedagogy,* Anis Bawarshi and Mary Jo Reiff argue that

> a dynamic view of genre [should include] not only knowledge of formal features but also knowledge of what and whose purposes genres serve; how to negotiate one's intentions in relation to genres' social expectations and motives; when and why and where to use genres; what reader-writer relationships genres maintain; and how genres relate to other genres in the coordination of social life. (19)

Their vision of understanding genre depends on examining how people develop, circulate, privilege, and revise genres in the real worlds of school and beyond.

Drawing on the work of Christine Tardy, Ann Johns, and others, Bawarshi and Reiff acknowledge that students are likely not to experience their learning of genre as significant unless the genres they are producing are real to them in the moment—that is, not as trial runs for actual uses and performances of genre. This means that students need to do more than learn to analyze and critique a genre's functions, features, and effects: students need to both contribute to and test the limits of their genres in which myriad disciplines traffic.

As I have argued in *Crafting Presence*, the essay—that most flexible and mutable of forms—thrives on formal experimentation and is the genre to which writers across disciplines turn when we are speaking to readers outside of our fields. The agreeable flexibility of the essay provides teachers and students with a genre that easily adapts to writers' changing needs inside and outside of the academy—or across the worlds of high school and college. Essays can range in form from literary experiments and idea-driven explorations, to op-eds driven by a desire to change minds and actions, to research-based work that builds new knowledge. Essays depend on experimentation and hybridity in writers' choices of content, structure, media, and linguistic inflections. We cannot create a sustainable creative nonfiction curriculum for high school without an entirely reinvigorated vision of the essay as genre and praxis—not as its inviolable foundation, but as lifeblood.

However, we only ought to make such efforts on the essay's behalf if the essay itself rewards such investment. A handful of writing studies scholars, including Wendy Bishop, Gordon Harvey, Paul Heilker, Lynn Z. Bloom, Candace Spigelman, and Douglas Hesse, have called for teachers, writing program administrators, and scholars to see in the essay a means to reconsider the goals and promise of writing instruction—both in high school and college. They each offer compelling reasons to do so. Wendy Bishop clarifies the motives of some of us: "those of us who (re)turn to the literatures of fact do so not to avoid investigations of discourse and community. Rather, we find nonfiction prose the appropriate investigative vehicle" (266). Paul Heilker, with refreshing candor, notes that he asks for students to read and write essays because they tend to yield pieces that both they and he can enjoy, and also because essay-writing can yield inherently meaningful work—work that they might want to keep, even after getting a grade. He writes, "I want to assign, foster, and read something that might last, that might have meaning and life outside the course requirements, even outside the university experience. Students' lives are inundated with ephemeral texts" (202). It is not sentimental to want students to engage in writing work that might endure or be worth returning to over time; in fact, some capacities we teach in writing courses (if by other names) are virtues: humility, patience, courage, compassion, and endurance. Essays require all of them.

Reading and writing essays in their various guises and humors provides curricular continuity upon which depends knowledge and skills transfer within high school, and from high school to college. As Kathleen Blake Yancey, Lianne Robertson, and Kara Taczak acknowledge in *Writing Across Contexts: Transfer, Composition, and Sites of Writing* (2014), college students "draw on what they learned about writing in earlier educational contexts, [which can include] middle school," even when they do not go immediately to college after high school (133). They also conclude, in light of Mary Soliday's findings, that to help students transfer their knowledge they should "compose in real world genres—so-called 'wild genres'—for real audiences" (134). Having a happy role for the wild in high school ought to appeal to those of us who, because of Thoreau, believe that "life consists with Wildness" (20).

Less quixotically, perhaps, teaching the essay as a wild genre rather than a thoroughly factory-farmed one would provide the means to create what David C. Perkins and Gavriel Salomon have called low road transfer, which they distinguish from high road transfer: "low road transfer reflects the automatic triggering of well-practiced routines in circumstances where there is considerable perceptual similarity to the original learning context," while high-road transfer "depends on deliberate mindful abstraction of skill or knowledge from one context for application in another" (25). The problem of transfer is one to which all teachers in any department should attend, of course. We do not have to give up on the possibility of fostering high-road transfer, while still getting more from low-road transfer across courses in which students already write essays. We would improve transfer if in every course where we asked high school students to read and write essays, we spent fifteen minutes of class time per week discussing, enacting, and reflecting on the essay's affordances as a genre. If this bar seems too low or too unambitious, high school teachers and administrators should ask where and how we communicate not only what we ask students to write, but why.

The emerging field of essay studies can provide high school teachers with some helpful language about the "why" of teaching essays—as well as other kinds of creative nonfiction. The work of Graham Good, Chris Anderson, Jocelyn Bartkevicius, Brian Norman, Cristina Kirklighter, Carl Klaus, Dinty Moore, Ned Stuckey-French, Robert Root and Michael Steinberg, Patrick Madden, Anders Monson, Phillip Lopate, and Crystal Fodrey has focused on rhetorical theory and pedagogy, the essay's historical development, craft, and literary analysis. Largely still missing from the literature are the perspectives of high school teacher-researchers about how we can reconsider essays for students in secondary school.

Essays offer approaches to reading and writing that embody some of the goals of a liberal education that must begin in high school, if not even earlier. As I write in *Crafting Presence: The American Essay and the Future of Writing* Studies, essays teach students to

- tack between self-expression and social commentary
- situate themselves in multiple contexts
- engage others' ideas and materials
- name and reflect on their values
- develop rhetorical awareness
- experiment with form and ideas
- craft new writerly presences in accordance with their materials, the publics they want to address or call into being, and the experience they want to create for their own readers.

Students will only have a chance of experiencing any creative nonfiction genres in ways that expand their capacities, and prepare them for a life of making choices about how they present and reflect on their worlds, if we design curricula for them.

Each community of teachers, in collaboration, will know best about what their students in any given year or cohort will be able to do as readers and writers of creative nonfiction. That being said, I want to propose the following features as starting points for any effort to design a creative nonfiction program, beginning with a focus on the essay:

Historical context: In any course where they might write creative nonfiction genres, students would learn the genres' history in different periods and cultures, and read both famous practitioners and innovators.

Shared pedagogical vocabulary: Over time, departments and schools would identify a limited vocabulary they would use to teach features of creative nonfiction across disciplines and years of study.

Sustained student inquiry: Students would reflect on creative nonfiction they read and write over time (e.g., in extended reading journals, annotated bibliographies, commonplace books.)

Published work: Every year, an editorial board of teachers and students would choose exemplary student creative nonfiction and publish it; teachers would use these publications as peer-mentoring texts for their current students.

Curricular articulation: Each academic year, faculty in each department would articulate and publish as a resource for their own classes' use and for their colleagues how the creative nonfiction genres they will teach intersect with other genres (e.g., blog posts, responses, research papers).

As the director of a writing program that provides first-year students at an R1 institution with their required essay-writing course, I am often asked by middle- and high-school teachers what they should be teaching their students in order to ready them for work at a university like mine. Here is what I have heard myself say:

> Your students will be ready to succeed in writing in college if they have begun to know that writing is not just a product, or a process to get to a product, but a set of practices as well as an academic subject that we can study for its own sake. They will benefit greatly if they have had experiences both responding to the work of other people in writing and having their own writing responded to, rather than simply graded. They will be well-prepared for college if they have ever had to come up with a problem to solve as a writer, in genres that they have studied well enough for them to describe their features and their purposes. They will have an easier time, if they have begun to cultivate across their classes relatively useful notetaking strategies, and if they have had multiple opportunities to revise their work. They should always know that there is no such thing as an academic paper, but many kinds of academic genres that

depend very much on the discipline in which they are working and often the faculty member who is assigning the piece. They would be well-served by any writing curriculum in high school if they knew that they had begun to work as writers using real-world genres that they can continue to study across their academic, professional, and social lives. They need most of all for each of their teachers to be reflective and explicit about the intrinsic value of anything that they write in school, so that the work they do for a grade has a shot at being more than simply that.

As recent history has told us, our well-prepared high school students are media savvy and ready to take up and circulate some of the most difficult debates of our time. Let us help to make more of them ready to show up when they know they have to.

Works Cited

Addison, Joanne, and Sharon James McGee. "Writing in High School/Writing in College: Research Trends and Future Directions." *College Composition and Communication*, vol. 62, no. 1, 2010, pp. 147–79.

Adler-Kassner, Linda, and Elizabeth Wardle. *Naming What We Know: Threshold Concepts of Writing Studies*. Utah State UP, 2015.

Anderson, Chris, ed. *Literary Nonfiction: Theory, Criticism, Pedagogy*. Southern Illinois UP, 1989.

Applebee, A. "Common Core State Standards: The Promise and the Peril in a National Palimpsest." *English Journal*, vol. 103, no. 1, 2013, pp. 25–33.

Applebee, Arthur N., and Judith A. Langer. "A Snapshot of Writing Instruction in Middle Schools and High Schools." *English Journal*, vol. 100, no. 6, 2011, pp. 14–27.

AWP: Guide to Writing Programs. www.awpwriter.org/guide/overview, accessed 18 July 2022.

AWP: Our History and the Growth of Creative Writing Programs. www.awpwriter.org/about/our_history_overview, accessed 18 July 2022.

Bartkevicius, Jocelyn. "Welcome to Our Country: Four Men Toss Around the Nonfiction Football." *Fourth Genre: Explorations in Nonfiction*, vol. 16, no. 2, fall 2014, pp. 147–60.

Bawarshi, Anis, and Mary Jo Reiff. *Genre: An Introduction to History, Theory, Research, and Pedagogy*. Parlor Press, 2010.

Bazerman, Charles. "Genre and Cognitive Development: Beyond Writing to Learn." In *Genre in a Changing World*, edited by Charles Bazerman, Adair Bonini, and Débora Figueiredo, Parlor Press, 2009, pp. 283–98.

Beaufort, Anne. *College Writing and Beyond: A New Framework for University Writing Instruction*. Utah State UP, 2007.

Bishop, Wendy. "Suddenly Sexy: Creative Nonfiction Rear-Ends Composition." *College English*, vol. 65, no. 3, Jan. 2003, pp. 257–75.

Bloom, Lynn Z. "Once More to the Essay: The Essay Canon and Textbook Anthologies." *Symplokē*, vol. 8, no. 1/2, 2000, pp. 20–35.

Charon, Rita. "Narrative Medicine: Attention, Representation, Affiliation." *Narrative*, vol. 13, no. 3, Oct. 2005, pp. 261–70. doi.org/10.1353/nar.2005.0017.

———. *Narrative Medicine: Honoring the Stories of Illness*. Oxford UP, 2006, pp. xvi, 266.

Clark, Irene L., and Andrea Hernandez. "Genre Awareness, Academic Argument, and Transferability." *The WAC Journal*, vol. 22, Nov. 2011, pp. 65–78.

Common Core State Standards. National Governors Association Center for Best Practices, Council of Chief State School Officers, Washington D.C., 2010.

Council of Writing Program Administrators, et al. *Framework for Success in Post-Secondary Writing Instruction*. 2011, wpacouncil.org/aws/CWPA/asset_manager/get_file/350201?ver=7548.

dcpublicschools. *David Coleman | Common Core | Summer 2011*. 2011. YouTube, www.youtube.com/watch?v=aTCiQVCpdQc, accessed 18 July 2022.

Dennihy, Melissa. "'Forget What You Learned in High School!': Bridging the Space between High School and College." *Teaching English in the Two-Year College*, vol. 43, no. 2, Dec. 2015, pp. 156–69.

Devitt, Amy J. *Writing Genres*. Southern Illinois UP, 2004.

DiMarzio, Erica, and Ryan Dippre. "Creative and Critical Engagement: Constructing a Teen Vision of the World." *The English Journal*, vol. 101, no. 2, 2011, pp. 25–29.

Fodrey, Crystal N. "Teaching CNF Writing to College Students: A Snapshot of Pedagogical Scholarship Before Assay." *Assay: A Journal of Nonfiction Studies*, vol. 2, no. 1, Jan. 2015.

Good, Graham. *The Observing Self: Rediscovering the Essay*. Routledge & Kegan Paul, 1988.

Harvey, Gordon. "Presence in the Essay." *College English*, 1994. pp. 642–54.

Heilker, Paul. "Twenty Years in: An Essay in Two Parts." *College Composition and Communication*, vol. 58, no. 2, Dec. 2006, pp. 182–212.

Hesse, Douglas. "Imagining a Place for Creative Nonfiction." *English Journal*, vol. 99, no. 2, 2009, pp. 18–24.

———. "The Place of Creative Nonfiction." *College English*, vol. 65, no. 3, Jan. 2003, pp. 237–41.

———. "The Place of Creative Writing in Composition Studies." *College Composition and Communication*, vol. 62, no. 1, Sept. 2010, pp. 31–52.

Hodgson, Elizabeth. "Orientation in English Composition." *The English Journal*, vol. 3, no. 4, 1914, pp. 233–37.

Keats, John. *Keats's Poetry and Prose: Authoritative Texts, Criticism*. W.W. Norton, 2009.

Kirklighter, Cristina. *Traversing the Democratic Borders of the Essay*. SUNY Press, 2002.

Klaus, Carl H. *The Made-Up Self: Impersonation in the Personal Essay*. U of Iowa P, 2010.

Leigh, S. Rebecca. "The Power of the Sketch(Book): Reflections From High School English Students." *Journal of Adolescent & Adult Literacy*, vol. 55, no. 6, Mar. 2012, pp. 539–49.

Lewis, W. D. "The Aim of the English Course." *The English Journal*, vol. 1, no. 1, 1912, pp. 9–14.
Lopate, Phillip. *To Show and to Tell: The Craft of Literary Nonfiction*. Free Press, 2013.
Madden, Patrick. "More Good News for Nonfictionists." *Fourth Genre: Explorations in Nonfiction*, vol. 16, no. 2, fall 2014, pp. 183–87.
Miller, Carolyn R. "Genre as Social Action." *Quarterly Journal of Speech*, vol. 70, no. 2, 2014, pp. 151–67.
Miller, Carolyn R., Amy J. Devitt, and Victoria J. Gallagher. 2018. "Genre: Permanence and Change." *Rhetoric Society Quarterly* 48 (3): 269–77.
Miller, Mike. "Breaking the Thin Glass: Alternative-Genre Responses to Standardized Writing Tests." *English Journal, High School Edition*, vol. 107, no. 3, Jan. 2018, pp. 100–05.
Moore, Dinty. "Why We Call It 'Creative Nonfiction.'" *Creative Nonfiction*, no. 56, summer 2015.
National Assessment of Educational Progress. *2011 Writing: Grade 12 National Results*. www.nationsreportcard.gov/writing_2011/g12_national.aspx?tab_id=tab2&subtab_id=Tab_1 - chart.
Norman, Brian. *The American Protest Essay and National Belonging: Addressing Division*. SUNY Press, 2007.
Perkins, David N., and Gavriel Salomon. "Teaching for Transfer." *Educational Leadership*, vol. 46, no. 1, Sept. 1988, pp. 22–32.
Polikoff, Morgan S. "Is Common Core 'Working'? And Where Does Common Core Research Go From Here?" *AERA Open*, vol. 3, no. 1, Jan. 2017, doi.org/10.1177/2332858417691749.
Root, Robert L., and Michael Steinberg. *The Fourth Genre: Contemporary Writers of/on Creative Nonfiction*. Pearson, 2012.
Russell, David R. "Rethinking Genre in School and Society: An Activity Theory Analysis." *Written Communication*, vol. 14, no. 4, Oct. 1997, pp. 504–54.
Soliday, Mary. *Everyday Genres: Writing Assignments across the Disciplines*. Southern Illinois UP, 2011.
Spigelman, Candace. *Personally Speaking: Experience as Evidence in Academic Discourse*. Southern Illinois UP, 2004.
Stuckey-French, Ned. "Our Queer Little Hybrid Thing." *Assay: A Journal of Nonfiction Studies*, vol. 1, no. 1, 2014.
Sullivan, Patrick. "The UnEssay: Making Room for Creativity in the Composition Classroom." *College Composition and Communication*, vol. 67, no. 1, Sept. 2015, pp. 6 34.
Taylor, Laurel. "More Than a Reading Assignment: Using Nonfiction Texts as Mentor Texts." *English Journal, High School Edition*, vol. 105, no. 4, Mar. 2016, pp. 49–54.
Thaiss, Chris, and Terry Myers Zawacki. *Engaged Writers and Dynamic Disciplines: Research on the Academic Writing Life*. Boynton/Cook, 2006.
Thoreau, Henry David, and Jeffrey S. Cramer. *Essays: A Fully Annotated Edition*. Yale UP, 2013.
Tremmel, Michelle. "Laying Our Burden Down: Saying Final Goodbyes to Theme Writing." *Journal of Teaching Writing*, vol. 30, no. 1, June 2015, pp. 55–76.

———. "What to Make of the Five-Paragraph Theme: History of the Genre and Implications." *Teaching English in the Two Year College*, vol. 39, no. 1, Sept. 2011, pp. 29–42.

Wallack, Nicole B. *Crafting Presence: The American Essay and the Future of Writing Studies*. Utah State UP, 2017.

———. "Focused Freewriting: How to Do Things with Writing Prompts." *Writing-Based Teaching*, edited by Teresa Vilardi and Mary Chang, SUNY Press, 2009, pp. 25–52.

Wardle, Elizabeth. "'Mutt Genres' and the Goal of FYC: Can We Help Students Write the Genres of the University?" *College Composition and Communication*, vol. 60, no. 4, June 2009, pp. 765–89.

Weber, Ronald. *The Literature of Fact: Literary Nonfiction in American Writing*. Ohio UP, 1980.

Yancey, Kathleen, Liane Robertson, and Kara Taczak. *Writing Across Contexts: Transfer, Composition, and Sites of Writing*. Utah State UP, 2014.

Chapter 12. Creative Nonfiction Accents the National Day on Writing

Douglas Hesse
University of Denver

Alec Baldwin wants to make sure he pronounces my name correctly. We're standing beside a stage on the top floor ballroom of the Mandarin Oriental on Columbus Circle in New York City, for a truncated dress rehearsal of the Norman Mailer Gala presentations, October 4, 2012. Baldwin is the master of ceremonies, and I'm presenting $5,000 checks to high school, college, and two-year college winners of creative nonfiction contests I've organized for the National Council of Teachers of English (NCTE). Baldwin is shorter and slimmer than I expected him to be, more *Hunt for Red October* than *30 Rock*, and he's taking all his responsibilities very seriously. I'm nervous as hell. This is the fourth time I've presented at this event, but I still feel an imposter among the star power assembled.

A few minutes earlier I'd met Mohammed Ali. A small group of prize winners and presenters had been ushered into a small side room where Mr. Ali was seated in the middle of a couch, wearing sunglasses and looking remarkably frail, sitting silently and absolutely still, his Parkinson's entering its final phases. A photographer quickly posed us while Ali's wife looked on, and then, as quickly, we were ushered out. I introduced a red bow-tied Garrison Keillor, who was there to give a fiction writing prize, to North Carolina high school English teacher Kay McSpadden. Keillor was intrigued by the title of her winning story, "Why Women Moan in Bed," and further humored that her husband was a Presbyterian minister. Joyce Carol Oates received an award.

The previous year's Gala event had been perhaps even more surreal. In the reception space outside the Mandarin Oriental ballroom, I apologetically backed into Tony Bennett, who was there to see Keith Richards get a Distinguished Biography award from Bill Clinton, for his recently published memoir, *Life*. I stood at the podium ten feet from Richards at a front table, his gray hair shocked up with a bright red headband, wearing tinted glasses, a loose dark suit with an unbuttoned white shirt, and a long silk scarf around his neck, hanging to his waist. It was unnerving. Also receiving awards that night were Elie Wiesel, Arundhati Roy, and Gay Talese. Roy provided a tense moment during her acceptance speech, when she took time to chastise Wiesel for Israel's policies with Palestinians; the Israeli ambassador to the U.N., Ron Prosor, was in the audience. The highlight of the evening was Clinton telling how Richards had graciously come to visit his family and signed a copy of his book for Hilary's mother, Dorothy Rodham, long a Stones fan. The former president reported her telling him, "I always did like those bad boys," a comment that got huge laughter. For his part, Richards played around. Holding up his award medallion, he observed that he was in a room full of famous writers and joked that he didn't see what was so hard about writing books, "You hacks." But then he turned serious and acknowledged the crucial effort of his co-author, James Fox, whom he then invited to speak.

When I gave the first NCTE Mailer Writing Awards, hosted by current and former *New Yorker* editors David Remnik and Tina Brown on October 20, 2009, Toni Morrison was the most luminous celebrity, but she wasn't alone. The room was filled with "glittery literati," as the *New York Times* reported the next day (Cohen). Oliver Stone. Salman Rushdie. Annie Lebovitz. John Waters. Ken Brown. Joan Didion. Jhumpa Lahiri. Don DeLillo. Doris Kearns Goodwin was the final speaker. Calvin Trillin was the master of ceremonies, and while he didn't ask how to pronounce my name, he did make a crack about Colfax Avenue in Denver, which he noted *Playboy* magazine had called "the wickedest street in America." As much as Denverites want that story to be true, it isn't. I replied with something flustered about Kansas City, Trillin's home town.

I'm gushing. I'll beg your pardon and explain why an English professor was handing big checks to students at celebrity dinners where plates started at $2,500. Then I'll explain what all of this signified at an historical moment for the NCTE, when the organization reached what I judge its apogee in celebrating everyday writing across America. For about a decade, starting around 2005, NCTE was seeking to expand public understanding of writing and its teaching. In addition to sponsor research and pedagogy for English teachers, the Council more overtly entered the realm of advocacy, opening a Washington, DC, office to influence policymakers and interact with other disciplinary organizations. With the help of a Ball Foundation grant, executive director Kent Williamson created the National Center for Literacy Education, coordinating two dozen other organizations, mathematicians to social scientists. NCTE sought to shape wider public perceptions of writing, including not only as something done for school and work but also in public and private lives, for a range of personal and interpersonal reasons. *Writing in the 21st Century*, an NCTE report written by Kathi Yancey, provided the intellectual framework for public efforts that found their apogee in the Mailer writing awards and the National Day on Writing.

The first Mailer gala was held on the first National Day on Writing, organized by the NCTE, and the event capped a nationwide series of events all centered on gathering and celebrating writing by "plain Americans" from all walks of life, plumbers to police, nurses to students, in lofty but also, especially, workaday/everyday genres: notes, social media posts, journals, documents. The National Day on Writing was born in an 800-word proposal that Kent Williamson brought to the NCTE executive committee in August 2008, as agenda item 22 of its summer meeting. Kent explained having been contacted by a staff member from the National Association of Secondary School Principals, who wondered if there was such a thing as a national writing day. The answer was no, but the idea generated interest among some NCTE leaders and staff, enough that Kent roughed out a few thoughts. President Kathi Yancey put it on the agenda for formal consideration, and the executive committee approved the concept and asked for preliminary planning.

With an initial desire to have a national day devoted to writing occurring as early as late January 2009, time was rather of the essence. Kathi and Kent put together a committee consisting of Sharon Floyd, Jennifer Ochoa, Kathi, Kent, and me, with NCTE staff including Barbara Cambridge, Millie Davis, Mark Rowe, Sharon Roth, and Mila Fuller. Charged to bring a recommendation to the executive committee by September 1, we had our first phone call on August 19, which I took from a Denver kitchen in shambles from remodeling. The group brimmed with ideas that quickly organized around two poles. One cluster was the day itself, which would feature having people write, of course, but also other activities: advocacy, celebrations, and the like. The other cluster concerned possible activities leading up to the day itself.

In his early proposal, Kent speculated that "the Council could reach out through its membership to invite not just teachers and educators, but all whom they touch (including students, parents, and other community members) to post their writing through the NCTE website to a national log or archive." He mused further that we might "mine the [resulting] database of collected writings to draw instructive lessons for policymakers during the 2010 Advocacy Month, and may well use the project as the rallying point for our first policy symposium or press conference in DC . . . cultivating grassroots support for future legislation or public initiatives that NCTE may choose to sponsor on 21st century literacies or writing" (Williamson, National Writing Day). Our committee embraced this general idea. One line of conversation focused on whether to have a theme for all this writing or simply make an open call. The other line focused on logistics and frameworks. I suggested that rather than an archive or database of writings, we might use the language of a National Gallery of Writing, replete with halls, wings, and salons. Maybe we could have different people open and curate different parts of the gallery, their main job being to encourage submissions and provide some minimal screening.

We ended that first meeting by agreeing each to do quick writing, which Kent gathered and circulated before a second meeting (Williamson, "Agenda"). During that second conversation, we settled on recommendations to the executive committee that included creating a National Gallery of Writing. We also, not trivially, settled on The National Day on Writing—not "of." The choice struck many as clunky, but our reasoning was that we didn't want to imply people should write that day only; in fact, one emerging interest was in bringing to the national consciousness how thoroughly writing pervaded all daily life, every day. The preposition "on" was to signify that this day would call attention to writing, that writing would be its feature and focus. People very well might write that day, but we wanted people on that day to think *about* writing. Years later, I'm not sure our subtlety was worth the effort.

By the time Kathi Yancey delivered her president's remarks at the November NCTE convention, much of the framework was established, as was the day's purpose. Kathi explained:

> This project affirms individual writers at the same time that it creates a major resource showcasing writing at the beginning of the 21st century . . . [It] places the knowledge of NCTE members at the heart of a very dynamic, large-scale enterprise. Second, it allows us to serve a much wider public while also gaining recognition as a community that has much of value to offer society (and needs to be supported!). And finally, it has the potential to "de-mystify" writing for those who don't think of themselves as writers while subtly making the point that writing is a skill that no segment of society can do without. (NCTE, "Minutes" 6)

With the help of Verizon and other partners, NCTE created www.galleryofwriting.org,1 an ambitious portal for gathering and displaying writing, and began building the national infrastructure to gather submissions. A brochure published in spring 2009 explained "three types of display spaces." One was the Gallery of the National Council of Teachers of English, "a broad mosaic of writing" hosted by the Council. A second was the Gallery of National Partners, several spots hosted by the many corporate and educational partners who joined the enterprise, from Verizon to the National Writing Project. Third, and most capaciously, was the Gallery of Local Partners. Any group could apply for a salon in this last gallery, the brochure inviting families, classes, schools, churches, clubs, workplaces, cities, or whatever. For example, I formed a Colorado Gallery of Writing, which I explained in an op-ed for *The Denver Post*, published October 17, 2009, inviting all Coloradans to send their writing. As you can see, NCTE's impetus was radical openness and inclusivity. In fact, a key point of the National Day on Writing was to make visible and celebrate writing in all facets of life, from the grand to the mundane. We wanted everyone to recognize themselves as writers. Kent asked me to write a few invitational words for the launch brochure and the website, and I embraced the vision in, a little pretentiously, the voice of Walt Whitman.

> Let's imagine America writing.
>
> Let's imagine essayists and auditors, poets and nurses, tweeters and technicians, blogging beauticians, church bulletin scribes, advocates and analysts, authoring.

---

1. This website no longer exists nor, sadly, as I'll explain below, do any of its contents. All the writing gathered in the gallery seems lost—or the dozens of hours I spent plumbing the Internet Archive's Wayback Machine simply illustrate my ineptitude. In any case, NCTE has no files.

Let's imagine memoirs and memos, rants and remembrances, oral histories, letters to the future, postcards from the past, profiles profane and sacred, instructions, directions, reflections, retorts, factual and fancied.

Let's imagine a living American gallery of writing checked with salons, fitted by school or site, by genre or by identity, but most importantly by you, salons in which a homeless man's story hangs next to the finance major's wedding vows.

Let's imagine school kids linked to college students, teachers to professors, and all to city halls, shelters, board rooms, all linked by writing.

Let's gather writers who'd never thought themselves that: mothers, bus drivers, fathers, and veterans. Let's have sharings, coffees, contests silly and celebratory, so that the national gallery of writing has myriad outposts, local and physical. Let's open our writing centers to our communities.

Let's imagine October 20 and all this embodied in a National Day on Writing, a day when we cut the digital rope on our Gallery, when the Norman Mailer Writers Colony gives creative nonfiction awards to high school and college writers in a gala ceremony sponsored by famed New York writers, students whose work has been supported and selected by NCTE members. Actually, that day is planned. What's needed to make it happen is you. Please help.

After a complex series of emails, October 20 emerged as the celebratory day itself, with a strong factor being the Mailer/NCTE Writing Awards, the logistics of that star-studded day creating a very narrow window. While the day had been set by early spring 2009, it received extra imprimatur on October 8 in Senate Resolution 310, sponsored by Robert Casey (D-PA), which declared October 20, 2010 as the National Day on Writing and called on "educational institutions, businesses, community and civic associations, and other organizations to promote awareness of the National Day on Writing and celebrate the writing of their members through individual submissions to the National Gallery of Writing." Barbara Cambridge, in NCTE's Washington office, was fundamental to this effort. Several of us around the country garnered similar resolutions. My colleague Geoffrey Bateman persuaded Governor Bill Ritter to establish October 20 the National Day of Writing in Colorado, his staffer drafting the proclamation making known their preposition preference.

The day itself was a whirlwind. NCTE had set up the day's activities in studio space at the New York Institute of Technology, at Columbus Circle in New York

City. At 4:00 p.m. that afternoon, Kathi Yancey and I were live, doing a webcast on college writing. With naive faith in America's airlines, I flew into LaGuardia earlier that afternoon and barely had time to check into a hotel on 57th Street and walk over to NYIT. Kathi and I talked about current developments in college writing. Prior to our hour-long session, numerous NCTE luminaries were live, including Cathy Fleischer and Linda Adler-Kassner, Lucy Calkins, Carol Jago, Ernest Morrell, Marilyn Valentino, and Bonnie Sunstein, who share a video, "What is a Writer." Interspersed throughout the day, which ran ET 9:00 a.m. to 8:00 p.m., hosts shared postings from the National Gallery of Writing. But a few outsiders spoke, too. The featured presenter at 11:00 a.m. was listed as "Presidential candidate Obama on the importance of writing (10 minutes)" (Williamson, "just to give you").

After the broadcast, I went back to my hotel, changed into a tux, and walked a mile south to Cipriani, on 42nd Street, location of the Mailer Gala. Cipriani was an impressive space with marble columns, inlaid floors, lofty arches, and dramatic lighting, designed for the kind of ostentatious impression befitting the building's origins as the Bowery Savings Bank and well repurposed for lending grandeur to events. I was barely in the door when the evening's architect, Larry Schiller, introduced Bonnie Sunstein, Susan Reece, and me to William Kennedy and Toni Morrison. Morrison told us she'd once been an NCTE member.

Schiller was the effusive broker of the Mailer-NCTE connection. When I first met him on the phone, I took him as an energetic impresario whose torrential stock of anecdotes must have been exaggerations at best. I knew he'd been a close friend of Norman Mailer, who'd made Schiller his literary executor, but really, those Forrest Gumpish stories and those exuberant plans? I confess I was proven utterly wrong. He did, in fact, photograph Marilyn Monroe and publish a famous book of pictures, *Marilyn and Me*. He really did direct seven movies and miniseries, winning five Emmys, including for *The Executioner's Song*, based on Mailer's book on which he collaborated. He really did collaborate with OJ Simpson during and after his trial to co-author a book presenting Simpson's views. He really did write a book about JonBonet Ramsey, *Perfect Murder, Perfect Town*, then was executive producer of a television movie based on it. Clearly, in working with Schiller, I was traveling miles above my small-town Iowa apogee as Sky Masterson in *Guys and Dolls* and president of the high school science club. Schiller made me dizzy.

Several months after Norman Mailer died, in November 2007, Schiller had approached Kent Williamson with an idea to sponsor student writing contests, both to encourage young writers (he told me of how important a contest had been to him in his formative years) and to perpetuate Mailer's legacy. He had a lot of money and ideas, but he didn't have the network or wherewithal to organize a national contest. He perceived that NCTE, with its longstanding student writing awards series, would be a good partner. Kent invited me to join a few other members in an exploratory conversation with Larry. Afterwards, I told Kent that I saw considerable advantages to a partnership, which would connect members and students to what seemed a high-profile literary crowd. However, I cautioned him that Mailer's reputation among NCTE members was complicated at best. After all, Mailer had cultivated an alpha-male persona of tough machismo that was ripe for critique and conflicted with some values held by teachers, especially at the college level, even if Mailer's progressive bona fides were solid. I thought the advantages outweighed the risks, but I wanted the NCTE leaders to understand Mailer's problematic reputation. I also noted that he was a writer few high school students or teachers were reading and that, when Mailer was assigned in college, it was generally a few essays or excerpts from books like *Executioner's Song*, as examples of technique. I found (and still find) him an important journalist and nonfictionist, even if I also share some of the dismay for his persona.

In the end, NCTE and Schiller agreed to collaborate, and in an NCTE executive committee vote on January 31, 2009, I was asked to organize the contest. I selected a small group that included longstanding members Bonnie Sunstein and Susan Reese. I figured that the world didn't need another fiction or poetry contest, and it surely didn't need students submitting traditional academic papers. I suggested to Schiller that creative nonfiction would be a meaningful focus for student writers, who could send everything from memoirs and personal essays to literary journalism, and that this umbrella would also recognize Mailer's significant contributions in the genre. Larry agreed. Working with Kent and with the deputy executive director of NCTE, Mila Fuller, who with Marcia Loeschen would manage the day-to-day logistics of the contest, I drafted contest guidelines and a call for submissions that was printed in brochure and featured in NCTE communications. From it, Schiller developed advertisements he placed in the *New York Review of Books*, *Publishers Weekly*, and elsewhere.

We considered various judging approaches, including ones that would screen at the high school, district, and/or state levels, providing filters before works would enter the national pool. In the end, we settled on the most open process possible: high school students would submit directly to the contest, with no supervision or oversight beyond providing information through which we could contact teachers and parents, the former for recognition, the latter for permissions. College students were free to certify their work as their own and to give (or withhold) permissions to publish. Submissions were online, students uploading files that were converted to pdfs. We wanted to welcome and trust students, especially seeking writing not done as part of any class. We also wanted to avoid bureaucracy, especially for teachers. While I lobbied for this approach, I'll confess that it scared me. What if we got 10,000 submissions? After all, the whole judging system I developed depended on a multi-step process. A large group of readers at the first round would each read 30–50 pieces, sending a fraction to a second round. No rubrics or elaborate systems. Simply identify the five works you thought best. Teams of second-round readers chose pieces to send to a third round, who would choose finalists and honorable mentions. The finalists would be judged by prominent writers invited by Schiller. (That first year, those judges were Ted Conover, Adrian Nicole LeBlanc, Anne Fadiman, Barbara Lounsberry, Lee Gutkin, and Melissa Fay Green.) While I was confident we could identify 100 first-round judges, I was less certain we could find twice that number if we were deluged by entries. Fortunately (or not, depending on how you look at it), that year had about 800 high school submissions and about 350 college submissions, which I allocated to various layers of judges, sending five finalists to the marquee final judges.

The high school winner that year was Laura Swanagin, a senior at the Alabama School for the Arts, who wrote a moving, braided personal essay, "Luna," in eight segments, each headed with a fact about the moon—for example, "The Orbiting Period," "Impact Craters," and "Maria (lunar planes) and terrae (highlands)")—that introduced poetically laconic images of a family undergoing divorce. As someone who'd read Swanagin's brilliant piece, I remember that night at the Cipriani dinner table, Emily sitting amidst all that glamour with her two parents, together celebrating a daughter for a poetic piece focused on the family's dissolution. It was a poignant moment, knowing this seventeen-year-old had written lines like, "Maybe my father will stop crying, and maybe my mother will fall in love."

The college winner was John Gilmore, a student at Utah State, who not only received a check for $10,000 and publication of his entry, "Final Cascade," in *Creative Nonfiction 39,* but also a paid residency at the Norman Mailer Writers Colony. Schiller and his colleagues enjoyed—and slightly fretted about—the fact that the winner shared a last name with Gary Gilmore, the subject of *Executioner's Song,* confessing that they'd carefully researched any connections (there were none). I sat at a table with Gilmore and his wife, Maryssa, who was studying mortuary science.

As much as I'd like to offer pages of profoundly engaging student writing, space and the complexity of permissions allow me to give but the smallest flavor. As you read them, I hope you'll appreciate both what students chose to share about their lives and the importance of providing them open opportunities to write about whatever experiences they saw fit. Here, for example, is the title of one high school student submission: "Things about My Parents I Forgot to Tell the Woman Who is Deciding Custody of My Brother, Sister, and Me."

Here's another student, from a piece about eighth grade:

> We were learning about parts of speech in English class when we got a new seating chart. I was placed by Brad, who always had everything he wanted and wrote in shiny black mechanical pencils.
>
> He snickered at me, one day. "You know that nobody really likes you?" He said it as if I was stupid for not ever knowing.
>
> Again, I couldn't speak.

"Circle the verbs in the sentence!" the teacher instructed. I look at my paper, eyes blurring.

Likes is a verb. And so is hate.

A high school student from an immigrant family:

> When I hear things like, "Look—girls your age are getting married and soon it will be your turn," those comments are like rockets landing in my ears. I find a place to be alone and think to myself, "All this hard work, these top grades, these compliments, for what? For me to remember when I'm seasoning the soup."

A college student writing about a relative:

> In the kitchen he was already prepared. Two paper plates, a bottle of ketchup, a jar of mustard, one bun, one fork, one knife. Uncle Steve turned on the microwave and pulled out a pack of Hebrew Nationals.

> Uncle Steve was a belated victim of the Vietman War, an unwitting agent of Agent Orange. He had newspaper clipping and a handful of medals detailed his service framed atop the fire mantle. He would die in the Long Beach Veterans Hospital at age 54, as it would turn out. He would go in for shoulder surgery and forget to retrace his steps.

A high school with an exuberant sense of style and pacing:

> My hometown is made of break walls surrounding a harbor where young children jump off and a man who once gave me an eagle feather got drunk and floated out on a mattress to the middle of the harbor at three in the morning and was torn through with the hull of a speed boat driven by a man whose daughter was my best friend and the owner of the bar. They'd chatted that night, the killed man and the killer, and the killer told the killed man to leave his bar because he was closing down for the night and the killed man had had too much Jack Daniels to stay. That boat came up in between that man's legs, and all he had left was that wife, those kids, and that eagle feather.

Over the years, Schiller convinced us to add a creative nonfiction contest for two-year college students and a fiction contest for high school teachers. Separately, he created a college poetry contest, and with his encouragement, the British edition of *GQ* magazine created a fiction contest for British students. That winner flew over for the gala.

The NCTE Mailer awards were last given in 2016, after a blazing seven years, their demise coming through a combination of circumstances. I'm partly speculating, because I stepped down as coordinator in 2014, when I was elected vice president of NCTE, but I watched several factors firsthand. By 2015, the annual gala had fairly much run its course; always an expensive undertaking to maintain its high profile, the event relied on substantial underwriting and the continued willingness of high-profile attendees to write big checks to support a top-tier (and expensive) event, with lots of concomitant travel costs for the student winners. Schiller contacted me, as program chair for the 2015 NCTE convention in Minneapolis, to see if we could make the student awards there, in a plenary session for which he could supply a big-name writer as part of the draw. That was impossible, for various reasons, though I was able to offer two options at the convention, neither of which appealed to him. In the end, he arranged a more modest event (at least by his high standards) at the Pratt Institute in Brooklyn on December 10, 2015, where Salman Rushdie was the featured honoree, Gay Talese made opening remarks, Billy Collins introduced teachers who won fiction awards, and the executive director of NCTE, Emily Kirkpatrick, gave the student prizes. In related conversations during 2015, Larry wondered if renaming the awards after more currently popular writers would bring greater attention, sharing some names that I agreed would have more cache than Mailer's. There was a contest again in 2016, with winners chosen, but there was no awards dinner, and in January 2017, Schiller asked to suspend everything for a year. They never restarted. The last sustained conversation I had with Larry was in spring 2017, after he invited me to a May 2 gala preview of an exhibit of 77 photographs he curated for John F. Kennedy's Centennial, at the American Art Museum (Gangitano).

NCTE has continued other writing contests, including the longstanding Achievement Awards in Writing for high school juniors. Students submit two pieces: themed writing and best writing. The 2022 theme included this line from H.G. Wells' *The Island of Doctor Moreau*—"I hope, or I could not live"—followed by this prompt:

> Pessimism is an easy habit to form but not a healthy one to maintain. With hope as your guide, look forward and imagine a better future.
>
> Your task will be to do one of the following:
>
> Create a piece that paints a picture of a hopeful future.
>
> OR
>
> Identify a global, national, or local problem that affects you or others you care about but that you feel hopeful you could change somehow. Describe the problem and offer a solution.

In contrast to the structured parameters of the "themed" component, illustrated in the prompt I've just quoted, the "best writing" contest is open. Students are told, "You may produce any genre, or kind, of writing (e.g., personal essay, graphic novel, news article, love letter, eulogy, oral history, photo essay, scientific report, letter to a politician, local petition, speech)." Students are encouraged to submit writing done outside of school assignments, though the call for submissions hopes that teachers might find the awards useful for teaching. This openness is somewhat tempered by the requirement that teachers screen submissions at the school level before they enter the national competition, with schools able to advance only one entry per five hundred students. Across the country in 2021, there were but 284 nominees, out of some 24,000 American high schools, and from these, 136 students (from 26 states) received Certificates of Superior Writing. No doubt a pandemic and strange mixes of remote learning had some effect on the seemingly low numbers.

What genres did students submit? How much creative nonfiction? The contest site for 2022 offered examples from three award-winning students from 2020, and of the six pieces, three are poems, one is a novel excerpt, and two are personal essays. In one of them, student Pedro Juan Orduz explains:

> In tenth grade, we read *Oranges Are Not the Only Fruit*. I didn't particularly care for the book, but the assignment we got for it was a personal literary essay. I had never written a personal essay before, so the format intrigued me; in fact, I had never really sat down and written about myself before—not in the context of long-form prose . . . I thought deeply about what stories to share and what stories not to, about what really affected my life and what was just a funny or tragic anecdote, about what was an actual reason for my behavior and what was my mind making up excuses to avoid self-examination. Even though it was not my best assignment that year, it's the one I remember most, and the one that had the greatest formative impact.

Orduz reflects on the valuable opportunity to write about his own life in the tradition of the personal essay, a genre unfamiliar to him, and I suspect to others. High school and college writing teachers would do valuable work in helping students understand and write such pieces, as I suggested in a primer to high school teachers (Hesse, "Imagining"). I served as one of the judges for 2022, reading work from nine impressive students, each of whom submitted at least two works, some of them three or four. By far, the genre most frequently represented was poetry (thirteen of twenty-six pieces), with fiction (six) and creative nonfiction (five) a distant second and third. Only two of the submissions were traditional "school" essays.

As for the National Day on Writing, it continues, at least as I'm writing in 2022, though the character is quite different, muted and truncated, a shadow of its founding aspirations. Probably such transitions are inevitable, as initial energies become unsustainable. Taking over a broadcasting studio for an entire day of programming, with updates to and from the field, isn't very realistic. Still, even without the high-profile actions of the founding years, it was possible to sustain some form of the national gallery of writing, a serious effort to gather and curate the range of writings that "common" Americans were producing as part of their daily lives, both everyday/workaday writings and creative works, both fiction and nonfiction, that they chose to pursue out of interest, not obligation.

Instead, around 2016, NCTE shifted the focus of the day to celebrity authorship and to social media. NCTE hired "author and social media thought leader C.C. Chapman" to host podcasts featuring writers and celebrities, along with a new website, whyiwrite.us, which seems to have been deployed last in 2019 (Froman). Celebrity writers were obviously present at the Mailer writing awards, as my opening illustrates, but the student writers were accorded equal space on the program, and their works stood alongside the more famous authors'. In the early years of the National Day on Writing, "the people's writings" were paramount in the national gallery, representing a range of purposes and genres, whatever people chose to submit through open calls. In later years, the invitation to write remained but the visibly sanctioned subject matter and genre had dwindled to declaring "why I write" and tweets, or tweet-length postings. The October 25, 2017, issue of INBOX precisely documented 93,956 tweets (about 40% of them original). A message "recap" included images from classrooms and pointed to a "Writer's Story Campaign" with a dozen short YouTube videos. The 2018 INBOX newsletter report celebrated a "national write-in with Jacqueline Woodson," and noted 49,129 tweets using #WhyIWrite, with 19,747 of them original (NCTE, "INBOX"). That newsletter featured four images, two from school classrooms and two from authors Clive Cussler and Jose Antonio Vargas, along with a link to another 137 Twitter screen captures. America's day on writing is now marked primarily by participation counts.

Perhaps such analytics are the only way we really know how to mark or represent the day, such is the power of quantitative representation. In fact, we could go a level deeper and count how many total words were generated, or how many phonemes. We could run everything through corpus linguistics software, calculating word frequencies. Perhaps we could report vowels and consonants. Apologizing for my sarcasm, I understand the rhetorical necessity, if you're a sponsoring organization, to have some quick way to represent a campaign announced as national, and numbers provide it. Reports on the first National Day on Writing certainly include numbers. But the main feature was the gallery of language artifacts collected and displayed. I suppose someone could report on a visit to the Art Institute of Chicago or the Tate by commenting on the total number of works they contained, or the number per salon, or the number of blue-dominant versus white-dominant, and such a report could provide helpful information, but we'd likely find a solely numerical report unsatisfying in conveying the nature of the place. Better would be describing in situ the Chagall windows or Whistler's "Symphony in White, No. 2," but evoking a gallery's spirit by describing its contents poses the challenge of time and scale: How many paintings do I need to describe to give some reasonable rendering? A gallery has countless functions; curating cultural works, allowing people to see them, and providing audiences for makers are three of them.

NCTE's National Gallery of Writing was most important, I think, because it invited "common" people to share a piece of writing true to them, regardless of genre, purpose, or merit, knowing that others could view that submission, in juxtaposition with others perhaps very different. My favorite museum in Denver—the Kirkland—has fine paintings and sculptures, certainly, but also a Model 30 Electrolux Vacuum Cleaner and a 1909 electric water kettle. The National Day and the Gallery celebrated writing as making, period, in all its manifestations. And while there's no denying the motivational and consequential effects of knowing 50,000 others are participating in a day on writing, the individual consciousness and attention are significant, too. The website of London's Tate museums provides a "Guide to Slow Looking," and perhaps a better way to celebrate the National Day on Writing would be to look at writing others have shared, to browse but linger on some few. Alas, the Gallery has disappeared into the Great Byte Beyond.

These days, NDoW happens in two spaces: Twitter and individual classrooms or writing centers. During the pandemic, the latter activities were largely virtual. In October 2021, NCTE retweeted a few dozen events from schools around the country, from individual classrooms to university libraries and writing centers to a two-week national environmental writing camp to a small consortium of northeastern college writing centers. NCTE's 2021 advice for preparing the day consisted of four bullet-pointed activities teachers might assign their students, along with a reminder to share the hashtag #WhyIWrite.

#WhyIWrite has become the non-school space of NDoW, taking on a life of its own, in some ways standing for the NDoW, primarily through a lively hashtagged exchange, with NCTE explaining that "Since 2009, the hashtag #WhyIWrite has encouraged thousands of people to lift their voices to the things that matter most to them" (Fink). That hashtag was a minor element in 2009, but since then it emerged pretty much as the brand. "National Day on Writing" has a copyright notation, perhaps because the day's origins in NCTE have gotten diffuse, and the Council wants credit for a good achievement. I've had conversations with teachers who assumed that the Day was created by the National Writing Project or thought nothing about its origins at all. Much of NCTE's effort to expand wide consciousness about writing in all manifestations, including as a self-sponsored personal and creative activity among 21st century literacies, has faded. Copyrighting a designation is a blunt way to assert commitment to broad public writing. Organizations change, obviously and naturally, and in the late 2010s, NCTE shifted its energies to reading and literature, with the effect of rendering itself less visible and central as a broader sponsor of writing, though it may shift yet again.

In 2019, a separate website, whyiwrite.us, included a fill-in-the-blank template, complete with a choice of color schemes, from which respondents could create a badge to then share on social media:

> EVERYONE is invited to declare and share their #WhyIWrite perspective with a new digital social badge. The #WhyIWrite social badges will help to illustrate the multifaceted ways in which writing is a part of our lives via a single phrase—"I am a (job title/position) and I write to (what/how writing supports who they are and what they do)." Download your badge and post to your own social media to help amplify the #WhyIWrite message to an even wider audience. Help us demonstrate, especially to students, the many ways and reasons writing drives how we live and work every day. Imagine how powerful this tapestry of examples will be. Create your badge today! (NCTE, "Welcome")

I appreciate the gesture toward the program's roots in recognizing the everyday writing of Americans, including in their work. It recalled Kathi Yancey's 2008 hope to "de-mystify writing for those who don't think of themselves as writers" (NCTE, "Minutes" 6). But instead of asking people to share their writing, it asked them to share *about* their writing, with the motivation, moreover, of getting a metaphorical gold star to put on metaphorical lockers and Trapper Keepers. And while I value reflection, respect motivation, and acknowledge declarations as a genre, the enterprise was artificial in ways the 2009 effort skirted. The imperative then was primarily to gather "found" writing, making visible the kinds of things people already had at hand, part of the natural course of being. It didn't preclude writing something new or special, but the spirit was to celebrate writing as it was happening, in all its guises, rather than to gather templated answers to a prompt.

I hope we might re-embrace the effort to push against writing as something that authors or professionals do, something that schools oblige of students, or that amateur creators do in poems or fiction, as the usual arty stuff by arty types. The Mailer celebrations put students alongside celebrated authors, as podium equals (if, obviously, not publicity equals.) The National Gallery of Writing (even the name was intentional) invited everyone to present themselves as a writer. Certainly, the effort to elevate the ubiquity of writers and writing has political value for organizations like NCTE; demonstrating writing's pervasiveness implies the importance of a professional organization devoted to its sponsorship, study, and teaching. And, certainly, a renewed effort to invite, curate, and celebrate writing has scholarly value for analyzing and representing vast varieties of written artifacts. But it also has the invitational value of recognition and respect, a democratizing aspiration, with NCTE valuing makers and making.

If the Day on Writing prized the everyday—the writing that happens spontaneously in going about life—the NCTE Mailer creative nonfiction contests privileged the polished: writing crafted intentionally by an artisan. It was striking that, among all the available genres of creative nonfiction—literary journalism, profile, travel writing, and so on—memoirs and personal essays overwhelmingly dominated submissions through the duration of the contest, and those were the pieces that inevitably won. I remember the most stylistically adroit piece I read during the first year was a deft, complex, new journalistic account of "hell night" at a local restaurant that annually hosted a ghost-peppered, Carolina-reapered menu designed to mete spicey pain on masochistic diners. The piece went forward as one of five finalists but didn't win.

More common—and judged more successful—were pieces that were less journalistic and more self-referential. I've explained elsewhere that creative nonfiction exists on an axis of self-full to self-less. Self-full pieces make the author's experiences central; they thoroughly foreground what the writer did and thought. Think memoirs or personal essays. Self-less pieces contain little to none of that, focusing instead on event or idea, keeping the author in the background, less as agent than as voice, though surely and keenly as voice (think literary journalism). The NCTE Mailer awards overwhelmingly drew self-full pieces, nearly all of it earnest, some of it immature or formulaic ("and the lesson I learned from this experience was"), but much of it well-wrought. Of course, it could be that memoir and personal essays were what students knew and were assigned. But it could also be that these genres are what they liked to read and wanted to write. The NCTE invitations gave them license and opportunity to put their lives at the middle of things. The message of the National Day on Writing was that all writing and writers mattered and ought to be gathered and preserved. The message of the NCTE Mailer Creative Nonfiction Contest was that writing about the world as you see it—especially as you lived it—was worth doing with attention and care.

~~~

The second-to-last ceremony I attended for the NCTE Mailer Student Awards in Creative Nonfiction was in 2013 at the New York Public Library. There was a usual fine crowd, and I had my picture taken with John Waters. The night's most interesting moment came while I was standing backstage with the student winners. Beside us in a wheelchair was Maya Angelou, who was receiving the night's biggest award. As we waited, author Samuel Delany was giving a lengthy introduction of Junot Diaz, who was getting a medallion. Suddenly, Angelou loudly shouted, "Boring." Her attendant/companion stage-whispered, "Dr. Angelou, you shouldn't say that," to which she said, perhaps even more loudly, "I don't care; he's boring!" I turned to the high school winner standing beside me and said, "Well, there's something you don't see every day."

My last event was in 2014, the awards having long been decoupled from the National Day on Writing. For the first time, I wasn't a presenter, instead sitting in a back corner with the high school nonfiction winner and his family. At the table beside us was Monica Lewinsky, attending as a guest of *Vanity Fair*. It turns out

Lewinsky had been friends with Norman Mailer in Provincetown, and shortly after that evening, *Vanity Fair*, for whom she's been a contributing editor since then, published her short piece about that friendship. I wondered if the high school writer sitting next to me knew anything about Lewinsky beyond her being yet another probably famous person in the room. I wondered if he'd write about that evening and what story he'd tell if he did. I wondered whether he'd keep writing essays at all or if this would become a one-time experience that happened years ago, perhaps remembered as a fond aberration in a writerly life that turned elsewhere, including away from writing.

Works Cited

Cohen, Patricia. "To Honor a Battler, Literary Peace Breaks Out." *The New York Times* C.1, 22 Oct. 2009, www.nytimes.com/2009/10/22/books/22mailer.html, accessed 7 Feb. 2022.

Fink, Lisa. "Recognizing the National Day on Writing 2021." National Council of Teachers of English, ncte.org/blog/2021/10/national-day-on-writing-3/, accessed 23 Feb. 2022.

Froman, Jonas A. "Let's Get All Scripty: #WhyIWrite Kicks of 2016 on Thursday." HuffPost, 19 Oct. 2016, www.huffpost.com/entry/lets-get-all-scripty-whyiwrite-kicks-off-2016-on_b_58011c55e4b06f314afeb31e.

Gangitano, Alex. "Smithsonian JFK Exhibition Shows a 'Unique Moment in American History.'" Roll Call, 2 May 2017, rollcall.com/2017/05/02/smithsonian-jfk-exhibition-shows-unique-moment-in-american-history/.

Hesse, Douglas. "Imagining a Place for Creative Nonfiction." *English Journal*, vol. 99, no. 1, Nov. 2009, pp. 18–24.

———. "Put Forth Our Best Writing Selves." *The Denver Post*, 16 Oct. 2009. https://www.denverpost.com/2009/10/16/put-forth-our-best-writing-selves/.

———. "Mailer/NCTE Awards Gala Caps National Day on Writing." *The Council Chronicle*, Nov. 2009, p. 10, library.ncte.org/journals/CC/issues/v19-2/12101.

Lewinsky, Monica. "Happy F**in' Birthday (with Apologies to Norman Mailer)." *Vanity Fair*, 16 Dec. 2014, www.vanityfair.com/culture/2014/12/monica-lewinsky-on-norman-mailer.

National Council of Teachers of English (NCTE). "Achievement Awards in Writing," ncte.org/awards/achievement-awards-in-writing/, accessed 23 Feb. 2022.

———. "INBOX: 10 years of #WhyIWrite." Received by Douglas Hesse, 23 Oct. 2018.

———. "Minutes of the NCTE Annual Business Meeting for the Board of Directors and Other Members of the Council." San Antonio, TX, 21 Nov. 2008.

———. "National Day on Writing, National Gallery of Writing." [Flyer], 2009, douglashesse.com/wp-content/uploads/2022/04/National-Day-on-Writing-2009-Flyer.pdf, accessed 18 July 2022.

———. "Welcome: Writing is an important part of life." *#WhyIWrite*, 2019, Internet Archive, web.archive.org/web/20210509084124/https://whyiwrite.us/, accessed 5 Mar. 2022.

Orduz, Pedro Juan. "Writing: My Key to Asserting Myself." National Council of Teachers of English. ncte.org/wp-content/uploads/2020/07/Pedro-Juan-Orduz-submission-2020.pdf, accessed 23 Feb. 2022.

Tate Galleries. "A Guide to Slow Looking." www.tate.org.uk/art/guide-slow-looking, accessed 4 Apr. 2022.

United States Congress, Senate. "Senate Resolution 310: A resolution expressing support for the designation of October 20, 2009, as the National Day on Writing." 8 Oct. 2009, www.congress.gov/bill/111th-congress/senate-resolution/310/text.

Williamson, Kent. "just to give you an overview of some of the programming scheduled for the National Day webcast . . ." Received by Douglas Hesse, Kylene Beers, Kathi Yancey, Carol Jago, and Millie Davis, 18 Oct. 2009.

———. "National Writing Day: How NCTE Sections, Conferences, and Other Groups Can Work Together to Affirm Our Beliefs about Writing and Provide a Dynamic Portrait of 21st Century Literacies." Agenda Item 22, NCTE Executive Committee Meeting, Aug. 2008.

———. "Agenda for tomorrow's call (10 eastern, 9 central)." Received by Douglas Hesse, et al. 25 Aug. 2008.

Yancey, Kathleen Blake. *Writing in the 21st Century: A Report from the National Council of Teachers of English.* NCTE, Urbana, IL, 2009, cdn.ncte.org/nctefiles/press/yancey_final.pdf.

Chapter 13. How Young Can You Go? Age and Experience and the Personal Essay's Limbo Pole

Jenny Spinner
SAINT JOSEPH'S UNIVERSITY

The U.S. Census Bureau assigns the category of middle age to anyone aged 45 to 65. The essayist that Graham Good describes in his preface to *The Observing Self*, a historical study of the essay genre, appears to occupy the upper end of that category. Here we find an English gent, wearing a "worn tweed jacket in an armchair," "smoking a pipe by a fire in his private library," and "maundering on about the delights of idleness, country walks, tobacco, old wine, and old books" (vii). Good's characterization is meant to demonstrate just how out of touch so many genteel essayists were, writing at the turn of the 20th century, especially amid the gathering clouds of World War I. Ned Stuckey-French, in *The American Essay in the American Century*, suggests that this gentleman essayist both reflected and attempted to maintain the positions his archetype embodied: "upper-middle-class values, Christian morality, the classical unity of truth and beauty, and a belief in the progress of (Anglo-American) civilization" (14). In other words, he was not just an essayist; he was a way of (white, upper-middle-class) life, drawing to himself, to the genre, imitators who looked, talked, and thought like him. The result was a genre whose entrenched poster child was a salt-and-pepper-haired maunderer.

More than a decade ago, when my own hair was still firmly pepper, I internet-searched my way to a Blogspot page titled "young essayist." The background on the blog's home page featured the sort of room someone much older might occupy, or at least someone whose tastes skew vintage: fine arts paintings in gilded frames, an oval mirror, an antique wooden wall phone, and a lamp with a silk, fringed shade. But the blog was empty. "No posts," a gray page banner read. I occasionally checked on the site over the next few years. Still: "No posts." The blog has since disappeared, likely abandoned or removed for inaction. *Young essayist?* it calls into the void. *What could you possibly have to say?* The answer, apparently, is nothing. Such a question seems absurd in our own contemporary age in which the essay now invites and celebrates a multiplicity of identities—including under-fifty essayists like Roxanne Gay and John Jeremiah Sullivan (born in 1974), Ta-Nehisi Coates and Zadie Smith (1975), Jenny Zhang (1983), Jia Tolentino (1988), and Morgan Jerkins (1992), to name just a few. All of them have plenty to say. But the essay's history, as it has been consistently framed and delivered, and especially its pedagogy, packaged as advice to the genre's novices, reveal a persistent problem, even if it is merely one of perception: The literary essay seems best suited to middle-aged ruminators, those who have put some decades behind them.

For many older writers and teachers of the essay (define "older" as you wish), achieving the essay's most notable markers—deep reflection, self-examination, and knowledge—is especially challenging for younger writers. "We would not want to think of the essay as the country of old men," writes Elizabeth Hardwick in her introduction to the *Best American Essays 1986*, "but it is doubtful that the slithery form, wearisomely vague and as chancy as trying to catch a fish in the open hand, can be taught. Already existing knowledge is so often required" (xv). In "On the Necessity of Turning Oneself into a Character," Phillip Lopate outlines ways that "student essayists," as he calls them, can strive to write the kinds of enduring essays that their literary models have achieved. One such strategy, turning oneself into a character, involves presenting oneself as a person "of a certain age, sex, ethnic and religious background, class, and region, possessing a set of quirks, foibles, strengths, and peculiarities" (72). In this vein, age is not an insurmountable barrier to writing essays. After all, students might well turn themselves into the young characters they are. But the key, as Lopate explains, is for them to look at those selves critically, and deeply, to identify their flaws and present them to their readers. The underlying question is whether young writers can turn themselves into middle-aged reflectors as well. In her essay "Letter to a Young Essayist," Eva Brann argues that "an ardent young essayist is an oxymoron, like, say, a 'spirited bureaucrat,'" suggesting from the start that her letter is just a bit of rhetorical dark comedy. Brann's real audience appears to be older tutors and teachers who share her views about young essayists and who would not lose heart at such a dispirited opening declaration: *Dear Young Essayist, Yours is an impossible existence.* Brann argues in the letter that the young essayist's dilemma is really tied to the nature of the essay genre itself:

> Poets and novelists have a double birth: their congenital gift and their self-generating industry. Essays are not born but almost altogether self-made. They may not have in them a propensity,

but a propensity is not a talent. They are the aboriginal un-geniuses in the land of literature.

It is not that essayists cannot achieve genius, she seems to suggest, but with age and experience as genre requisites, they simply must live long enough (past the age of most high school and college students, certainly) to cover their blank slates. By contrast, fiction writers are apparently the teenage boys in that land of literature, enjoying their creative peaks early before fizzling out. In a 2010 essay titled "How Old Can a 'Young Writer' Be?" *New York Times Book Review* editor Sam Tanenhaus offers this "essential truth" about fiction writers: "They often compose their best and most lasting work when they are young." His thoughts occasioned by a *New Yorker* issue featuring 20 writers under the age of 40, Tanenhaus points to a 2009 interview that novelist Kazuo Ishiguro did with *The Guardian* in which Ishiguro suggests that fiction writers reach their pinnacle of creativity before they are 30. "There's something very misleading about the literary culture that looks at writers in their 30s and calls them 'budding' or 'promising', when in fact they're peaking," Ishiguro told the interviewer. In his 50s at the time of the interview, and two decades past the year in which he was awarded the Booker Prize for *The Remains of the Day*, Ishiguro agrees that in some ways he has already peaked as well. The only way out of such a decline, he says, is to "change and write different kinds of things" (Aitkenhead). It is not entirely clear what Ishiguro has in mind by "different kinds of things." Maybe the essay? But maybe not yet. For now, Ishiguro continues to pump out novels, publishing his eighth in 2021 at the age of 66.

In this construction, if poets and novelists are the stuff made of young dreams, the essayist is the stuff made of second chances, midlife crises, and back-up plans. "I don't suppose many young people dream of becoming essayists," opines Lopate in a 2013 essay for *The New York Times*. "Even as nerdy and bookish a child as I was fantasized about entering the lists of fiction and poetry, those more glamorous, noble genres on which Nobels, Pulitzers, and National Book Awards are annually bestowed" ("The Essay, an Exercise in Doubt"). While I, too, was a nerdy and bookish child, I was happy to imagine myself an essayist from the time I was 19 years old and took a college course on the contemporary essay that marked my life. I did not receive the message that I should consider doing something else, until a course in my first semester as an M.F.A. student in nonfiction during which my professor, a famous novelist, dismissed my work in front of my older classmates, declaring that nobody cared about my infantile experiences, and advised me to grow up. Perhaps as a counter to my own argument here, it took a few more years before I realized he was right, but also really truly not right. My essays were not subpar because I was young; they were subpar because at that point, I hadn't read enough or written enough or worked hard enough as a writer. I would have been a subpar poet and fiction writer, too, although I suspect my professor's criticism then would have been tied to talent rather than to age. At least there was hope for me as an essayist; apparently all I had to do was get older. In his introduction to *The Art of the Personal Essay,* Lopate observes, "While young people excel at lyrical poetry and mathematics, it is hard to think of anyone who made a mark on the personal essay form in his or her youth" (xxxvi). Lopate offers James Baldwin and Joan Didion as two exceptions, with the caveat that Baldwin and Didion "both adopted precociously world-weary personae" (xxxvi). For Lopate, one of the signature traits of the essayist, the ability to organize—examine, reflect, make art of—the mess of life for oneself and for a reader inevitably comes with age:

> It is difficult to write analytically from the middle of confusion, and youth is a confusion in which the self and its desires have not yet sorted themselves out. A young person still thinks it is possible—there is time enough—to become all things: athlete and aesthete, solider and pacifist, anchorite and debauchee. Later, knowing one's fate and accepting responsibility of that uninnocent knowledge define the perspective of the form. (xxxvi)

Middle age is the time in which that confusion starts to sort itself out, suggests Joseph Epstein in his introduction to *The Norton Book of Personal Essays:* "The personal essay is perhaps intrinsically a middle-aged or older writers' form in that it calls for a certain experience of life and the disposition to reflect upon that experience" (15). For both Epstein and Lopate, the artful reflection on the lived experience—which Doug Hesse refers to as "emplotted experience" (208)—also requires temporal distance as it moves from mind to page. In that sense, both the living and the thinking about it are measured in years, and young essayists cannot simply reflect their way out of this dilemma. They can only pass the time.

It is hard to imagine how such messages are received by young essayists, first dipping their toes into the essay genre by way of these well-known anthologies. *You might benefit from reading essays (collected in anthologies edited by wiser, older essayists), but you are unlikely to write them, at least not yet.* The Antiguan American writer Jamaica Kincaid received that message as a student of the essay. In her introduction to the *Best American Essays 1995,* Kincaid describes her first encounters with the essay by way of men "of substantial standing in their societies, men who had time to contemplate an idea, who knew that their opinions might influence events in their day" (xiii). Kincaid's reaction both to reading these essayists and to being asked to imitate them? "I felt angry, I felt sad, I felt I could never have command over words, I felt I would never have an idea, I felt no matter how big I got, I would always remain small," she writes (xiii). Yet for many essayists, those big ideas—knowledge acquisition in its most formal sense—are a defining characteristic of the genre. In her introduction to the *Best American Essays 1992,* Susan Sontag roots the greatness of the essay as a literary form in the sermons and public lectures of Jonathan Edwards and Ralph Waldo Emerson, declaring that the best essays display "sheer intelligence of the highest order" (xvii). No wonder young writers like Kincaid react as they do to such framings, internalizing *I am not there; I may never be there.* While Kincaid later finds value in her exposure to essayists like Francis Bacon, she still finds unsatisfying, even alienating, this presentation of form to her as *the* form—as if the only way into the essay is by way of (white, male) privilege, experience, and age, and the ideas that accompany them.

This notion that age and experience (no less whiteness and maleness) are prerequisites to the kind of interior reflection that the literary essay demands has trailed the essay from its modern beginnings. In 1580 when Montaigne published the first edition of the *Essays,* he was then in his late 40s. By contemporary standards, he was entering middle age. In sixteenth- and seventeenth-century France, however, where life expectancy was 25 to 30 years and a 15-year-old had only a 50 percent chance of reaching the age of 50, Montaigne was lucky to still be alive, and he knew it ("Montaigne on Age"). In his essay "Of Age," he writes, "my idea is to consider the age we have reached as one few people reach. Since in the ordinary course of things men do not come thus far, it is a sign that we are well along" (237). The subjects of Montaigne's essays range widely—from sleep to cruelty to drunkenness to war—and yet, they herald the sort of middle-aged gentleman's concerns that essayists, male and female, would embrace for the next several hundred years. William Cowper was 25 in 1756 when he published "Complaints of an Old Bachelor" (Cowper attached himself to widows during his 68 years of life but never resolved his young man's complaints). Alexander Smith was 33 in 1863 when "Of death and the fear of dying" appeared. Robert Louis Stevenson was a ripe old 27 when he published "Crabbed age and youth" in 1877. By comparison, in our own modern times, Roger Angell was in his 90s when he published "This Old Man" in 2014. Edward Hoagland was in his 70s when "Sex and the River Styx," an essay that explores the sexuality of the "dirty old man," first appeared in 2003. Helen Garner was 77 when, in 2020, she wrote "The Invisible Arrow" about being an old writer.

In "Emerson and the Essay," William Gass notes that many of the earlier practitioners of the essay projected an image of "effeminate and sickly" men, "full of resentment and weakness, procrastinators, passive as hens, nervous, unwed" (26). Such a characterization further distances the essayist from virile youth. Moreover, it is a characterization that many (young) women essayists, at least in the first three centuries of the modern essay's life, readily adopted. In other words, the essay as a de-masculinized, middle-aged man's space helped to open a space for women essayists as well. In 1838, Gail Hamilton, for example, put a pipe between her lips and donned the essayist's tweed jacket in "Happiest Days." Her essay is a rollicking condemnation of the notion that childhood is the happiest time of one's life. Notably, Hamilton claims, it is the wisdom and experience that come with age that make growing older the real treasure, not remaining young. Like Lopate, Hamilton finds that "Every year evokes *order from confusion* [emphasis added], till all things find scope and adjustment. Every year sweeps a broader circle for your horizon, grooves a deeper channel for your experience" (435). Hamilton was 25 when she published "Happiest Days." Elisabeth Woodbridge Morris was just over 40 when she wrote "The Embarrassment of Finality," a humorous meditation on how she wished to spend her last moments. "Live as if each moment were my last? Not at all! I choose to live as if each moment were my first, as if life had just come to me fresh," she decides (60). Morris lived another 50-some years after she wrote this essay. It is too simple to counter that Montaigne and his descendants, having necessarily reached the age of maturity far ahead of young people today, also necessarily focused on middle-aged topics. No, the essay itself, at the moment Montaigne made his 40-something self the matter of his book, seemed destined for middle-aged thinking and reflection, no matter the essayist's age; once established as such, those who came after ran with it, knees creaking all the way. Even in the *Best American Essays 2015* volume, editor Ariel Levy remarks on just how many of the essays she considered for inclusion in the volume had to do with aging—perhaps, she suggests, because the essay genre is occupied by so many baby boomers (xvii). Levy, an essayist in her 40s, remarks that she appreciates "sitting on the shore watching the pros do what they've been practicing for decades," although she also recounts the "joy" she feels—though "in a different way"—reading a younger essayist who is just beginning a career but manages to mount the barrier of youth to "get it right" (xvii).

Perhaps ironically, the idea that experience, fine-tuned with age, could share the genre's platform alongside other types of knowledge was novel in Montaigne's time. In his essay "Of Experience," Montaigne upends prevailing philosophical notions by suggesting that experience matters when it comes to constructing knowledge. He uses experience to justify his act of writing (about himself), but he also seems to suggest that this experience validates the reader paying attention. In other words, the reader can trust Montaigne because Montaigne's reflections are attached to the life he has lived and the experiences he has accrued. Those experiences make him an expert of himself, but that self-expertise, he argues, is also legitimate knowledge. And here, Montaigne nods to Plato:

> So Plato was right in saying that to become a true doctor, the candidate must have passed through all the illnesses that he wants to cure and all the accidents and circumstances that he is to diagnose. It is reasonable that he should catch the pox if he wants to know how to treat it. Truly I should trust such a man. For the others guide us like the man who paints seas, reefs, and ports while sitting at this table, and sails the model of a ship there in complete safety. Throw him into the real thing, and he does not know how to go at it. (827)

In many ways, this analogy of doctor-patient is important to understanding the dilemma for young essayists. We trust the author because the author has lived the experience. We trust the author because the author has thought their way deeply into—and usually out of—the experience. Thus, an essay that begins "Years ago" or "When I was younger," seems to situate itself on much firmer ground than the one that begins, "Earlier this year" or "When I was a sophomore." Young essayists then have an ethos problem from the beginning. Who are they, whirling around in their chaos and confusion, their brains (according to science) not fully formed until the age of 25, who are they to tell us anything? In the natural order of things, young people sit at the feet of their elders, not the other way around. Perhaps that is why so much advice to young essayists is to go out and live some more—then come back when you have something of value to offer.

In her introduction to Lee Gutkind's *In Fact: The Best of Creative Nonfiction*, Annie Dillard provides a list of tips for young novices dabbling in the genre, from focusing on mechanics ("Learn grammar." "Learn punctuation.") to buying books from independent booksellers rather than from chain stores. But many of Dillard's tips mirror the sort of "go out and live more" advice young essayists are often given: live a year in a different part of the country, buy books and read for pleasure, register and vote. And, significantly, she tells young writers: "Don't write about yourself." Why? Because, she says, "Boring people talk about themselves" (xv). Dillard's advice is not without merit. Live more, do more, think more, write more—certainly such advice can only serve to benefit an essay, and a life. And Dillard's are certainly livelier tips than those offered by Brann to the essayists she doesn't believe exist: "Drink green tea. Occupy the bathtub. Carry a notebook. Seize on a phrase" (Brann). But surely "boring" touches a nerve in young people already plagued with worry that their lives are too boring (not enough age and experience) to create essays. And this current generation of young people in particular carries additional baggage that must feed their self-doubt: statistics show that compared to previous generations, they are slow to get their licenses, move out of their parents' houses, seek paying jobs, get married, start families, and achieve other traditional milestones that mark adulthood (Twenge and Park). In fact, there is some suggestion that young people—and their parents—have so internalized this concept of delayed adulthood that it has become a self-actualizing promise (Henig). It is not a big leap to wonder if something similar might apply to essay writing. Young people hear "you are too young to write essays," and so they don't dream of being essayists. As teachers of nonfiction, as critics and essayists ourselves, we need to assure them instead that not living, doing, thinking, or writing as much as they might eventually live, do, think, or write does not preclude a good essay. We can only write from where we are, and where we are is no less adequate than where anyone else is. And while perhaps Dillard would also advise adults to avoid writing about themselves, her advice here to young people seems particularly suspect. In the creative nonfiction classroom, we feed our students a steady diet of essays in which older essayists (and not boring ones) spend a great deal of time—whole essays, whole books even—writing about themselves, and writing well. Why should our young essayists not do so too?

The long and short of it is that people younger than 45, 35, 25 are perfectly capable of writing profoundly good essays, no matter how old they are or what experiences they have thus acquired. Furthermore, the spaces we invite them into in order to create these essays, the critical discussions and craft talk we simultaneously present, must suggest they are not too young to bend themselves under the essay's limbo pole. After all, their metaphorical young bodies are far more likely to do so without falling to the ground or throwing out their backs. And so, if the young essayist is indeed capable of writing essays, the problem may be instead with the (old) receiver. In a review of books by several contemporary essayists—Davy Rothbart (born 1975), Sloane Crosley (born 1978), John Jeremiah Sullivan (born 1974), Sheila Heti (born 1976)—Adam Kirsch finds the work of these essayists (save Heti) lacking. The essay of old (by the old?) engaged with the world, he argues; the new essay, on the other hand, "is exclusively about the self, with the world serving only as a foil and an accessory, as a mere staging ground for the projection of the self." For Kirsch, the failings of this new essay are tied to the generation producing them, a generation, he says, "now on the cusp of 40, an age when it is no longer charming for one's heart to be an idiot." In other words: time to grow up. There are similar arguments to unpack in the concluding paragraph of Laura Bennett's "Generation Whine," in which she examines the work of two 20-something bloggers, Emma Koenig and Ryan O'Connell, and decides—with some caveats and complexities—that Koenig and O'Connell are stand-ins for an entire generation of 20-somethings who are caught in the "self-affirming echo chambers of social media":

> [R]eading Koenig and O'Connell, it is hard not to think that such smart, funny, articulate, motivational twenty-somethings are wasting a decade's worth of creative energy, that they would be better off living outside their own heads for a while. But they want to be artists, and they want to be heard, and they are adrift between their own creative ambitions and the pressure that the culture at large has foisted on them: to be . . . the voice of their generation or at least a generation; to speak for everyone simply because they have a blog and so they can; to take their experiences, and make them ours. (Bennett)

The idea that this kind of self-inventory and personal reflection is mere naval-gazing (wearisome, whiny, narcissistic) has plagued the essay for centuries. But attaching it particularly to young people with us versus them language is problematic. There is nothing wrong with laying the sidewalk of one's experiences for others to traverse in order to find their way to some kind of shared emotion or new understanding. It is advice I tell my students: Give me something from your experience for myself, even if it's simply a means of understanding what I don't share with you. That these experiences are rooted in youth, tied to a younger person's experiences and concerns, makes no difference. Several years ago, one of my students wrote a powerful essay about being raped not once but three times in her college career. As a result of these traumas, she became addicted to the show "Law and Order: SVU" and begins using what she learns from "SVU" to try to make sense of her own experiences. The essay didn't succeed because she was young—though it captured some truth of what it means to be a young woman in college—and it wouldn't have failed because she was young. It succeeded because it was a thoughtful, lyrical, unnerving, self-conscious essay. It would have failed if it were not those things.

In their seminal creative nonfiction textbook, *The Fourth Genre,* Robert Root and Michael Steinberg note that the essay genre encourages "self-discovery and self-exploration" (xxv), two concepts that seem especially suitable to youth, marked as it is by that process of discovery and exploration. Sondra Perl and Mimi Schwartz use those same terms in their textbook, *Writing True,* arguing that all nonfiction shares a "desire for self-exploration and discovery, whether writing about yourself or others" (9). It is hard to square Dillard's advice to avoid writing about oneself with the craft advice to explore and discover oneself. Both sets of authors also settle on "personal presence" (Root and Steinberg) or an "engaging voice" (Perl and Schwartz) as another defining characteristic of the essay, again, a feature that seems well within reach of younger writers. After only a couple of weeks with a class of creative nonfiction writers, many of us are able to assign blind submissions to their rightful owners because we can already hear them, can recognize their voices on the page. But when it comes to the voices they are reading, it is fair to say that many of the examples we offer capture the voice of the middle-aged, the old—and while those voices and experiences can certainly resonate, it is also worth thinking about offering our students not only literary models in other voices but craft talk models as well, written from vantage points other than that of the "wise elder."

I have had to re-examine my own craft advice in light of this awareness. For example, I used to advise creative nonfiction students not to write in media res, advice that, in retrospect, seems comical given that the entire genre is proffered as best suited for human beings in media res. I was simply passing along advice that had once been given to me, about how time (that is, years and experience) allows for the kind of deep reflection that underlies good essays. It made sense to me given how difficult reflection can be in the midst of chaos, no matter one's age. And then my father died. Several weeks after his death, I began to write about those wrenching final days of his life, about the pain that consumed him, about his last words—"Why? Why?" before he choked on his last breaths. I knew if I didn't write the details down, I would forget them—because the part of me that had to go on from those days needed them erased in order to do so. In some ways, it was too soon to write my father's death, and I knew it. Still shell-shocked, still horrified by my father's rapid wasting from pancreatic cancer, I could make no sense of it. The only discovery I could manage was the fact that I could indeed make no sense of it. Instead of acknowledging what Lopate sees as a default of youth, I turned it into an asset. I let what I didn't know, the chaos and confusion, drive the essay. It was named a *Best American Essays 2003* Notable Essay. In many ways—and I tell my students this—I will write my father's death over and over for the rest of my life. That first essay was a beginning, written in my youth. I took another stab in 2016 with the publication of an essay I titled "The Stairs." Was it better? I don't know. Certainly different. Because I was different. The key to writing that original essay, though, was not age (I was in my 20s) but a forced detachment from the experience as I wrote: that is, I had to examine my words not as experience, as the thing itself, but as art. I had to dive deeply into my own mind, into my feelings, in order to emerge with art. I traveled the distance of Hesse's "emplotted experience" rather than the distance of time in order to make that essay work.

Perhaps that sort of mental travel—rather than physical travel through time—is embedded in the concept of the "old soul." In Taoism, the old soul is the last stage or lifetime in the journey of reincarnation, encompassing now the memories, experiences and knowledge acquired in all past lives. This final lifetime, though, is not necessarily linked to age, and perhaps for that reason, people latch onto the idea of old souls "trapped" in young bodies—as if the young body is some kind of impediment to the old soul's full life. Nevertheless, at least at the level of pop psychology, old souls are often defined by their maturity, their propensity for introspection and reflection, and their sensitivity. In that sense, the characteristics of an old soul are not so different from that of the essayist. Significantly, though, while the soul may be old, the body does not have to be. Again, I know from my experience as a creative nonfiction professor that young people are capable of writing essays that demonstrate with equal finesse the kind of old-soul writing that the actual old souls themselves produce. Put another way: young people are capable of writing, and being, essayists. For really, it is something of the old soul that drives the essay. And yet, I have since wondered, maybe the concept of the old soul doesn't do enough to celebrate the possibilities of the other stages of life's journey that are also rich with experiences, even if they do not yet contain all experiences, or enough experiences, for full enlightenment. The essay's call to deep thinking and reflection is not tied to middle age and middle-aged experiences but to the desire to be on a journey, to think at all, to relentlessly mull things over. And young people have something of great value to offer to the essay genre.

In a now out-of-print collection titled *Twentysomething Essays by Twentysomething Writers,* then 20-something editors Matt Kellogg and Jillian Quint celebrate in the volume's introduction the way that the included writers tackle the issues that their generation faces: "With hope, intelligence, irreverence, and urgency, they show that we are not to be taken lightly (but not too seriously, either), that we're finally ready to sit at the proverbial Grownups' Table" (vii–viii). Point taken, and humor aside, the idea of (the goal of) a Grownups' Table undermines that value of what 20-something essayists can and are contributing to the essay genre. Anne Fadiman, in the introduction to her student Marina Keegan's collection of prose and poetry, *The Opposite of Loneliness,* published posthumously after Keegan's death in a car accident five days after her graduation from Yale, notes that Keegan's writing differed from that of her classmates:

Many of my students sound forty years old. They are articulate but derivative, their own voices muffled by their desire to skip over their current age and experience, which they fear trivial, and land on some version of polished adulthood without passing Go. Marina was twenty-one and sounded twenty-one: a brainy twenty-one, a twenty-one who knew her way around the English language, a twenty-one who understood that there were few better subjects than being young and uncertain and starry-eyed and frustrated and hopeful.

In other words, Keegan, like my own student who wrote of sexual violence in college, rejected the voice of the middle-aged essayist that her classmates thought they had to assume in order to write essays and chose instead to write in her own. The literary obituaries for Keegan understandably mourned the possibilities of what Keegan's writing might have become had she lived. Shortly after the publication of Keegan's posthumous collection, Emma Cueto wrote,

> it is somewhat tragic to read her work, which is already very good, and know that she would have gotten better. The writer in these pages still hasn't quite honed her voice or her craft just yet. Almost, but not quite. And it's enough to break your heart.

However tragic the untimely death of a promising writer, let us reject, however, the notion that to hone the voice of an essayist, one must grow old. After all, who better to capture with raw sincerity—isn't that a hallmark of an essay, too?—the experiences of being young than the people who are living it. They may write those experiences again when they, too, reach middle age, but they won't be the same essays. Our task as teachers of creative nonfiction is to help young essayists write the essays they are meant to write now—to embrace their meaningful contributions to the essay genre, and even to reimagine what the genre is capable of holding and telling in voices well shy of middle age.

Works Cited

Aitkenhead, Decca. Interview with Kazuo Ishiguro. *The Guardian*, 26 Apr. 2009, www.theguardian.com/books/2009/apr/27/kazuo-ishiguro-interview-books.

Bennett, Laura. "Generation Whine." *New Republic*, 5 Oct. 2012, newrepublic.com/article/108186/generation-whine.

Brann, Eva. "Letter to a Young Essayist." *The Imaginative Conservative,* 20 May 2013, www.theimaginativeconservative.org/2013/05/letter-to-a-young-essayist.html.

Cueto, Emily. "The Most Tragic Book You'll Read All Year." *Bustle,* 8 Apr. 2014, www.bustle.com/articles/20348-the-opposite-of-loneliness-by-marina-keegan-shows-a-promising-young-author-who-never-got-to.

Dillard, Annie. "Introduction: Notes for Young Writers." *In Fact: The Best of Creative Nonfiction,* edited by Lee Gutkind, Norton, 2005, pp. xi–xvii.

Epstein, Joseph. "The Personal Essay: A Form of Discovery." *The Norton Book of Personal Essays,* edited by Epstein, Norton, 1995, pp. 11–24.

Fadiman, Anne. Introduction. *The Opposite of Loneliness* by Marina Keegan, Scribner, 2014, pp. xi–xx.

Hamilton, Gail. "Happiest Days." *Gala-Days.* Ticknor & Fields, 1863, pp. 411–436.

Hardwick, Elizabeth. Introduction. *The Best American Essays 1986.* Ticknor & Fields, 1986, pp. xiii–xxi.

Henig, Robin Marantz. "What Is it about 20-Somethings?" *The New York Times,* 18 Aug. 2010, https://www.nytimes.com/2010/08/22/magazine/22Adulthood-t.html.

Hesse, Douglas. "Essays and Experience, Time and Rhetoric." *Writing Theory and Critical Theory,* edited by John Clifford and John Schlib, Modern Language Association, 1994, pp. 199–200.

Kellogg, Matt and Jillian Quint. "A Note from the Editors." *Twentysomething Essays by Twentysomething Writers,* edited by Kellogg and Quint, Random House, 2006, pp. v–viii.

Kincaid, Jamaica. Introduction. *The Best American Essays 1995.* Houghton Mifflin, 1995, pp. xii–xv.

Kirsch, Adam. "The New Essayists, or the Decline of a Form?" *New Republic,* 18 Feb. 2013, newrepublic.com/article/112307/essay-reality-television-david-sedaris-davy-rothbart.

Levy, Ariel. Introduction. *The Best American Essays 2015.* Houghton Mifflin Harcourt, 2015, pp. xv–xviii.

Lopate, Phillip. Introduction. *The Art of the Personal Essay,* edited by Lopate, Anchor Books, 1994, pp. xxiii–liv.

———. "On the Necessity of Turning Oneself into a Character." *To Show and To Tell: The Craft of Literary Nonfiction,* edited by Lopate, Free Press, 2013, pp. 17–25.

———. "The Essay, an Exercise in Doubt." *The New York Times,* 16 Feb. 2013, opinionator.blogs.nytimes.com/author/phillip-lopate/.

Montaigne, Michel de. "Of Age." *The Complete Essay of Montaigne,* translated by Donald M. Frame, Stanford UP, 1958, pp. 236–238.

———. "Of Experience." *The Complete Essay of Montaigne,* translated by Donald M. Frame, Stanford UP, 1958, pp. 815–857.

"Montaigne on Age." *Population and Development Review,* vol. 38, no. 2, pp. 369–372.

Morris, Elisabeth Woodbridge. *Days Out and Other Papers.* Houghton Mifflin, 1917, pp. 53–60.

Perl, Sondra and Mimi Schwartz. *Writing True: The Art and Craft of Creative Nonfiction,* 2nd ed. Cengage, 2014.

Root, Robert L., Jr. and Michael Steinberg. *The Fourth Genre: Contemporary Writers Of/On Creative Nonfiction,* 3rd ed. Pearson, 2005.

Sontag, Susan. Introduction. *The Best American Essays 1992.* Ticknor & Fields, 1992, pp. xiii–xix.

Stuckey-French, Ned. *The American Essay in the American Century.* U of Missouri P, 2013.

Tanenhaus, Sam. "How Old Can a 'Young Writer' Be?" *The New York Times,* 10 June 2010, www.nytimes.com/2010/06/20/books/review/Tanenhaus-t.html.

Twenge, Jean M. and Heejung Park. "The Decline in Adult Activities Among U.S. Adolescents, 1976–2016." *Child Development,* 18 Sept. 2017, pp. 1–17.

Chapter 14. I Am Going to Write About You

Kerry Reilly
University of Colorado at Boulder

> My grandfather told me I should make a habit of thinking about unsolved questions until the answers came of their own accord; in that way I should benefit more. The questions piled up, and the answers were more and more pieces of the mosaic that made up the great picture of the world.
>
> – *Thomas Bernhard*, Gathering Evidence

Dear current and future students, myself included,

Maybe you will look to me for answers, but I am not sure I have them. What I do have are stories. Before I earned an M.F.A. in nonfiction writing, I went to graduate school to study literature. Signed up for an essay writing class because I thought it would be a break from thousands of pages of reading and literary analysis. On the first day, the professor told us each to go home and write an essay. I was ashamed to admit I did not know what an essay was. For hours, I wandered the stacks of the library, flipping through pages by Michel de Montaigne, Virginia Woolf, Samuel Johnson. Johnson calls an essay "a loose sally of the mind; an irregular indigested piece; not a regular and orderly composition." The *Oxford English Dictionary* defines an essay as "an attempt." The latter helped assuage my perfectionistic tendencies and so I began attempting to write a piece about my Aunt Mimi, an artist who was diagnosed with paranoid schizophrenia in her early thirties, a typically late age for onset. I wrote short sentences, filled with images that were seared into my mind. I attempted to make meaning out of what had happened to my aunt. My attempt asked more questions than it answered and left me with more questions than it asked. Was I invading Mimi's privacy? Paying tribute to her? Humanizing one of the cruelest illnesses a brain can develop? Who, if anyone, might this essay hurt and who might it help? For days, I walked around campus feeling quiet and blue, my first writing hangover. Not long after, the piece was accepted for publication. By the time it appeared in print, Mimi was living in a facility and did not have access to or interest in literary journals. My mother had died four years before. My aunt, the third sister, told a cousin the piece was accurate, but too upsetting to read.

Dear Dorothy Allison,

You are standing at the podium, bellowing the words of your characters, intoning wildly and convincingly. I have read *Bastard Out of Carolina* and *Two or*

Three Things I Know for Sure, the fictional and nonfiction accounts of the abuse you endured as a child. My mother, siblings, and I suffered similarly under the roof of my father. When the reading ends, I, a tongue-tied, 20-something graduate student escort you across campus, past the trees with tight, green buds, to the building where refreshments are being served in your honor. I thank you for writing your books and ask if it is hard to be so brave. You stare ahead through wire-rimmed glasses and tell me you do not have a choice, that writing saved your life.

Dear Brigid,

Remember how you wedged yourself behind the refrigerator to practice your rented clarinet? All we could see was the black bell of the instrument peeking from behind the side with the alphabet magnets that spelled the names of our dogs, cats, soccer teams: Dudley, Daisy, Blueberry, Big Red, Blazers, Angels, Angelettes. "Twinkle, Twinkle, Little Star." Your nine-year-old fingers pressed the silver keys in fits and starts. Your breath squeaked through the bamboo reed. You hated when people looked at you. For years, you wore a Sherlock Holmes hat, tilted the brim to hide your eyes. Sometimes, you untied the laces at the top; earflaps drooped like a hound's ears, skimming your cheeks and jaw. Decades later, you stand on a platform in a middle-school cafeteria, not far from where we grew up on Long Island. Using only your voice, you keep a roomful of unruly middle-schoolers in line. Like you, I am a teacher, but nearly two thousand miles away. A student from Malaysia tells the class he would like to go camping, but he is afraid. "The only real danger is exposure," a young Coloradan tells him. I know this is true of wind, lightning, rain, but sometimes it feels true about revealing the things that went on in our home. None of you asked me to blow the roof off our house.

Dear Dad,

I published an essay in *The New York Times*, a piece I wrote as one of many attempts to understand how you used the same sad, terrifying script with your second family as you did with us, your first. Two divorces. You estranged yourself from all seven of your children and stepchildren, then moved to an island off the west coast of Ireland where, at 63 years old, you died of alcoholism and an infected heart. When I flew alone to bury you, I found your rented cottage crowded with soggy cardboard boxes. Unpacked clothes and worthless documents speckled with mold. Yet two glazed pots graced your rainy door. They were bursting with yellow and orange marigolds the landlady told me you had planted. Blazes of color that cut through relentless December fog.

"There is always something beautiful in a tragedy," said my long-ago student Zita. She wrote an essay about a frail, bullied boy who lived in her apartment building in Poland. Zita would sit on her windowsill and listen to the boy play the piano. One day, when she came home from school, an ambulance was slowly leaving the driveway. The boy had jumped from the fire escape. Years later, Zita could not stop thinking about the music or the fact that she had not stood up for him on the playground. There is always something beautiful in a tragedy. Piano notes. Marigolds. The fog, jumble, and heartbreak of experience broken into clear and manageable pieces.

Dear Mairin,
 You, brave, stoic sister, chose that pseudonym, "beloved, star of the sea." You taught me to read and write at the shiny dining room table that sits in your home today. You read entire novels and biographies to me before I could sound out the words. When I remind you of this, you wave my words away with your hand. You do not want any credit for turning me into a teacher or writer. "Why don't you have your students write about The Declaration of Independence?" you asked me when I first started teaching nonfiction writing. "You're not a trained therapist," you said, worrying my students' stories might be too much for them, for me, perhaps for you to hear about. Before I published the essay in the *Times*, I sent a copy to you and everyone in it. You all gave the go-ahead. But after the piece appeared, you told me you were glad we had different last names. You thought you could be fired from your job if people knew what went on in our home. Brigid said, "I want my superintendent to read the piece because I want him to know how brave I am." My mind agreed with Brigid, but my nerves agreed with you. There is power in remaining a mystery. I had given up that power for both of us. Chosen the place and time. Chosen a different kind of power for myself and took you along for the ride. Took our siblings and stepmother for the ride. Took the people in our town along for the ride. Our quiet brother, Peter, was working in a shop in town, stood behind the counter as people who had known our father walked in to tell him they had read the piece, that our father finally got what he deserved. People we knew and did not know overwhelmed us with old and new stories about the tragedy of our father. Offered strong opinions on whether I should have written and published the piece. What justice. What a betrayal. Said he must be "rolling in his grave." But none of us wanted him to be rolling in his grave. The story is more complicated for us. Our father has caused us nightmares. Yet in our own ways, all we want is peace.

Dear Declaration of Independence,
 My students are welcome to write about you. They are welcome to write about moths. Trips to the lake. Gap years. The time they missed the penalty kick. Parents' divorces. Coffee shops. Accidents. "Anyone who survived childhood has enough material to write for the rest of his life." I tell my students Flannery O'Connor said this.
 Years ago, I had a student who rushed into class everyday wearing dirty Carhartt overalls. He wrote about his job as a gravedigger, how he and his fellow diggers made crass jokes about the people who were going to be buried in the holes they dug. Until the day his high school friend fell off a roof and died. The student's

boss had offered to give him the day off, but he declined. He said it was the most important grave he had to dig.

Dear Winston Churchill,
    You hated the portrait commissioned by Parliament on your 80th birthday. You did not deny its likeness, but you wanted to look regal, standing tall in your Robes of the Garter. Instead, artist Graham Sutherland captured you seated, in a rumpled suit and bowtie, posture both vulnerable and defiant. Columbia University art historian Simon Schama said, "What Sutherland saw before him was a magnificent ruin." Critics call the work a masterpiece, but only photos of it survive. At your request, your wife, Clementine, took it out to the yard and burned it.
    "Like the angels, you are likely to be simplified," Amy Leach writes in her essay, "Memorandum to the Animals." I wrote about the fact that the neighbors did nothing when Mairin and I ran to their house in the middle of the night, begging for help because our father was in a rage. "How could you?" Mairin said after the piece was published. "They gave me a Waterford bowl for my wedding." But the piece was not about the Waterford bowl or the ways we shrieked with joy as we jumped in their icy pool, then sat at their long kitchen table, eating hot dogs and Fritos. An essay can only be about so many things, I tell my students. We all hope readers know this, but sometimes they do not seem to know this. Last year, I received an email from a student who had written about being sexually assaulted on campus. She had entered the essay in a contest and was proud to learn she had won. Still, her email said: "Imagine walking into a bar with a bruise on your face from being beaten or blood on your outfit from being assaulted. People no longer see you as you want them to see you. And many times, they don't see you at all. They just see the blood and the bruise."

Dear fancy, adjustable office chair,
    My husband bought you for me because I kept telling him I could not get comfortable at my desk and this was the reason I was not writing. I read your manual, adjusted the back and armrests to the most ergonomic angles possible. Still, I did not feel at ease. A pseudo-protective fog kept descending over my desk. I was trying to write about a course of electric-shock treatments I underwent in my 20s, after my mother died. I had kept the treatments secret even from some of my closest friends. "Silence is not going to solve it anymore, Quentin," Arthur Miller writes in his autobiographical play, *After the Fall*. I believe this to be true, but still had decades of shame and silence-training to shatter. Decades of fear that I would be judged and scrutinized for what had happened to me and how I had responded, and not enough strength to handle it if I was.
    "No one will be able to fuck with me!" I said to my husband over and over as I worked on the electric-shock treatment essay, all false bravado, and then the piece was finished and I started to look with compassion at the girl I had been. I started

to feel strong, like a whale covered with barnacles and scars from shark bites and boat propellers, but still able to swim a hundred miles a day.

Dear current and future students, myself included,

I am not a trained therapist, but I will do my best to read and listen carefully, and I know where to send you for help and support if you need it. Maybe some of you will write to redeem what has seemed unredeemable. To attempt to control and make sense of things that were beyond your control, to tinker from the relative safety of your desks, with words, which I will tell you Charles Simic calls "splendid poverties." But still, some of us will ask ourselves, which stories are ours to tell? We will try to choose carefully, but sometimes we will go ahead without really being sure. After the *Times* piece was published, I heard from a Princeton University football player who thanked me because his father was similar to mine and the essay made him feel less alone. A woman in South America said the same. A classmate from elementary school said she had no idea. And then there was another neighbor who sent my sister and me home after we banged on her door shaking very late one night. I saw her at the wake of a friend. She touched my arm, led me to a corner, apologized, and we hugged and talked.

Chapter 15. The Next Anthology: The Personal Essay in the Digital Age

Ned Stuckey-French
FLORIDA STATE UNIVERSITY

Over the past few years or so, during which the essay has seen a renaissance, new platforms and technologies for publishing and disseminating them have emerged. Attention to marginalized voices and efforts to center those voices resulting from the radical activist movements of the 1960s have likewise contributed to the newer relevance of the personal essay and the first-person voice to students of writing and to school curricula.

Given these two historical trends, how do we understand the essay's present moment and what does that moment call on those of us who write and teach essays to do?

The Essay Renaissance

In 1976 Edward Hoagland bemoaned the fact that "though two fine anthologies [*Best American Short Stories* and the *O'Henry Prize Stories*] remain that publish the year's best stories, no comparable collection exists for essays" (24–25). A decade later Houghton Mifflin launched the *Best American Essays* series under its Ticknor & Fields imprint with Robert Atwan as series editor. The series experienced immediate and continued success, which has led its publisher to add related series (science and nature, travel, spiritual, and sports writing, and "nonrequired reading") that feature essays. At the time Hoagland published his piece, New Journalists such as Truman Capote, Joan Didion, Norman Mailer, Gay Talese, and Tom Wolfe had already been working for the better part of a decade to invigorate feature writing by importing techniques from fiction: a strong first-person point of view, thick description, figurative language, sustained dialogue, and dramatized scenes. Wolfe offered a theory of and rationale for this approach in four manifesto-like introductory chapters to the 1973 anthology *The New Journalism*. Work by the New Journalists soon found its way into essay anthologies, stretching the boundaries of the genre and challenging the still prevalent view of the essayist as "a middle-aged man in a worn tweed jacket in an armchair smoking a pipe by a fire in his private library in a country house in England, in about 1910, maundering on about the delights of idleness, country walks, tobacco, old wine, and old books" (Good vii).

Out of the political movements of the 1960s came not only calls for more relevant curricula and the establishment of African-American and women's studies programs, but also for new courses and curricula. Development of these programs and others like them led to the recovery of silenced, ignored, and lost texts, an opening of both the composition and literature canons, and a more engaged, process-oriented approach to the teaching of writing. One of the resulting developments was growth in creative writing programs: according Mark McGurl, in *The Program Era: Postwar Fiction and the Rise of Creative Writing*, their numbers went from a "handful . . . in the 1940s [to] some 150 graduate degree programs (offering the M.A., M.F.A., or Ph.D.)" in 1984, and "as of 2004 . . . more than 350 creative writing programs in the United States" (24).

As McGurl's subtitle suggests, the new creative writing programs emphasized fiction (though poetry was generally there from the outset as well). The essay, on the other hand, was relegated institutionally to first-year writing and composition classes. In schools where such courses were staffed by adjuncts and graduate assistants, beginning teachers were supplied with "readers"—textbook anthologies filled with model essays, discussion questions, and exercises designed to walk them through their first teaching experience. The situation was not new. According to Lynn Z. Bloom, the essay had suffered a "fall from canonical status to school genre" around 1900 ("Once More" 25).

In the 1980s things began to change for the essay. By 1986, the year Houghton Mifflin launched the *Best American Essays* series, the Association of Writers and Writing Programs (AWP) already noted that "the fastest growing creative writing programs are in nonfiction" (Rose 238). Of the 388 graduate programs in creative writing that AWP now lists (as of 2022), 267 of them offer degrees in creative nonfiction, with memoir and essay dominating, all under the unfortunate umbrella of "nonfiction," which, as Scott Russell Sanders has pointed out, is

> an exceedingly vague term, taking in everything from telephone books to *Walden*, and it's negative, implying that fiction is the norm against which everything else must be measured. It's as though, instead of calling an apple a fruit, we called it a nonmeat. (123)

Up until the early 1990s, the essay had been an afterthought in most literary magazines, often appearing as criticism or discussions of craft. Suddenly, it seemed, a number of journals appeared that were devoted exclusively to the essay, many holding onto the nonfiction tag: *Creative Nonfiction* (1993), *Fourth Genre: Explorations in Nonfiction* (1999), *River Teeth: A Journal of Nonfiction Narrative* (1999), *Under the Gum Tree* (2011), *Hippocampus* (2011), and *Assay: A Journal of Nonfiction Studies* (2014). The *River Teeth*, *Creative Nonfiction*, and NonfictioNow conferences are all focused exclusively on the essay, and the AWP conference, attended each year by upwards of 12,000 writers, teachers, publishers, and students, began to host more panels on the essay. Creative nonfiction, as Wendy Bishop put it in a 2003 issue of *College English*, was "suddenly sexy."

The history of the University of Iowa's Nonfiction Writing Program is representative of both the essay's late arrival and its improved status within the academy. In 1922, Iowa became the first university in the United States to accept creative work as the thesis for an advanced degree. In 1936, the university set up the Iowa Writers' Workshop, the nation's first degree-granting creative writing program. Focusing exclusively on fiction and poetry, the Workshop pioneered the now-ubiquitous workshop approach, a pedagogical technique in which an experienced writer-teacher guides a discussion of a student manuscript, relying heavily on comments from the student's peers. The Workshop's graduates have won dozens of Pulitzers, National Book Awards, MacArthur Foundation grants, and other honors, and it has consistently ranked as the top program in the country.

In 1976, 40 years after the Workshop was founded and the year Jix Lloyd-Jones became chair of the English Department at Iowa, six of the department's professors founded the Nonfiction Writing Program that offered what was called a Master of Arts in English/Expository Writing, or M.A.W. degree. Students tailored their final projects to fit their interests, doing everything from research-based feature writing to memoirs to film criticism. In 1984, Carl Klaus became the director of the program, helped change the degree to a Master of Fine Arts (M.F.A.), and brought in published essayists as visiting faculty. In 2004, Robin Hemley became director, set up the biannual NonfictioNOW Conference; established the Overseas Writing Workshop (which enabled students to write and study in countries such as Cuba, the Philippines, and Australia), hired new faculty, and continued to bring writers to campus as visiting faculty. The program has been prominent since, its graduates publishing scores of books, landing strong teaching positions, and winning Guggenheim, Whiting, Lannan, and MacArthur Foundation fellowships as well as numerous awards.

The Essay in the Digital Age

The digital transformation has changed the way we read and write. Books, magazines, copyright, research methods, libraries, the whole publishing industry—all of these are different now, as is the way we read, write, collect, and teach essays.

In 1984, Phillip Lopate announced on the front page of *The New York Times Book Review* that "The Essay Lives—In Disguise." In fact, it has always been, as Hoagland put it, "a greased pig" (25), sometimes camouflaged as a column, a feature story, an op-ed, or a profile. The essay is not so much a genre as a "galaxy of subgenres," the word "essay" preceded by one of a "passel of adjectives: *personal, formal, informal, humorous, descriptive, expository, reflective, nature, critical, lyric, narrative, review, periodical, romantic,* and *genteel*" (Stuckey-French). Digital technology has compounded the problem—or alternately, it has increased the essay's possibilities.

Essayists have experimented with multimodal composition for years. John T. McCutcheon illustrated George Ade's *Stories of the Streets and of the Town* during the 1890s. A couple of decades later, Don Marquis drew cartoons for his "archy and mehitabel" columns. Radio essays date to that medium's origins. Nonfiction writers as different as James Agee, W.G. Sebald, Susan Sontag, Roland Barthes, and Michael Lesy have used and meditated on photography. But the proliferation of digital technologies in the early 2000s has set off an explosion of new forms. The transformation from film and video provides an especially stark example of what is happening.

In 1992, Lopate published "In Search of the Centaur: The Essay-Film." It examined the work of filmmakers, including Americans Orson Welles, Ross McElwee, and Michael Moore and French filmmakers associated with the New Wave such as Jean-Luc Godard, Alain Resnais, and especially Chris Marker, and then offered a five-part definition of the essay-film. This hybrid genre must, he argued, "have words, in the form of text either spoken, subtitled or intertitled"; "represent a single voice"; "represent the speaker's attempt to work out some reasoned line of discourse on a problem"; "impart more than information" (for Lopate, the domain of the documentary) and instead advance "a strong, personal point of view"; and finally, its "language should be as eloquent, well-written and interesting as possible." Lopate also worried the question of why there were so few examples of the essay-film. He attributed the scarcity to, among other things the "intractable nature of the camera," which tends to capture more in its "promiscuous images" than the filmmaker anticipated or perhaps wants. People who are drawn to movie-making, Lopate asserted, seem to be those who "revere images, want to make magic, and are uncomfortable with the pinning down of one's thoughts that an essay demands."

Film critics immediately took Lopate to task for what they saw as a logocentric view. Paul Arthur pointed out, for instance, that because "film operates simultaneously on multiple discursive levels—image, speech, titles, music—the literary essay's single determining voice is dispersed into cinema's multi-channel stew" (59). While this debate simmered, the digitization of the film industry proceeded apace. Home video moved from VHS to Blu-ray to DVD to streaming. Webcams became standard in laptops and then in mobile devices. In a 2010 issue of *Blackbird*, Virginia Commonwealth University's online literary journal, John Bresland introduced a "suite" of six video essays with a defining piece titled "On the Origin of the Video Essay." He spoke to Lopate directly, arguing first that the "promiscuity of film isn't a weakness of the essay-film," but is instead "a feature" or "complication" in the way "that pianos complicate singing." And as for the hybridity of Lopate's centaur, Hollywood's hegemony, and the problems of distribution, Bresland argued that they were fundamentally a thing of the past:

> Film is visual; the essay is not. Film is collaborative; the essay is not. Film requires big money; the essay costs little and makes less. Essays and film, Lopate notes, are two different animals, and I agree with him on one condition: that it's 1991. That's when Lopate wrote "In Search of the Centaur" for Threepenny. The internet was just a baby then, nursed by dweebs. Then, financial

considerations reigned. If you wanted your film made, you first needed grants, financing, distributors. Today, to make a small-scale personal film, you can shoot the thing on an inexpensive digital camera and upload it to any number of free video sharing sites . . .

Today artists have access to video editing tools that ship free on computers. A generation ago, such capability didn't exist at any price. Now all it takes for a young artist to produce a documentary is an out-of-the-box Mac, a camera, and the will to see an idea through to its resolution. The act of writing has always been a personal pursuit, a concentrated form of thought. And now filmmaking, too, shares that meditative space. The tools are handheld, affordable, no less accessible than a Smith-Corona. You can shoot and edit video, compelling video, on a cell phone.

Brave new world, right? But what do we call it?

We're calling it the video essay. ("On the Origin")

Bresland argued from the position not just of theorist but also practitioner. His suite included a breakthrough video essay of his own titled "Mangoes," a provocative meditation on gender, parenthood, and class that utilized quick cuts, voiceover narration, reenactments, found footage, interviews, and black-and-white photography. In his introduction to this (now widely taught) piece, Bresland revealed,

My own modest obstruction in "Mangoes," self-imposed, was to acquire video, record sound, and compose a score using only a cell phone. In the end, I cheated. But just a bit. For the most part, "Mangoes" is authored on an iPhone.

Over a decade ago, Bresland's touchstones were YouTube and the iPhone, and the digital revolution has continued to accelerate. Many digital natives who arrive in our classrooms each fall are already proficient, to varying degrees, in assemblage and multimedia composition: text, sound, image moving and still, links as sources or illustrations Many of them are already blogging, podcasting, designing games, creating videos and Instagram essays.

A decade ago at Florida State University where I teach, we launched a new track for our undergrad English majors, an alternative to our existing literature and creative writing tracks. We called this third concentration editing, writing, and media (EWM) and summed up its mission with the (now antiquated) tag line "Writing for 21st Century." It was meant to be a pilot project with a soft rollout, but students loved it and within two years it was the most popular of our three tracks. EWM majors take a core set of traditional literature and writing courses but supplement those with courses (some required, some electives) in areas such as visual rhetoric, digital design, line editing, and the history of text technologies. They work in our two digital studios and create e-portfolios. Most do an internship and pursue careers in book and magazine publishing, public relations, advertising, and arts administration. Many go on to graduate school. The EWM track is currently home for more than half of our approximately 1400 undergraduate English majors.

Florida State is hardly alone in developing a program like this. Some colleges and universities have established them as independent departments or programs: University of Kentucky's Writing, Rhetoric & Digital Studies, Bentley University's English & Media Studies, Massachusetts Institute of Technology's Department of Comparative Media Studies & Writing, and Seattle University's Digital Technologies and Culture. Others offer something similar as a concentration within English or another major: University of Massachusetts Amherst, Mount Mary University (WI), Emmanuel College (MA), Auburn University, University of Massachusetts Boston, Miami University (OH), St. Edwards (TX), New Mexico State, University of Rochester (NY), and University of Wisconsin-Stout.

Among graduate programs, the digital essay has had a slower uptake. Important work is being done by Claudia Rankine at Yale University, Eric LeMay at Ohio University, Ira Sukrungruang at the University of South Florida previously and more recently at Kenyon College, Joe Wenderoth at the Univeristy of California at Davis, Ander Monson at the University of Arizona, Brian Oliu at the University of Alabama, José Roach Orduña at the University of Nevada Las Vegas (UNLV), and Kristen Radtke at UNLV's Beverly Rodgers and Carol C. Harter Black Mountain Institute. But creative writing seems so far to have left much of the work in program and course development to colleagues in film, journalism, and media studies, even as it has developed online venues for creative work that employs new media. Journals such *Ninth Letter* at the University of Illinois, *DIAGRa.m.* at the University of Arizona, *Tri-Quarterly* at Northwestern University, and *Slag Glass City* at DePaul University are among some of the magazines publishing digital essays. Iowa's Nonfiction Writing Program has sponsored much of this work. Bresland (and his wife Eula Biss with whom he collaborates), Radtke, and Orduna are all Iowa graduates. Robyn Schiff, Nick Twemlow, and Jeff Porter have done multimodal work.

The Next Anthology

Program and curriculum development are essential to the genre's development and growth but so too is publication, including historically through anthologies, which have long played a critical role in helping define the canon and did so again during the essay renaissance.

As Lynn Z. Bloom has persuasively argued, the post-World War II essay canon had been constructed primarily in first-year writing anthologies. These collections emphasized shorter, more accessible essays that could be used by beginning teachers to model familiar modes of writing (exposition, narration, persuasion, description) for beginning writers. According to Bloom this made for a canon that was primarily pedagogical rather than critical, historical, or national. But as the essay renaissance began and nonfiction worked its way into burgeoning M.F.A. programs, essay writers and scholars of the essay began to create anthologies that were organized historically and that included more complex essays by more diverse writers.

A multitude of print anthologies helped fuel the essay renaissance. Important examples of the period included Carl Klaus, Rebecca Faery and Chris Anderson, eds., *In Depth: Essayists for Our Time* (1989; 1993); Gerald Early, ed., *Speech and Power: The African-American Essay and Its Cultural Content from Polemics to Pulpit, Vols. I and II* (Ecco 1992, 1993); Sandra Tropp, ed. *Shaping Tradition: Art and Diversity in the Essay* (Harcourt 1992); Phillip Lopate, ed., *The Art of the Personal Essay: An Anthology from the Classical Era to the Present* (Anchor Doubleday 1994); Robert Sayre, ed., *American Lives: An Anthology of Autobiographical Writing* (U of Wisconsin P 1994); Joyce Carol Oates and Robert Atwan, eds., *The Best American Essays of the Century* (Houghton Mifflin 2000); John D'Agata, ed., *The Next American Essay* (Graywolf 2002); D'Agata, ed., *The Lost Origins of the Essay* (Graywolf 2009); Michael Martone and Lex Williford, eds., *The Touchstone Anthology of Contemporary Nonfiction: Work from 1970 to the Present* (Simon and Schuster 2007); Richard Labonté and Lawrence Schimel, eds., *First Person Queer: Who We Are (So Far)* (Arsenal Pulp Press 2007); Carl Klaus and Ned Stuckey-French, eds., *Essayists on the Essay: From Montaigne to Our Time* (U of Iowa P 2012); D'Agata, *The Making of the American Essay* (Graywolf 2016); and Marcia Aldrich, *Waveform: Twenty-First-Century Essays by Women* (U of Georgia P 2016).

These anthologies introduced readers to new voices by reaching back historically—even beyond Montaigne to the classical period—and by being more attentive to gender, ethnic, and racial diversity than most earlier anthologies had been. In some instances, they crossed national borders to explore the genre in its global context. In addition to broadening their content they also curated the material differently. Traditional first-year writing anthologies had usually organized their tables of contents by genre or rhetorical mode, theme or topic, or alphabetically by author, and offered editorial apparatus that emphasized writing prompts and discussion questions (see Bloom "Once More"; Root). The new anthologies were more likely to organize their contents chronologically, include multiple essays by individual essayists, offer headnotes that gave substantial biographical and historical context, include a full bibliography and index, and provide a scholarly introduction.

The digital revolution that has captured imaginations and spawned many new literary forms has at the same time played havoc with textbook publishing. Many writers teaching nonfiction prefer to have students buy multiple essay collections by single authors or to create ad hoc anthologies for their courses. Blackboard, Canvas, and other online platforms make it easy, indeed de rigueur, for teachers to set up password-protected classroom sites where they can easily and legally create their own digital course library. These innovations have hit the whole textbook industry hard, but have posed particular problems for print anthologies aimed at classrooms. Publishers push editors and authors for new editions every two or three years in an attempt to outmaneuver used booksellers. They raise the prices with each new edition to shore up their margins against sagging sales. At the same time, authors' agents raise permissions costs. Editing an anthology, which had never done much to help one's case for promotion and tenure, has become even less attractive. Faced with an accelerated editing process, dwindling advances, and the moral dilemma of textbook costs to students already burdened by high tuition and student loan debt, many would-be editors find less incentive than ever to take on this task—and increasingly fewer opportunities to do so.

Despite these pressures, anthologies continue to be published (often as trade books rather than text) used in classrooms, and play a role in forming canons. But new conditions call for new anthologies. How might we collect and curate essays in formats appropriate to the digital age? How can print and electronic texts complement each other?

My focus here is not on the question of print versus screens per se. Both are here to stay, at least for the foreseeable future. We know the pros and cons. Text on a screen is easily customizable; it allows you to carry thousands of books in your pocket, access databases like Project Muse, follow links, take screenshots, do searches, and make annotations. Print, on the other hand, is better for reading longer works and for reading deeply with retention. Print books don't come with distractions like social media or limitless surfing. You carry the whole of the material book with you rather than face single contextless virtual pages. My concern is with how we might construct an essay anthology that straddles the two realms, combines valuable aspects of print and electronic books, makes full use of today's technology-enhanced and virtual classrooms, offers students classic essays from the past and also cutting-edge digital work, and perhaps even leads textbook publishers into the new age. Such an anthology might exist in a print form but be supplemented by a digital component that can be accessed from a mobile device, as publishers are doing with composition textbooks

To be honest I'm not sure that what I have in mind should be called an anthology. When I show students a new book trailer or mash-up or animated memoir or bit of film criticism full of quick cuts, they ask, "But is this a video essay?" And I'm not sure, but it leads to a good discussion that gets us talking about genres as lying along a spectrum rather than as a set of pigeonholes in a fixed cabinet. It is hard to find names for things that are truly new. So perhaps this thing I am talking about is a new kind of anthology, but it might feel more like a set of concerns and ideas about anthologies in the digital age. In any case, here are some the problems and questions that face us.

The Teach Act of 2002 (in particular, section 110) allows instructors at accredited nonprofit institutions of learning to use digital materials, including video and PDFs that have not been bootlegged, in distance-learning classrooms and on password-protected classroom sites, such as Canvas and BlackBoard. Instructors can use these for the duration of the class as long as they make it clear to students that the work is protected by copyright and is not to be copied or shared beyond the classroom.[1]

Understanding this, instructors have long shared links, PDFs, and other materials. At present instructors use crowdsourcing calls on Facebook and other social media platforms to gather ideas and links, but a more systematic approach would be helpful. Libraries, online literary journals, and those of us who teach the essay might begin to create digital archives that collect some of these materials for use in our courses and research. The curation role is central. Anthologies are important for both their inclusion and their exclusion. With the now billions of websites on the internet and the soaring use of YouTube, Instagram, and TikTok, finding examples to use in class presents a nearly paralyzing array of choices, requiring vast amounts of time. Options are wonderful, but an editor-curator function is, too. More sites like Fandor, where Kevin Lee, a great video essayist and curator of the form, posts would be a help with this Sisyphean task.[2]

Crowdsourcing can often seem like a catch-as-catch-can way to find new essays online or share teaching ideas but they remain necessary and Facebook pages such as Creative Writing Pedagogy and the late William Bradley's Essaying the 21st Century make possible the platforms for such calls.[3] Sites such as Dinty Moore's, *Brevity's* Nonfiction Blog and Ander Monson's Essay Daily provide links, craft advice, podcasts, "visual essays," posts from conferences, roundtable discussions, reviews, and news about contests and calls for submissions.[4] As literary magazines publishing essays put their archives online, sometimes for a subscription but often free, readers and teachers can move among several of them and create their own anthologies.

Collection and anthology sites are essential and invaluable for creating a community of writers, scholars, and teachers, but they are not exactly anthologies. A digital archive, which attempts to preserve materials in a readable, searchable, and contextualized format, is more akin to an anthology. A few digital archives of essays exist. Most notably there is Patrick Madden's Quotidiana, which contains scores of essays by dozens of essayists beginning with Seneca.[5] Compiled and updated over several years by Madden and his graduate students at Brigham Young University, Quotidiana is beautifully curated with biographical notes, searchable and downloadable files, and even portraits of each essayist. The essays all date from before 1923 and so are in the public domain. This archive is an

---

1. https://www.copyright.gov/title17/92chap1.html#110
2. https://www.fandor.com/browse-movie
3. https://www.facebook.com/groups/509120669155567/
4. https://brevity.wordpress.com/ and https://www.essaydaily.org/, respectively.
5. http://essays.quotidiana.org/

invaluable aid for scholars and teachers focused on the classical essay. Quotidiana emphasizes the Anglo-American tradition but tries to introduce African, Asian, and Native American voices as well and includes 33 women essayists.

With the help of my graduate assistants and undergraduate interns I created a digital archive, Essays in America, of more contemporary essay materials. It contains 32 essays by 20th- and 21st-century American essayists ranging from Randolph Bourne and W.E.B. Du Bois to Maxine Hong Kingston and Jo Ann Beard. The entries include a short biography of the essayist, discussions of the form of each essay and of its subsequent appearances in collections and anthologies, a bibliography, and scans of each essay as it first appeared in magazines, as well as surrounding ads, illustrations, cartoons, contributors' notes, tables of contents, subsequent letters to the editor, and other materials that might help inform readers about the essay's original rhetorical context. When possible, there is a link to or PDF of the essay in its entirety, but copyright provisions have not always allowed that.

Another site that offers important digital archives that focus primarily on print essays is *Assay: A Journal of Nonfiction Studies*. Founded by Karen Babine, *Assay* is published twice a year; each issue contains articles and conversations about essays and the teaching of essays. The site also contains two important archives that are continually updated. The first of these is a syllabus bank and the second is a searchable archive of all the titles that have appeared in the *Best American Essays* series since its inception in 1986. Again, because of copyright provisions, one cannot link to the essays themselves, although the archive is searchable by author, title, and year.

But what about new digital essays? Here the archives are scattered and this is where scholars, teachers, and students could really benefit from an archive that collects some of the most innovate work or at least links to it. Currently one must either search online journals, such as *Tri-Quarterly Online*, *Ninth Letter*, and *Blackbird* that often publish such work, or go to the individual artists' websites. Important video essayists such as Claudia Rankine (who often collaborates with John Lucas) and John Bresland (who often collaborates with Eula Biss) collect their work at their websites, but also upload work at Vimeo.[6] Similarly, Brian Oliu's groundbreaking video game essays might at first seem only to be scattered among various online magazines before one discovers that he has his own YouTube channel, Uploads from Brian Oliu.[7] Scripts of video essays that have been created as video essay are rarely available online, though they would be of tremendous use in the classroom. The best substitute is to view video adaptations of print essays. Two good comparisons that help illuminate the adaptation process involve essays by Brian Doyle and Ryan Van Meter. Doyle's essay "His Last Game"

---

6. http://claudiarankine.com/ and https://bresland.com/, respectively.
7. https://www.youtube.com/playlist?list=UUbiRmDQKiTDa89z9faDxeNg

appeared originally in *Notre Dame Magazine*,[8] was later made into ten-minute film by director Avery Rimer, and is available online at hislastgame.com. Van Meter's essay "First" appeared in *The Gettysburg Review*[9] and a video adaptation of it by Sarabande Books served as a book trailer for his first collection, *If You Knew Then What I Know Now*.

Two accomplished graphic essayists and memoirists, Alison Bechdel (dykestowatchoutfor.com) and Kristen Radtke (KristenRadtke.com) have exquisite websites that showcase their work. Both regularly update their sites and link to interviews, YouTube videos, and blog posts in which they discuss their creative process. Two innovative digital essayists, Eric LeMay (ericlemay.org) and Ander Monson (otherelectricities.com) do something similar at their websites, where they collect their work but also link to scattered podcasts, interviews, videos, and craft pieces. These craft pieces and discussions of process, like the scripts of video essays, can be very helpful in learning how to create these new subgenres. An especially illuminating example of this kind of back-and-forth between print and digital is the history of Monson's essay "Solipsism," which appeared first on his website. Then Wendy Sumner-Winter worked with him to redesign the piece for *The Pinch*, a print journal she edited at the University of Memphis. The print version caught the eyes of editors Robert Atwan and Adam Gopnik, who chose it in 2008 when it became the first online piece to be included in the *Best American Essays* series. Monson's original essay and the version he and Sumner-Winter created for *The Pinch* are both online.

This to-and-fro between print and digital gets only more complicated when we begin to consider podcasts, mashups, and Instagram, Google Maps, and various hermit crab essays that inhabit other forms such as online syllabi, BuzzFeed listicles, and who knows what else. The goal is not to contain or limit the diversity of the internet within a few or, heaven forbid, a single online anthology, but what I hope to propose here (and perhaps even enact here) is the idea that an online clearing house or anthology or some such animal is needed and even possible.

How do we cultivate a respect for traditional forms while leaving ourselves and our students open to innovation and the possibilities digitization offers? What can we learn from people who are digital natives? What is multimodal composition? What is a digital essay? And what might an essay anthology look like in the digital age? Embedded in that last question are several others. For example, what purpose can or should anthologies serve? Teaching convenience is one rationale, reading pleasure a second, canon formation a third. It may be that professors would rather pick and choose their own works, that readers are plenty happy either with Best American series or reading favorite periodicals, and that canon formation is best left to critics or social circulation. Perhaps anthologies in a digital age are largely going the way of, say, *The Reader's Digest*, in the age of

---

8. https://magazine.nd.edu/stories/his-last-game/
9. https://tinyurl.com/ss38pxvs

print. Still, to the extent that their remains a combinatorial or curatorial role for anthologies—an anthology function—especially in the still emergent period of digital/multimodal essays and all their affordances, it seems desirable to embrace some means of identifying works that deserve attention, even acclaim.

Works Cited

Arthur, Paul. "Essay Questions: From Alain Resnais to Michael Moore." *Film Comment*, vol. 39 no. 1, Jan./Feb. 2003, p. 58–62.

Association of Writers and Writing Programs. *The AWP Official Guide to Writing Programs* www.awpwriter.org/guide/guide_writing_programs.

Bishop, Wendy. "Suddenly Sexy: Creative Nonfiction Rear-Ends Composition." *Creative Nonfiction*, a special issue of *College English*, vol. 65, no. 3, Jan. 2003, pp. 257–275.

Bloom, Lynn Z. "The Essay Canon." *College English*, vol. 61, no. 4, Mar. 1999, pp. 401–430.

———. "Once More to the Essay: The Essay Canon and Textbook Anthologies." *symploke*, vol. 8, no. 1–2, 2000, pp. 20–35.

Bresland, John. "Mangoes." Video Essay Suite. *Blackbird*, vol. 9, no. 1, spring 2010.

———. "On the Origin of the Video Essay." *Blackbird*, vol. 9, no. 1, spring 2010. Revised and reprinted in *Essayists on the Essay: From Montaigne to Our Time*, edited by Carl Klaus and Ned Stuckey-French, U of Iowa P, 2012, pp. 180–84.

Essaying the 21st Century. Facebook group. www.facebook.com/groups/509120669155567.

Good, Graham. *The Observing Self: Rediscovering the Essay*. Routledge, 1988.

Hoagland, Edward. "What I Think, What I Am." *The Tugman's Passage*, Random House, 1982. Appeared originally in *New York Times Book Review*, 27 June 1976.

Lopate, Phillip. "The Essay Lives—in Disguise." *The New York Times Book Review*, 18 Nov. 1984, pp. 1, 48–49.

———. "In Search of the Centaur: The Essay-Film." *The Threepenny Review*, vol. 48, winter 1992, pp. 19–22.

McGurl, Mark. *The Program Era: Postwar Fiction and the Rise of Creative Writing*. Harvard UP, 2009.

Root, Robert. "Once More to the Essay: Prose Models, Textbooks, and Teaching." *Journal of Teaching Writing*, vol. 14, no. 1–2, 1995, pp. 87–110.

Rose, Mary. Associated Writing Programs. Telephone conversation (2 Nov. 2000), quoted by Douglas Hesse, "The Place of Creative Nonfiction," Creative Nonfiction, a special issue of *College English*, vol. 65, no. 3, Jan. 2003, pp. 237–241.

Sanders, Scott Russell. "Interview with Scott Russell Sanders." Interview conducted by Robert K. Root, *Fourth Genre*, vol. 1, no. 1, spring 1999, pp. 119–32.

Stuckey-French, Ned. "Our Queer Little Hybrid Thing." *Assay: A Journal of Nonfiction Studies*, vol. 1, no. 1, fall 2014.

Wolfe, Tom and E. W. Johnson, eds. *The New Journalism*. Harper & Row, 1973.

Chapter 16. Why I Write, Read, Teach, Edit Nonfiction

Laura Julier
Michigan State University

Of course I stole (the stem of) my title from Joan Didion, who stole it from George Orwell. I don't in any way aim to stand in that line of succession, but only, as it were, to borrow for myself a way to begin. Because for this purpose, at this time, I might just as well tell this story as if it began there, in 1976, in Los Angeles, when I was a relatively new recipient of a B.A. in English, newly divorced, working at a Kentucky Fried Chicken on Pico Blvd. just down the street from the 20th Century Fox studio lots, trying to figure out what the heck I would make of my life. I was working ten hours a day with a bunch of 15-year-old kids, leaving that job to drive five miles into the Hollywood Hills to care for an elderly woman with a deeply unsettling and otherworldly history, who was invalid and imperious and routinely told me I was too timid.

Somewhere, somehow, in some spare hours probably between the lunch hour rush at KFC from the studio and the time when all the teenagers arrived to work after school, I hid from the lecherous store owner, and in the corner where the squat round pots of acrid coffee burned down, I read. Somehow, somewhere, I'd picked up *Slouching Towards Bethlehem*, the particular texture of the pages of which I can still recall to my fingers, the way the font was laid out on the page, spaciously, with generous margins and gutters, but more importantly—much more importantly—the way the voice on the page seemed to resonate in my head, as if it were my own voice, as if it were something I recognized, shaped by my own life, although our lives held absolutely nothing in common except the English degree.

It wasn't as if I hadn't ever before immersed myself in the words of a writer: I had been reading and absorbing and chewing up words from pages and the worlds they created for as long as I could remember. Worlds that I can call up again wholecloth now decades later, words that challenged and absorbed me in figuring out how they worked. It was an English teacher in junior high school who, recognizing that I was hungry for more, had set me the task of explicating a passage from *Portrait of the Artist as a Young Man*. Who'd thereby set an example to me of how a sentence might take hours and hours to pull apart, to understand how a sentence might craft a world. It was a different English teacher who threw a Gerard Manly Hopkins poem at me, requiring sense be made of it, and although I failed at his task, I still remember the poem, still remember how deeply I longed to be a writer myself who could make words do the things they do in "The Windhover."

In the late 1960s, universities were abandoning requirements and prerequisites, inventing courses that took untraditional, even radical, approaches to their subjects, so it was not unusual—but thoroughly in line with my hunger for the worlds that words might open up in a single poetic line—that I was able to spend not one but two entire semesters at the University of Buffalo swimming in the complete works of James Joyce and two semesters reading not only Yeats' poetry but also his philosophy and drama. In another course, we were reading and rereading *King Lear* with five different theoretical lenses, from Freud to Foucault to R.D. Laing, and I was completely engaged and mesmerized. But I can remember sitting day after day, as the spring semester days warmed and lengthened, counting down as one after another student spoke, keeping track of the dwindling number left who, like me, had not yet spoken. Then noticing that I alone remained, and imagining how if I did speak, everyone would turn to see who it was who had suddenly used her voice. And so, I didn't. I spent the entire term silent, afraid and ashamed of what I might say, and took the lower grade as a result.

In Didion, however, I encountered not a fictional world, not words in service to inventing a world, but the (somewhat different) work of following a mind at work on the world, the work of nonfiction essays, one after another, which grabbed me in a way that seemed as if I'd already and always known it. And not a man's voice but a woman's, describing and following experience shaped by intense perception and self-doubt, in equal proportion.

And there, sitting in a corner in my little red-and-white striped KFC uniform, completely absorbed by her voice that felt like my own, I realized that although her voice seemed (as I would later learn so many critics made a point of saying) fragile, neurotic, and wounded, it was nonetheless *there* on the page, between covers of a book, taking up space. That while I heard Didion's voice in my head, in the classrooms the voices had been all male.

I applied to graduate school to earn another degree, not for the sake of the degree but to reclaim some of that time lost as an undergraduate, because, well, I wanted more poets. And I started teaching because that's how you support yourself in graduate school. As an M.A. degree student, I read my way through the surveys of centuries, preparing for exams. Although the reading lists directed me to D.H. Lawrence's novels, I veered off course and discovered *Studies in Classic American Literature*. William Carlos Williams' *In the American Grain* interested me even more than his poetry. What *was* this? Was there a way to talk about it with the same critical, analytical vocabulary and approaches used in courses on poetry, fiction, or drama? Apparently no one I knew or encountered at that time cared.

I thought I was a poet. I had written poetry, published poetry, consumed poetry. When I was prompted to write essays, however, I knew that speaking and exploring and making sense of experience in the forms offered by the essay was where and how I felt most naturally drawn. I hadn't known it to begin with, when

I'd had this vague desire to write and to study writing, but what I was being drawn to was (what was then called) literary nonfiction.

I found Annie Dillard and Alice Walker, James Baldwin and Richard Selzer, John McPhee and Lewis Thomas, but those writers weren't yet appearing on any syllabus or any exam reading list or any list of canonical writers in any Norton anthology. And while I was discovering the ways in which essays were not regarded as significant enough—Virginia Woolf's novels, but not *A Room of One's Own* or *The Common Reader*, for instance, and Adrienne Rich's poetry, but not *On Lies, Secrets, and Silence*—I nonetheless read them hungrily.

~~~

Does anyone really ever have a good reason for beginning Ph.D. study in English? I heard many stories, but none of them included a clear-headed notion of what the work would involve and why one would choose that work. When I went seeking a Ph.D. program, I still couldn't articulate what I was looking for, and I made at least one false start. By then I had acquired some research skills, and I used them. I made a pain in the ass of myself to every director of graduate studies of every doctoral program in the country that seemed remotely interesting, using push-pins on a AAA map of the US to keep track. I asked to meet and interview graduate students. I kept hearing that the University of Iowa's English department was a very "humane" place—that was the word used over and over, by people who did not know one another.

What convinced me to study at Iowa were the conversations I had when, on a blustery day in early March, I visited the university's English-Philosophy Building (more colloquially known as EPB). I arrived while the office was still closed for lunch break; I leaned against the brick walls in the dark hallways, waiting. A man in a wrinkly raincoat opened the door, switched on the lights, and disappeared around a corner—to a closet, I imagined, assuming he was the janitor. But he was, in fact, Richard Lloyd-Jones (known familiarly, I would later learn, as Jix), chair of the department at that time. He invited me to take a seat in his equally dim office and spoke to me (as did every other graduate student or faculty member I met that day) about the distinguishing feature of the department: that no matter their academic training or specialty, no matter which of the programs then under the very capacious umbrella of the English department—rhetoric, American studies, African-American studies, comparative literature, women's studies, writing studies, the Expository Writing Program (the first name for what became the Nonfiction Writing Program), the Writers Workshop—each and all cared deeply in some sense about the way language works.

In the halls and seminar rooms of EPB and at public readings, those many renowned writers and scholars shared scholarship and fertilized one another with questions, weaving together disciplines, creating new programs and curricula. Each understood and supported the notion that the work of an English department was language, in whatever form, towards whatever purpose, for any number of audiences. That trivium was self-evident throughout all those programs under its umbrella, which also included a set of first-year writing courses in the Rhetoric Program.

When I studied theories of writing with Paul Diehl, we were talking about stylistics but also teaching writing to underprepared students, and he would veer off into expounding about how poetic metrics inflected and influenced the prose of any writer, of writers who were stylists, of writing you could find anywhere, even in advertisements. In Wayne Franklin's seminar on colonial American literature, we read *Of Plimouth Plantation, Incidents in the Life of a Slave Girl,* and Fanny Kemble's diary, attending to the prose cadences created by word choice and the rhetorical devices that contributed to particular representations of self. I was immersed, that is, in conversation about the craft of nonfiction. In a seminar on composition theory, the eminent British writing theorist James Britton had us looking at nonfiction prose to understand the rhetorical strategies, the language patterns, and the kind of self encoded by those choices, all designed to shape how one teaches writing, be it first-year writing or upper-level expository writing or graduate seminars in literary nonfiction.

For a year or two I also worked as an editorial assistant for *The Iowa Review,* edited by David Hamilton, who solicited and published (in addition to the poetry and fiction expected in a literary journal) nonfiction pieces that were also literary criticism, very different from the pieces of literary criticism that appeared in more "scholarly" journals. This was writing about literary matters that in itself explored form, employed a distinctive voice in developing the writer as persona, crafted in sentences that were lyrical or proceeded associatively, or wove the personal and the critical in ways that reminded me of Williams and Lawrence and Rich.

Even the American studies scholar Sherman Paul, in his seminar on the Contemporary Long and Serial Poem, required critical papers that engaged the subject in the ways that Charles Olson and William Carlos Williams did: in lines of prose that were lyrical and cadenced, explicating literary works not with literary theory but with infusions of the personal, with myth, with references to and echoes of other writers' work, with more questions than assertions. With the voice of a writer not a critic. And because Sherman Paul's own critical approach to 20th century poetry and the seminar reading list were entirely male-centric, I set off on a search that led to the nonfiction of HD and Denise Levertov and more Adrienne Rich.

As a graduate assistant, I also taught university-required general education literature classes (with titles that included American Lives, Narrative Literature, and Literary Presentation of Women) that I could build around women's voices, and so I filled them with nonfiction by women. Although most of the sample syllabi we were provided listed fiction, for these students (most of them women) who were struggling with and discovering things about their lives, it was Woolf's and Rich's and Walker's essays that spoke loudest. And what the students themselves wrote were nonfiction pieces, what's now called personal criticism. Not merely personal narratives, although you could find such elements in their essays, they were personal responses to "In Search of My Mother's Garden" and "Living with Weasels" and "Notes on Lying," to name just a few, pieces which showed those students to be reading carefully and deeply while engaging the historical, cultural, and literary textures of the texts.

I also taught courses in the Expository Writing Program, which was, at that time, the name for courses in literary nonfiction. Students read, they imitated in exercises, and wrote essays that may or may not have been self-consciously influenced by the exercises. Those exercises were informed by the assignments I had myself written for Paul Diehl's course on metrics and stylistics, on Francis Christenson's article on cumulative sentences, on Raymond Queneau's quirky *Exercises in Style*—all texts and assignments and conversations I'd encountered in my courses. Nonfiction infused everything I experienced at Iowa.

~~~

In spite of the wide-ranging understanding of language that animated the scholarly and pedagogical commitments of the faculty, the requirements for the Ph.D. in English at Iowa were, like most at that time, entirely traditional and shaped by chronology and literature. The scholarly discipline of writing studies or composition studies was relatively new and had emerged by and large from scholars and practitioners of English education. If I wanted to study writing theory in a doctoral program, it would require additional courses beyond the required ones. It wasn't that I started out wanting to study how to teach, although I was a good teacher and wanted to be better. I didn't in any way yet understand the institutional history of these things, or the complicated ways that the cultural history of English education and the discipline of "English" in the US, issues of literacy, and the cultural forces of xenophobia and racism had all contributed to the ways we talked about and taught writing.

I was energized by those intersecting narratives, sought out the work of scholars who wrote to elucidate their essential untruths and oppressions. I wanted to learn about the differences between prescriptive and descriptive grammar. I cheered when Francis Christiansen wrote that those who complain about run-on sentences don't know what they're talking about, that real writers composed such sentences, illustrating this with example after example. I loved the work of picking apart sentences to drill down, trying to unearth the underlying structures of thought, of lyricism, of the music of language, of voice. That impulse went hand-in-hand for me with discovering the voices that previously had been suppressed in the literary canon, recognizing and hearing voiced the reasons for that suppression and the efforts to bring them to the forefront.

I doubled up my own course load so that I not only ticked off all the centuries of literature in the canons but also took all the available courses in writing, which is to say theories of writing, rhetorical theories, courses on the essay, and nonfiction writing workshops.

So, although the Ph.D. requirements looked the same as a traditional program in any other R1 university, Iowa made intellectual space, gave financial support, and provided teaching experiences that allowed me to range widely and take up nonfiction in various guises and contexts and for various purposes. I created syllabi around nonfiction writers, I included it in general education literature classes, in first-year writing courses, in upper-level nonfiction writing courses. I spent time dissecting the sentences of nonfiction writers in order to think about how to teach writing to undergraduates. I read nonfiction as a way to think deeply about the intellectual development of American letters, as a way of writing literary criticism. I was able to engage student writers at all levels in merging personal narrative and critical reflection, to question received cultural knowledge, and as a powerful means of fostering cross-cultural empathy—to bring as many alternative voices as possible into the classroom and into students' lives and awareness. This is to say that the courses I taught, the courses I took, the pieces I read and heard at public readings, and the pieces I wrote all intersected generatively, all led to a doctoral degree in nonfiction at a time when there was barely any such idea of it elsewhere as a field of study. At Iowa, under Jix, it was a natural and self-evident choice.

~~~

Mine, I later learned, is not an uncommon story. I came from a family that did not know much about higher education and saw little point to it. Especially for daughters. I was a child who for a whole host of reasons—cultural, personal, familial—did not land in the sightlines of a mentor. I made choices that ricocheted me into social situations very different from what I'd been born into; I did not know how to understand them or navigate them very well. Given the time, given the possibilities for women beginning to be visible in the places teenage girls might see them, those like me rebelled against expectations. I didn't have a clue how to turn an undergraduate degree in English into any sort of relevant job (no less career), and so there I was, hanging out behind the counter of that KFC, reading. I followed a thread to graduate school, but did not know what a discipline was, did not care what a graduate degree in literature or English was good for. Did not understand that choices I made would inevitably lead to certain opportunities or worlds opening up further. All I really knew was there was oxygen there.

All through my education, I hung on to the thread of nonfiction, even when I did not know it was the name of what led me. I learned at my first tenure-track job interview that I was unprepared to articulate what connected first-year writing instruction to the discipline of women's studies. I didn't realize that outside of Iowa it was not self-evident how the growing canon of literary nonfiction or the history of the essay (Virginia Woolf, George Orwell, E.B. White, Joan Didion,

Annie Dillard, Loren Eiseley, for instance) fit into or alongside the canon of American or British literature. I did not notice that no job ads, no position descriptions mentioned nonfiction in any form. I emerged from my graduate degree program like everyone else coming out of a graduate degree program, shaped by that program and the stories its faculty told, with ideas about what was worth doing, shaped by the courses they taught, the books and articles they wrote, and what I heard at conferences. I emerged believing I'd find these kinds of assumptions similarly self-evident and supported in other universities and English departments.

I was wrong. I landed in a faculty position at a different Big 10 university—not in an English department but in a first-year writing department with a rigid curriculum, a constricted notion of what it meant to teach writing, and a patronizing model for mentoring junior colleagues. Needless to say, it did not leave room at all for nonfiction either in its curricula or its understanding of writing. And so I found myself continuing that struggle to make space for nonfiction—in creating new courses, sometimes in other departments and disciplines, in designing a new major, in advocating for faculty hiring, and in arguing for my own merit raises and tenure and promotion.

~~~

There is another reason I stole my title from Didion. It is this passage from "Why I Write" I keep coming back to, have been returning to for over 35 years since I first read it:

> The arrangement of the words matters, and the arrangement you want can be found in the picture in your mind. The picture dictates the arrangement. The picture dictates whether this will be a sentence with or without clauses, a sentence that ends hard or a dying-fall sentence, long or short, active or passive. The picture tells you how to arrange the words and the arrangement of the words tells you, or tells me, what's going on in the picture. *Nota bene:*
>
> It tells you.
>
> You don't tell it.

Following words on a page, picking them apart to find out how they work to create an idea, a world, a way of seeing and thinking and knowing, following another mind at work—this is how I learned to think. This is how I learned to have a voice. How I learned (again Didion) that "writing is the act of saying I, of imposing oneself upon other people, of saying *listen to me, see it my way, change your mind.*" Didion goes on to call this "a hostile act," "the tactic of a secret bully, an invasion," which is, I grant, one way of thinking about it. Having grown up in a different time and place, in a different context, coming round to a feminist sensibility at the time that I did, I see it differently. Putting words on paper that say *listen to me, see it my way, consider this* is how I learned to speak up and speak out, learned to figure out what to say, and that I even *had* something to say. It was a way of pushing other culturally loud, dominating, and domineering voices out of the way so that I had space to speak.

And so it followed that in whatever context I taught writing, I found my way around and back to what first pulled me in as a writer and reader of nonfiction, which I came to understand as operating on two deeply interrelated levels. On one level, literary nonfiction (as essay, as memoir, as literary journalism, in any of its forms) allowed me to hear voices and stories that are alternatives to the dominant cultural narratives I had instinctively rebelled against my entire life. Rejected not those narratives themselves, but their valorization, the fact that they insisted on taking up all the air, pushing anything but a replication of themselves out of the way. There were, I knew, other voices and other stories, a world of alternative ways of seeing and understanding experience, of giving (or claiming) space for the full range of those other voices and stories. The impulse to represent these voices and stories in other genres was certainly evident: *Orlando, Their Eyes Were Watching God, Diving into the Wreck, The Bell Jar, Rubyfruit Jungle, The Color Purple, Woman on the Edge of Time*, and more all lined my bookshelves. Somehow, however, the stakes of telling a story of one's own, in one's own voice, seemed much higher. Those stories—in their own voices, about their own lives—resonated with a kind of authority and legitimacy that bore deeper into my soul.

On another level, what continued to feed me was what close attention to the choice and arrangement of words on a page can teach us: How shaping language shapes experience. How attention to the craft of an essay leads a writer and reader into a conversation about what difference it makes to say something one way rather than another. How stringing words together in a certain order creates a rhythm and a meaning that is nuanced and unique, and can open whole other worlds of knowing. How close attention to that act of shaping creates that which we call voice or persona.

You see this if you turn again to that opening of Didion's essay, where she explains why she stole Orwell's title, focusing on the sound of its "three short unambiguous words," all of which share the sound "I," a word and a letter she reproduces three times, in a column, that create and take up a swath of space on the page. Here begins an essay in which she tells us that a writer is aggressive, hostile, a "bully" bent on invading "the reader's most private space," and at the same time tells us that she cannot think, that she is "no legitimate resident in any world of ideas." So many readers have characterized Didion as fragile, and yet if you pay attention to the language, what you find is a writer very forcibly indeed imposing her "I" on readers, taking up space, saying "see it my way," literally. Which, then, is Didion? Which the creation, the persona? Which the assertion and which the evasion? How does Didion's arrangement of words create a sense of her self, her voice, and at the same time create a smokescreen behind which she hides?

It's that reflective and critical turn which seems to me crucial, whether writing a narrative of one's intellectual history, or a course syllabus, or a critical essay, or a lyrical place-based memoir. Seems to me, in fact, the unique power and requirement of the essay, and indeed all creative nonfiction.

And so what I have tried to do in teaching is to open up for writers an awareness of these differences. No matter what course I've taught, it always begins with some version of this exercise, inspired by that little book by Raymond Queneau: Go somewhere and observe something. Describe it happening. Or find a sentence someone else has written about something happening. Write it out. Now using the same words (although you may change the form of the words) and changing punctuation as often as you like, rewrite the sentence in as many ways as you can imagine. Most everyone can come up with ten sentences, some as many as twenty different versions, and some, if they choose well, get to 35. What difference does it make if the words unfold one way rather than another, I ask. And from there, we move into conversation about writers' choices and intentions, how one's meaning may be crafted—and perhaps most important of all, why one might take the time, make the turn, and care about it all.

Although it can seem as if my focus here and in the teaching of writing I have described is on the page, on the subtleties of syntax and arrangement, it is also the case that that very close attention to what is on the page is designed to excavate the possibility of multiple meanings and multiple perspectives. To uncover and create an appreciation for the ways that diverse experiences create differing perspectives on social and cultural knowledge.

<p style="text-align:center">~~~</p>

In the final decade of my academic career, I was named editor of the literary journal *Fourth Genre: Explorations in Nonfiction*. At the time I took over, it was one of only three journals in the US that published solely nonfiction. The writers who submitted work ranged widely: not only those long practiced in the forms of the essay, but also people who were incarcerated, elderly retired folks who had been urged to write their life stories. Journalists and anthropologists whose work wasn't finding acceptance by the traditional publication venues of their colleagues. Former Peace Corps volunteers who all seem to have been told by someone that their stories would do the rest of the world some good. M.F.A. students who had been told to get their work out there. Writers whose previous writing had been in a different genre and were now trying something different. Writers I knew, writers who claimed a connection to me, writers who were cocky or arrogant or desperate or flippant or inexperienced or perfunctory—as well as writers who clearly had no idea what *Fourth Genre* published, who simply and doggedly wanted their words to be heard by someone. I read more pages of prose in that decade than in all my years of undergraduate and graduate study. How to choose?

Schooled by Jix in the teaching of writing with writers of varied degrees of experience and expertise, I developed a practice and philosophy for editing a literary journal of nonfiction. I began by shaping the production work of *Fourth Genre* as a learning lab for students in the relevant undergraduate majors of professional writing, creative writing, and literature: students who were learning about editing and publishing and literary nonfiction, students who were writers aspiring to have their own work published somewhere at some point. I involved them in all the aspects of journal production: in conversations with the writers who submitted work (famous or beginning), with publishers and marketers and designers. Though most of the students were readers and lovers of words, some of them poets, some of them aspiring book editors, some of them graduate students exploring nonfiction as I had once done, almost none of them had extensive reading in or knowledge about the widely divergent range of nonfiction. They had discovered a couple of writers and books that had excited them, or they'd taken a course in which they'd generated personal essays. They were good readers. They were hungry. They were like I had been.

Editorial meetings, at which we considered submissions in order to winnow them down and make selections, were in essence workshops. As in the classes I taught, we workshopped by attending to the language very closely, attending to the ways words create meaning differently in each essay and for each of us as readers. I worked to move them to understand that the voice they heard coming off the page is not the same as the writer's. To find and follow a mind at work. To locate the persona of the writer through attention to the places where the mind turns back on itself. I directed their attention to the sentence level, to the rhetorical, syntactic, and lexical choices, to the structures of thought that mapped those habits of mind. To think about form serving the work of the essay. To understand the role of reflection, the way that an essay expects more than merely the rendering of experience, but rather that the writer make sense of it, in some way explicit or not. The ways in which tracing the machinations of a mind at work might reveal the thorniness and intractability of some of the most enduring of life's questions. To be or to find the best reader possible for each submitted piece, because as inexperienced readers of nonfiction, they tended to be drawn to the voices and stories that were most "relatable" (a favorite descriptor), most familiar. We worked at untangling a passage's (or even a sentence's) curves and twists, understanding the grammar, and what might lie beyond the grammar—a mystery that emerges as detail, structure of thought, and syntax weave and clear a path through questions and unexpected shifts to some new meaning. They also learned to accept that the meaning one makes of a sentence or essay is provisional, because the next reader brings something else to the conversation. Provisional because in hearing what another reader makes of the same words—in that difference—together we might find our way to yet another understanding.

In the many decisions about those submissions that fell to me alone—which in the end were almost all of them—I came to a principle of selection that harkened back to my first encounter with literary nonfiction, sitting with a 238-page book in hand, in a corner behind the counter of a KFC in LA, hearing a voice I desperately needed to hear but had never before encountered: given the limited number of pages I get to publish, to whose voices do I want to give space?

~~~

It's no coincidence that as academic or scholarly or intellectual work began (after the "rights" movements of the 1960s and 1970s) to interrogate the content, source, and bias of knowledge production, and started to develop ethnography as a methodology and standpoint theory as a critical lens and critique, the interest in and focus on story—as with narrative medicine and narrative theology, to cite just two examples—led to a surge in telling nonfiction stories.

Why else the explosion of interest, in the past 20 to 30 years, in memoir? Why else the explosion of M.F.A. programs over the past 20 years—from a handful in the early 2000s when I first researched them for a proposal at my institution, to over two dozen just three or four years later, to so many now that it's not worth counting. How else to explain the development of so many more nonfiction journals than existed when *Fourth Genre* was founded, not to mention the anthologies, the curricula, the venues for publication such as Modern Love in *The New York Times*. Not only *Harper's, Atlantic Monthly,* and *The New Yorker* but dozens of online sites and platforms, and the surge in flash pieces.

We seek places to tell our stories, and we crave the ability to tell and read stories that have been historically silenced, unheard, unread, unvoiced. Despite the recent ascendancy of repressive political and cultural forces born of fear, there is a surge in desire to embrace wider and wider varieties of identity and personal expression. Well-crafted, there is nothing so powerful to engage and change us than a story from inside what it means to be me.

How do we understand ourselves? How, now that there's a request and need for hearing formerly silenced voices, do we tell our stories? We need to hear them and we need them to help ourselves know and hear ourselves. Shaping story to shape culture. And most urgently, most easily forgotten: where and how do we provide spaces for them to be heard?

Forty years ago, while studying rhetorical theory with Jix, I wrote an essay (not a very good one by any means) about the teaching of writing, weaving my way among the basketful of researchers and theorists then current for scholars of composition and writing studies. There were, among them, child development specialists, linguists, poets, psychologists, high school teachers, journalists, and writers such as Orwell and his essay, "Why I Write," which Didion acknowledges in her first line was the basis for her own essay. I was surprised to reread my essay, which I found while clearing out my office, and which ranged across the various political persuasions and linguistic styles of all these theorists, landing on Michael Polanyi's ideas about the search for personal truth through what he called "the active contemplation of what is known." This, I went on to say, is the work of the essay, no matter its subject, the occasion which gives rise to it, the particularities of its form, voice, or syntax, or the conscious or unconscious motives of the writer.

For Jix, my attempts to work from rhetorical theory to a theory of the essay was fair game, and from what I could tell from his response, made sense. From Jix I learned how to be an essayist in the world. Or, to put it differently, I learned that the way I wanted to live in this world, everything involved in being the kind of human being I aspired to, might best be found by reading, teaching, writing, and editing nonfiction.

Afterword. Richard "Jix" Lloyd-Jones: A Biographical Note

Carl H. Klaus
UNIVERSITY OF IOWA

When I visited Jix in October 2014, two days before he died, he was prone on a couch, cared for by hospice, attended by family, and breathing with the help of an oxygen line, but he sat up so quickly and held forth so vigorously—about writing and teaching and colleagues of yore, as well as his Welsh heritage, centuries back—that he seemed capable of lasting for weeks or months or more. He had, after all, survived most of his life with only a small portion of lung, in the wake of bronchiectasis during his late teens. Despite that profound impairment, he was perennially active on numerous professional fronts in the fields of composition, rhetoric, research on writing, and writing pedagogy. And always accessible to colleagues and students no matter how many burdens.

For each of his writing courses, Jix designed a distinctive sequence of assignments, like a theme and variations—such an inventive and influential form of writing instruction that I and other colleagues took up sequencing in our own writing courses. Given his commitment to excellence in teaching, he also developed a special program for training and mentoring graduate teaching assistants. No wonder, then, that in 1970, Bob Scholes and I dedicated *Elements of the Essay* to Jix, referring to him as teacher of teachers, "doctorum doctor." Throughout his career at the University of Iowa, Jix was so devoted to teaching that he maintained a full course load in the English department while serving as director of undergraduate studies, then as chair of the department, director of the School of Letters, member of Liberal Arts College advisory committees and of the Faculty Senate.

Beyond his varied academic commitments, Jix also took part in major educational projects: during the 1960s, he taught in several federally funded institutes for high school English teachers; during the 1970s, he created a rhetorically based mode of writing assessment for the National Assessment of Educational Progress and oversaw its implementation; during the late-1970s, he helped to launch the Iowa Writing Project for the professional development of Iowa teachers; during the late 1970s and early 1980s, he served as associate director of the NEH Iowa Institute for directors of freshman composition programs at colleges and universities throughout the country. Collaborating with Jix on these and other projects, I often heard him distill his thoughts in striking assertions—"We are our memories." And provocative questions—"What is going on when not much is going on?"

So much was going on in his professional contributions—as co-author of *Research in Written Composition*, as principal author of "The Students' Right To Their Own Language," as chair of the College Conference on Composition and

Communication, as president of the National Council of Teachers of English—it's not surprising that he prized those moments when not much is going on, when the mind is free to take its own course, as it did in the poems he wrote throughout his life. Bearing witness, as in his prose, to the limits and the power of language: "Reporters will tell the facts that lie, / while I will make from lies a lively truth..."

Thanks to his influence, many others throughout the country have devoted themselves to research on writing and the teaching of writing.

Appendix. Word and Focus

Richard Lloyd-Jones
UNIVERSITY OF IOWA

> This is not a final draft, and indeed I have no idea what a final draft might be.
>
> – *Richard Lloyd-Jones, Jun 5, 2012, at 12:08 pm*

W.H. Auden suggested that if you want to identify a budding poet, you don't look for the message, but for the love of words. He also said that Time would pardon Kipling and Paul Claudel in spite of their ideas because they wrote well. Auden thus set a standard for teachers of English. The words themselves are what make writers. Having spent more than half a century exhibiting our language to students, I side with Auden.

Apparently I was intoxicated by words as a child. Adults were delighted by my four-year-old self enchanted by "bilaterally symmetrical." The term described a pattern on some sort of peg board and mattered very little as information, but I doubtless liked the effect that polysyllables had on my parents' generation. I treasured other big words, too, and used them liberally. Yes, I went on to write poetry, take part in school debating, and even act in school plays, and I thought the ideas were important, but the words bound me.

A church-going boy, I was hypnotized by the beginning of St. John's gospel, which was read aloud every other Sunday. "In the beginning was the Word, and the Word was with God, and the Word was God." I do not now recall whether I ever wondered about what it meant, but I liked it as a soothing punctuation for the service. I had to move the missal from the epistle side of the altar to the gospel side.

When I was warehoused in an army hospital I had time and no duty, but the hospital had a surprisingly good library. As a bored 18-year-old I found myself reading Bertrand Russell's history of philosophy and encountered some of the Greek philosophers who had influenced John. The "Word" was *logos*, the root of logic and all of those " ology" studies that involved learning. I was sufficiently stimulated that when I was discharged from the hospital and the army, I wanted the V.A. to "rehabilitate" me as a philosopher, but their advisers seemed to think that English would be a more practical (!) major. (Eventually I had three majors—English, philosophy, and speech—all word fields.)

Thus, I was generally captivated by the philosophical and myth-making Greeks, and I explored the implications of their use of "logos" and their fondness for stories—or in the case of Plato, conversations. In a bit I'll explain that concretely, but first I'll offer an abstract and somewhat paradoxical view of language they led me to. I mean more than natural language; I include mathematics, graphics, the arts generally, dress, and various codes. By insisting on this broader class I part from the Greeks and many 18th century grammarians by implying that languages are arbitrary but useful social inventions. Symbol systems. The Word is not the reality; it is merely a device indicating some aspect of a presumed reality. Words enforce reason upon chaos. That leads us to two propositions:

1. The power of language is that it enforces focus.
2. The limitation of language is that it enforces focus.

The teacher of composition is most likely drawn to the first proposition. We want our students to be clear and exact. Their papers should be efficient and have focus. I was fortunate in having my first teaching job in an engineering college. My students were juniors and seniors, sometimes former commissioned officers in contrast to my status as private, and I had no technical experience. (Hiring was an accident; I just happened to be in the right spot when the position opened and no one else was handy soon enough.) As a practical matter the students often had to explain to me what was self-evident to them.

"Beryllium? What's that?" "An alkaline earth metal? What's that?" And so it went. In high school I had learned about the periodic table, so eventually they would find a general class—a genus—that I could imagine. Then they had to lead me through the ways it was different from other elements and other metals, and so on. I knew the pattern of definition from Aristotle, so I could ask useful questions, and they could be politely patronizing in dealing with my ignorance. And like Plato, I sometimes over-played my level of ignorance, but they came to recognize the procedures of definition. You might reasonably expect that people who believe in the periodic table would imagine that Reality is neatly tabular. The biologists were especially susceptible to a belief in order. For them, as for the Greeks, words provided access to the World as it actually is. The *logos* is the pattern, the structure of reality. If you manipulate words (or numbers) correctly, you will learn the Truth. When Mark Twain has Adam and Eve name all of things of the world, he is assuming a kind of one-to-one relationship, albeit with a touch of irony. Plato's dialogues exhibit the same sense that exploring words is in fact exploring the world.

Even for engineering students such static definition is not enough, though. They live in a dynamic world and must examine actions, procedures, processes. Still, when they conceptualize an action, they arrest it so they can focus on relationships. They kill the tissue so they can put it on a slide under the microscope. Most likely, these are temporal relationships, but they start by making them static by naming the whole procedure or process and then by naming each sub-step of the action. Once the name is chosen, the action is contained as a "thing."

That name is not always self-evident. I recall a recipe for roast duck that began with the instruction, "Roast the duck in the usual manner." The discussion dealt primarily with making the stuffing. You can say that the recipe was mis-named, and so it was, but probably the author merely understood that the process was defined by a duck. The chef was thinking of a duck as a given, a kind of framework for the real point of the recipe, and she simply assumed many of the steps of roasting were self-evident. Take another homely example of painting your living room. Do you think it begins with your awareness that the room is shabby? Or with choosing the paint? Or preparing the surface? That is, what is your focus implied in the term "painting the living room"? By giving the process a name, you limit your understanding of it so that you can get on with the job.

One might imagine that the result of the naming process leads to a flow chart or a tree diagram. The boxes on the chart represent steps, actions, but in the discourse they are static, visible segments of the whole. We analyze the whole process into components. The steps, too, are named and thus frozen into the text. Altogether, they make a pattern, a *logos*. Representing our understanding in a visual diagram makes clear how the abstracting, the stop-action, makes a process inert, dead. Eventually a reader re-activates, re-animates, the cadaver so that actions may take place. In a strange way the two-dimensional drawing is made four-dimensional by adding another dimension of space and then time, by escaping the focus of language.

Some intellectual purist might insist that because a process consists of actions, a writer should begin by identifying appropriate verbs representing actions, and indeed one might muddle among various steps, but until one finds a framing name, one cannot really begin. A collections of notes does not make a tune, random acts do not make a procedure. Euclid alone sees beauty bare, said Edna St Vincent Millay, for Euclid saw patterns. When the writer finds the name, the process can be described by finding sub-names.

For teachers a practical manifestation of this need to find a context can be seen in how some raters of student essays use analytical lists of skills to be assessed. Rating is a process. But the raters begin by listing qualities to be valued: organization, spelling, punctuation, images, tropes, what-have-you. The qualities may be inherent in "student essays" or somehow related to what skills a teacher is promoting. Each category is assigned a scale of points and then the essay is scored category by category and the points are added to create a score for the essay.

Some raters follow the rules. Some adjust the rules to fit other purposes they understand. If, for example, the essays are used for placement in composition courses of varying difficulty, there are probably cut-off scores showing who will be assigned to advanced courses and who will be sent to some remedial neverland. In such circumstances some raters make a holistic decision of the value of the essay in suggesting appropriate placement and then arrange the scores in different categories so they will add up to the appropriate cut-off number. They see the focusing term as "placement," not as "essay writing." The change of focus changes the reality.

Focus is a function of purpose, but purposes are usually mixed or multiple. One may write simply to inform some reader at a lesser level of competence, one may write to persuade, or one may write simply to see what emerges from words put together. A tidy informative document may persuade a reader of its truth; a truly persuasive treatise must have information. And any writing is some sense exploratory. School writing often has no evident purpose other than persuading some rather that the writer is docile in following prescribed conventions, not a purpose likely to excite many students, but often quite practical. Docility is a virtue that delights parents and employers, so socially inventive behavior in writing or thinking may be less honored in mass education than is adhering to conventions. Critical reading and imaginative questioning of the status quo are honored in political speeches about education more than they are encouraged in the classroom itself or in the "world of work."

The difficulty for teachers at home or in school is greater than I have made it seem. After all, societies must have a common base of shared understandings. Languages serve commonality. Too much variation leads to rebellion and riot; too little leads to stagnation and bigotry. Purpose exists within a social context, so every writer is some sense a social critic while being an informer and a persuader.

Consider natural language, such as the one I am using, English. Each user of a language group, each person, has some variation from the base language. That personal variation is an idiolect. Related idiolects make up a dialect. Some privileged dialect is designated as "the language." In a democratic society there may be more than one view of what is "standard." For some 18th century grammarians (often bishops), the base language was a pre-Babel universal code, so for religious reasons they sought what they imagined to be the gift of God. Truly words represented reality, and somewhere there was a correct form. In an age that seeks to interpret the languages of apes and dolphins we are more likely to seek patterns that emerge from efforts of higher animals to form social groupings, and we accept the notion that some groups have more power than others.

Most likely we begin our sense of a proper language with our mothers and our immediate family. Our personal language is a sub-set of English different from the language of the larger community. "Mar-mar" and "wee-wee" and single word requests or piercing screeches may be intelligible to many adults, and may even be used within the family, but they are viewed with parental condescension. "He'll outgrow it." No, he'll adapt it and enlarge it for adult uses—perhaps the language he uses when he talks to himself, or more socially to a spouse. Consider how long-married people manage to know when to leave a party. It is the vocabulary of intimacy, a very private version of the common language. And it rarely makes trouble in a classroom because it is rarely discussed.

Trouble begins when we worry about dialects, the versions of English favored by groups within the larger population. A country comprised of immigrants and the children of immigrants borrows readily from other languages, and that is an accident of history, but the main reason for dialects is that three hundred million people cannot quite relate as bosom buddies. Earlier societies based on families and tribes that shared assumptions and quirks could adopt a common tongue, perhaps stratified by social rank, as in the King's English. Even within the relatively small geographic range of England, however, many regional variations grew out of neighborly interactions. In the US, despite national radio and television, we have not eliminated the dialects of hyphenated Americans or social status or even geographic isolation. Asian, Hispanic, Greek, Italian, Irish, African, Appalachian, Nordic, blue collar, suits, tweeters, teenagers, and so on. Indeed, if poll takers can name some sub-group of Americans from whom to discover an opinion, you can find a related dialect. What then is correct English?

"Correct" is what pleases people in a particular conversation. In an ordinary high school or college classroom that means Edited American English, a fancy way of naming what is expected among responsible people doing the world's work. In the show-and-tell of the primary classroom or the written "story" of what happened at a birthday party a teacher may reward almost any intelligible utterance or manuscript. Eventually children have to be led to the linguistic and editorial conventions of grownups, because being grown up is the fate of us all, and we want to be assimilated. Teenagers may create dialects of their own which they treasure into old age as a badge of remembered past. Pre-adults may cling to their linguistic inventions in daily use until they realize they have become adults and don't need to emphasize their separateness. Yes, a few rebel, but most stay close enough to the normal discourse that they can be understood even in moments of their rebellious irritations, and "normal" allows for considerable variation. Among some politicians the language of power may be "folksy." Among minorities the variations signal alliances. "Pleasing" is specific for a person in some context.

When I was growing up, textbooks made issues of shall-will, of between-among, of split infinitives, of who-whom, of that-which, and many more fine points of usage. Fowler or Strunk ruled. Some editors still insist, but in ordinary discourse even fussy writers often ignore the old distinctions. Languages shrivel. We cut off the dead branches and watch new ones grow. My senior students in engineering and in literature in some sense wrote correctly and yet in styles so different that one might have considered that they used different dialects. True to their languages they understood the world differently. Their focus allowed them to map "reality" differently. Consider how the language of medicine creates a body different from the one you live in from day to day. A physician has to be clever to translate the layperson's sense of ailments into clinical talk, so she can deal with it, and only a few of us make sense of the medical books. To be sure, most adults have some facility in several dialects. We may be lost in Cajun or Creole or Gullah or even "street-talk," but we manage to accommodate many of the assumptions of special occupations and different social classes. We can switch dialects.

When in 1965 I taught in a summer program financed by the Rockefeller Foundation for 80 or so teachers of English in the traditionally black colleges, I had to cope with complex expectations. Our participants—especially the older ones—had invested time and ego in mastering Edited American English (EAE). Some were puzzled that the staff—both Black and White—seemed comfortable with Black English Vernacular (BEV) in various farms, but the issue was dormant until we had James Meredith speak to the group. One of the teachers had had Mr. Meredith in class, and he spoke to us in BEV. The teacher was mortified not so much by BEV, but by the fact the four White instructors heard it. Her student, noted as he was, had violated the code expectations she felt marked the quality of her teaching. His focus was on excluding the white establishment. She and we heard the same sounds, but we interpreted the sounds differently. Incidentally, we all used the term "black," for African American came into vogue at a later time.

When we understand that language is the result of a social contract, we admit that even when we talk to ourselves someone is looking over our shoulder. I, a retired teacher, cannot help talking to a teacher, at least part of myself. Indeed, it is convenient here in talking to myself, in exploring what I think, that I evoke an audience of English teachers. I am the English teacher audience.

My words are English teacher words, but I am constantly exposed to the words of students who are expanding into language and society. What do they hear when I talk to them? How do they escape the limits of their family language? I recall fondly a brilliant honors student who was majoring in English and oriental studies. When she came to a final examination, which she thought silly, she filled a blue book with intricate pen-and-ink drawings of Chinese dragons. She also had a dim view of degrees even though she accepted a B.A. Eventually she wrote poems and made pottery. Maybe she essayed pots. Her languages—verbal and graphic—set her own limits, her own focus, and I was expected to enter her world. After all, I expected my students to enter my world.

Still, as a teacher, I cannot write an essay without trying to teach myself in a way that might teach others. Having lived eight and a half decades I have seen many wayward, unfocussed minds ramble associatively from notion to notion—I have made a few such excursions myself—but being a creature of a professional clan, a tightly bound family of scholar-educators, I am driven to make a point even when I don't have one. When I write to this extended family, I may have little information of consequence, yet in piffling, punning, decorating a phrase I remind myself and the others that we are a group and we play at trivia so we remember the bases of our common bonds. The point is merely that we exist, and that may not be "merely." At the moment of writing some sort of "I" exists even though in the next instant someone else will exist in my body. No writing can exhibit a whole self, if indeed that whole self exists. We are in some ways re-made in each situation, in each encounter.

Still all of my surface "selves" posit a world beyond language. As they focus their language in particular circumstances, they believe that they have captured an accurate view of a facet of the world. They also are constantly reminded that they have eliminated much of the world from their view, and the more they focus the more they cut out their alternate selves. Yes, focus denies the existence of much of reality. So, we have come to my second proposition about the limits of language.

Practical people ignore the reminders of the world beyond language, get on with their daily chores. Even faithful churchgoers may resist temptations to consider what the words might not reveal. They leave that sort of problem to mystics or poets or wayward minds. Even theologians sometimes play games with the surface of words rather than read beyond them. The rituals are soothing and imply some sort of assured order. Whenever some suggests a change in custom—say, wearing hats in church or not wearing hats—the congregation frets because their focus on order is disturbed. Translating the Bible—moving it farther from the pre-Babel purity—is a threat to conventional understanding. (If you are a 14th-century bishop in England it is also a threat to your temporal authority in the Church's hierarchies.) Even a new translation upsets modern churches. These changes force one to contemplate what might exist beyond the limits of focus.

Those who are curious to discover more about the world pushed out of focus by conventional languages constantly invent new ways to escape the limits of the languages they have inherited. Picasso and Duke Ellington, Darwin and Einstein, Keynes and Freud in their several ways tried to show us what we hadn't then noticed. Not one *logos*, but several. For most native speakers of a language, though, it is the poets and other creators of fictions who cause trouble. An old metaphor makes the point—the steel glass. In centuries past mirrors of real glass were rare—sheets of steel served to provide reflections of one's face. The sheets had twists and imperfections which rendered reflected images distorted. The distortions offered the means of satire and through satire remind one that conventions are not the whole of reality. Even when the harshness of satire is not intended, the poet deals in metaphor, a way of saying two things at once. Or, in another definition, the poet seeks an objective correlative, images that in some way give body to an abstract notion.

Perhaps I should explain. The distortions of satire—the twisting out of shape or out of focus—are in some sense false, but they serve to alert us to the exclusions of a conventional statement. If Swift suggests that we control population growth by eating babies, we may become aware of how incomplete is the planning of some social scientists. Students being forced into close reading of poems sometimes complain that teachers find too many implications, but even benign and trite love poems depend on multiple associations. Why is my love a rose? Is she red? Has she petals? Is she graceful? Why not a petunia? Or a columbine? Of course, my love is not really any of these things, but the poet tries to focus your attention on some particular quality. If the poem is much grander—say, the Aeneid—does it exist merely as "history" to tell about the founding of Rome, or is it a broader narrative dealing frustration, privation, and sacrifice against all sort of trials in order to achieve greatness? Of course, it is both and more because the poet hopes to reveal something important about the world beyond language.

T. S. Eliot's Prufrock struggles to say what he means and ultimately decides that he is unable to capture what he feels. In his love song he wants to tell the lady some overwhelming question, but in the end he has heard the mermaids singing and does not think they will sing to him. He is neither Hamlet nor Odysseus, no sailor on the Great Sea. But the whole portrait is a comment on the times, where daily life renders one unable to represent an underlying reality. The setting is a soiree characterized by arty but trivial chatter, a context in which a middle-aged man expresses his awareness of a world he cannot enter. Eliot has found objective events to suggest a reality beyond the events. That is the work of any metaphor.

By definition all metaphors are mistakes, just as the images of the steel glass are mistakes. The dog is obeyed in office? One does not really elect a cocker spaniel to be mayor, and a person is not a dog. But clearly, we are asked to consider the ways our mayor is like a dog. Some metaphors are so weary that we don't even hear them as metaphors. Your sentences flow? No, rivers perhaps flow, but the old phrase does not like raise the image of a river in your mind. Some mistakes are more powerful than others. "Survival of the fittest" and the "struggle for existence" conjure up images of war and for some people make evolution into biological empire building. The people who deal in the images of letters on a double helix have a calmer view of biological processes, but they are equally trying to find a new language for expressing reality.

So I am back to the word and human efforts to access something real. The history of religious thought is a study of metaphors. Through false claims of identity we enforce comparisons that might offer us a glimpse at the ineffable. We name that which can't be known—God—but the name itself tells us very little. We pile on abstractions—omnipotent, omniscient, benevolent, eternal—but that helps little. The preachers I have heard rarely delve into these questions, partly because they are really social workers using church doctrine to alter behavior, and partly because they sense that the congregation would be bored.

Some sneer at the ancients who named multiple gods—a god for every special need—and then arranged them in tribal families with all sorts of human failings, but after all they were just finding metaphors from their sensory world as a way of describing forces they could not apprehend literally. For us, human thought made a great leap when it rolled up all of the subsidiary gods in to one God. To be sure, many people then and now take the surface of the metaphor as though it were literal—a gospel truth—and then have to think up stories in order to explain the god's will. Indeed, some people take Biblical characters and treat them like Greek gods.

Find your own image to suggest what is beyond the Word. Eve, the Great Goddess, Aphrodite, Astarte, Mary—take whatever lady you fancy—and you are puzzling about the female principle. You may focus on Woman as the fertility partner, the mother, or the custodian of cadavers, but you have still not found reality. Yin-Yang, the anima and the id, the body and soul, Higgs boson, what-have-you. C. S. Lewis suggests that the person with greatest number of metaphors has the greatest access to the world as it is. Probably most of us most of the time walk comfortably along our customary paths. We put food and the table and then go to bed. When we least expect it, the poet sneaks out and the Word shimmers and we are not sure of what we have seen.

Decades ago someone preached sermons that I did not listen to (in a narrow church the altar was far from the pulpit but being somewhat deaf was also helpful). I counted the bricks on the farther wall, until for a few seconds St. John delivered his Word.

June 2012

Appendix. Poesis: Making Papers

Richard Lloyd-Jones
UNIVERSITY OF IOWA

This is not an academic paper; I revert to an older, more conversational style of raising some questions with you.[1] Let me claim the genre "essay," if not in the manner of Montaigne, at least with the tone of bemused speculation.

When I first started coming to meetings of the CCCC, we all lived in an Edenic world of conversations. We had diverse backgrounds—mostly built on a literary base—but we were drawn to NCTE and had large loads of composition students. We had practical problems to solve and wanted to know what others were doing. Indeed, our journal was primarily a record of our conversations. It was not unlike what now appears on the WPA email listserv.

At the time I was running a program of technical writing in a college of engineering, really just a pair of required junior-senior courses. I was the only tenure-track person; the other teachers were graduate students, mostly from the Iowa Writers Workshop and mostly poets. I was not allowed to hire new assistants until after registration was complete and enrollment was certified. To finesse the problem, I had a deal with Paul Engle, who never had enough aid for aspiring writers, to identify Writers Workshop graduate students who were able and who might relate to engineering students. Late on Wednesday I'd call him, saying, "I need X number of assistants," and Paul would send up X plus a few, and I'd pick my needed number to sit in the back of the classroom on Thursday and start teaching the following Tuesday. Oddly enough, the system worked quite well. Why?

Sometimes the writers did have specifically useful backgrounds: pre-med, factory work, military assignments, law degrees, even engineering degrees. But mostly the useful quality was that they believed in poesis, making things with words, the very root of poetry. In the 1940s and 50s poets were crafty, like blacksmiths and shoemakers and engineers. Even if they weren't bardic or courtly, they believed that poems were made. I recall coming on Phil Levine in his engineering cubicle writing trimeters. He said he had been writing a lot of iambic pentameters of late and needed to break out of the mold. Levine obviously had themes and ideas, and later critics have made much of them, but his concern was technique. Our sculptors shaped in steel and stone; our composers ordered sounds; our writers disciplined words and sentences.

---

1. A version of this essay was presented at a panel on "Composition, Creative Writing, and the Pedagogy of Craft" at the 1997 Conference on College Composition and Communication in Phoenix. It was published in *Writing on the Edge* Vol. 8, No. 2 (Spring/Summer 1997): 40–46.

This state of mind suited engineering students. They too made things. Scientists speculated, but engineers built. They built bridges—not metaphorical ones to the twenty-first century—but real ones from shore to shore. They made television sets, permeable membranes, traffic interchanges—and could be made to see that reports and contracts and instruction manuals are things to be made. They could even imagine that sentences had raw materials that had to be shaped, and the poets could relate to that. A few of the poets and a few of the engineers could be drawn into speculation about language, but people of neither group really wanted to be linguistic scholars, except incidentally. They wanted reports and poems that, like bridges, would carry the assigned load. They wanted the joints to hold.

I don't mean to suggest that these people were unaware that language exists in a world of people. Poets of that generation knew that great poets require great audiences because *Poetry* magazine reminded them, and they wanted at least the editor-as-audience to respond. These writers aspired to professional status and learned early about markets for their work. Great themes were fine, but competence was essential. I recall a now much-honored poet who was extremely sympathetic to the civil rights movement, even participated in a mild way, but who sniffed at the work of a poet of the movement—"Just a street poet"—because he saw only emotion, not craft, in the poems. The audience these poets sought respected craft.

Engineering students accepted the idea that writing was supposed to cause an effect in some other person, but they tended to imagine that all other persons were like the one they saw in the mirror. Fortunately, seniors had acquired specialties that created sub-audiences, so within a classroom they encountered "otherness" in a form they could respect. All of the engineering students could agree on the importance of well-crafted work. The poet-instructors, who were much aware of how their own careers depended on "others," had but a small leap to make in encouraging students to adapt to even less similar audiences, like the people in marketing or accounting or management. Maybe even clients.

You may see where my fragment of a narrative is leading. Poets and engineering students alike *had* their subject matter—they took it for granted. They *had* their audiences, even though they tended overly much to think that those audiences shared all of their world. They knew their authority for speaking, their identity. It just happened that facing each other they sometimes thought they shared none of these assumptions about subjects, otherness, or selfhood. They were just fellow strangers possessing alien kinds of knowledge being forced to do something together. They did believe in form, and to make the best of an awkward social situation they could demonstrate to each other how the other variables are revealed in form. Let me give an example to add flesh to that abstraction.

Our students operated a magazine of semi-technical articles they had written for classes. Few were making serious "contributions to knowledge," but they were assembling information about what industries and researchers were developing, so they had real news to report. It was technical journalism intended for people who were committed to technology but who lacked information beyond their own special interests. That audience may in fact be merely the "general reader," but the more limited term allowed us to deal emphatically with their problems of adapting vocabulary, illustrations, and reasoning to people unlike themselves.

At that time engineering-student readers and writers for our magazine were almost all males, *young* males. They thought *Playboy* was daring and exciting, and they wanted to put pin-ups in their magazine. Aside from explaining to them that engineers were not necessarily male, we could point out that the role of engineer was sexless, that gender was an irrelevant characteristic of the audience. They should not want to distract that audience by playing to animal drives not related to the technical subjects at hand. They should not want to muddle their own role as a technical authority by emphasizing their interests out of working hours.

In a rhetorical sense we were able to discuss self-identity as a construct, as something made. For English majors we might adapt Kenneth Burke and talk about it as though it were creating consistent roles in a play or a dramatic monologue or, for that matter, a simple lyric. For these student engineers it had to do with their aspirations, with learning to act like the best engineers. Most of them had come to believe in reliable design made economically to be useful in some particular set of circumstances. If you could show them how language demonstrated those virtues to others, they would struggle with the necessary craft, even as they struggled with calculus or the laws of motion.

The issue of "making an audience" was harder to sell. Even then, journalists were caught up in·market analysis, in discovering audiences. They assumed the readers had needs and limits of knowledge and perception, they could discover such needs and limits, and they could craft language to address them. Catering to such views we could effectively discuss whether one should turn a knob "to the left" or "counter-clockwise," whether it made any difference that the knob itself was "serrated" or "knurled," or whether the manager authorizing expenditures needed to know that there was a knob at all. We could send students to city council meetings to observe engineers trying to explain why a traffic signal would be a hazard even though the neighborhood folks thought it was essential. That is, practical writers like rhetoricians of old thought of audiences as people with pre-existing collections of motives to be moved from one intellectual place to another by reasonable information, roused emotions, or personal authority. And we were willing to play to that set of beliefs. I guess most of the time we shared it.

Still, literary writers have an obligation to make audiences. We sometimes tell our literature students that they must make themselves into "fit readers" of Shakespeare or Milton or Wordsworth. And we promise them that if they make the effort to belong to those worlds in language and fact, the poets will reward them with insight. We even claim that by becoming a fit reader, one enlarges oneself and becomes a person with greater possibilities. Literary language, the language beyond daily commerce with neighbors, makes us more than we were, not so much by increasing our knowledge as by providing a different way of seeing the world around us.

Sometimes it is easier to understand how Picasso, say, taught us how see differently, or Strindberg how to hear differently. We may like to remind people that J. S. Mill, a great logician and philosopher, thought he had lost his mind when he first read William Wordsworth because Wordsworth made demands of a new craft on the reader—craft we now think so ordinary that we relegate Wordsworth to literature for adolescents. Engineers may understand how their developments—say, the atom bomb or the interstate highway system—can re-structure the world they live in without quite recognizing that their detached manner of addressing audiences also re-shapes human relationships. It leads to a belief in mega-deaths, for example. I suggest that most of us would be happier in our literary roles if a generation or two of critics had not so admired technical and scientific prose.

I have been implying a common attitude toward form and design shared by poets and engineers as the basis for their becoming comfortable with each other over the course of a semester. Let me now turn that proposition over to suggest why it often has been counter-productive, and let me start with an example from literary criticism.

In the late nineteenth and early twentieth centuries there existed a group of critics loosely identified as "sonnet legislators." They knew sonnets had 140 syllables, alternately unstressed and stressed, spaced in ten syllable lines, grouped either in three stanzas of four lines and one couplet or in one octave and one sestet. They also had rules for rhyming, assonance, caesurae, alliteration, thematic development, and more. One critic, as I recall, had 1028 acceptable rhyme patterns. Their rules made them eliminate Milton and Wordsworth, Meredith and Rossetti, and many others we consider strong sonneteers. They would not have accepted Hopkins, although two-thirds of his poems are sonnets, and they'd have raged at E.E. Cummings, whose body of work is perhaps one-third made of sonnets. That is, their formalistic rules required them to condemn poems we may well honor. A few apologetically admitted at they saw good poems that were bad sonnets, but that was exceptional broad-mindedness.

My poet friends of the 1940s and 50s who were writing sonnets and sestinas, rondeaus and rondels, epigrams and epithalamia fortunately did not know about the legislators, so they varied the original forms to suit their fancy. The prescribed forms of versification offered resistance that kept them alert and demanded all of their talents, but they felt free to adapt and to build on the tradition. They were so crafty that many readers didn't even notice the craft or the basic form. By creating variations on the established moves they were becoming the Michael Jordans for the poetic world in spite of the critics, who are now mercifully unknown.

Classroom composition has not always worked out so well. We were, in the early days of CCCC, distracted by the "Minimum Essentials" movement that dealt almost entirely with scribal correctness and social conventionality. Three "errors" and the paper fails. The five-paragraph theme, which has its roots in

Aristotle and Cicero, simplified composition in a school classroom, but lost its connections with purpose and audience. The formula was easy to enact, and it could be elaborated into rules that required "the first sentence to state the subject with a predication that limits the paper, the second sentence to offer definitions, and the third sentence to list the contents of the following three paragraphs." And so on. It could be written by students who had no purpose other than obliging the teacher and getting out of school, and it allowed teachers a form of quick checking as a substitute for real reading.

In short, it denied what form was really supposed to provide, control for the writer's vision. It was a parody of craft, of poesis. It also made life tolerable for high school teachers who had 150 pupils a day and practically no time for preparation. And at the same time, Rudolf Flesch and Robert Gunning offered readability formulae that reduced adaptation for audiences to a matter of arithmetic. Both business and journalism paid big bucks to hire their consulting services. Flesch also did rather well telling us why Johnny couldn't write. To some extent the system was revived by E. D. Hirsch and his "relative readability." "Correctness" and "formulas" seemed to the public to represent orderliness and a suitable submission to the boss, so they had and still have public approval.

Such perversions of form led to overstatements of contrary positions. I recall people waving Ken Macrorie's *Uptaught* like Mao's little red book in order to energize a countermovement that stressed personality, ethical proof. Walker Gibson and Albert Guerard pushed the idea of voice as an expression of self, although with Gibson especially it implied an ontology of relativism, and with the people at Stanford it was more a matter of style. In England James Britton and others pulled together the ideas of various psychologists and linguists to suggest a "self" that is a product of language. The fights over Webster's Third, Black English Vernacular, and social class were also arguments about the mutability of language as well as about the special purposes of alternate forms-alternate in the sense of allowing crafty choices and styles, in suggesting social allegiances and values.

The people I've named were not responsible for the overstatements, but some uncritical readers overstated the case. It was rather like current fights about "whole language" and "phonics." The people who actually did the research are generally quite calm and reasonable, but supporters sometimes roar out "all or none." True faith leads to all sorts of false claims and outrageous attacks, and the general public in this cynical age tends to run with the people who view with the noisiest alarm. Oddly enough, people also buy the silliest nostrums, probably because they have learned to distrust the people they are presumed to trust.

You'll note that I haven't been saying that teaching craft is the only way to go. It's a blue-collar kind of approach to our trade, requiring lots of hand labor and apprenticeships, and we suffer enough from fellow academicals who seem to think we rank lower than the part-time clerks in the registrar's office. True cabinetmakers do fine work, but they don't make many slogans.

In my own academic context at Iowa, the rules that were established to protect the high prestige of the creative writing program (as well as studio art and performance music) also made it possible to develop a program for a broader range of writers. Journalists came to our courses as well as poets, graduates as well as freshmen, biologists as well as literary critics. They all came to perfect their crafts; we claimed that the craft we offered allowed them better to define themselves as crafters, to govern their own materials, and to relate to the rest of the human world. Our craft, we said, is as complicated as life itself and it engages any question a human can care to ask. We remain the most liberating of all the liberal arts. At times we have been denied by the National Endowment for Humanities, either because they claim we are "mere" mechanics or "mere" rhetoricians, or worse, incompetent therapists, public relations hacks, and badly trained philosophers. I prefer to classify us as poets, primeval makers, enabling the culture to know itself and connect its people into a productive wholeness.

Contributors

Bruce Ballenger is Emeritus Professor and former department chair at Boise State University, specializing in composition theory, inquiry-based learning, and creative nonfiction. He has authored seven books, including *Crafting Truth: Short Studies in Creative Nonfiction*, the best-selling textbooks *The Curious Writer* and *The Curious Researcher*, and more than thirty articles and essays.

Jocelyn Bartkevicius teaches in the M.F.A. and undergraduate creative writing programs at the University of Central Florida. Her work has appeared in such journals as *The Hudson Review*, *The Missouri Review*, *Crab Orchard Review*, *Fourth Genre*, and *Bellingham Review*, and has been awarded the Annie Dillard essay award, the *Missouri Review* essay award, the *Iowa Woman* essay award, and the John Guyon Literary nonfiction award. She is completing a memoir on burlesque and imperialism.

Nancy DeJoy has directed first-year writing at several colleges and universities, including Michigan State University. She is the author of *Process This: Undergraduate Writing in Composition Studies* and co-editor with Beatrice Quarshie Smith of *Collaborations and Innovations: Supporting Multilingual Writers Across Campus Units*. She has been an advocate for the inclusion of undergraduate voices in composition studies throughout her career and is committed to approaches to first-year writing that center participation (rather than adaptation) and contribution (rather than consumption). She is an accomplished installation poet; her TEDx talk, "Illuminating Survivor Voices," with over 30,000 views to date, advocates for the importance of poetic listening and inclusive approaches to working for social justice.

Rachel Faldet is Assistant Professor Emerita of English at Luther College. An essayist, she has edited several anthologies, including *Our Stories of Miscarriage: Healing With Words*.

Tom Montgomery Fate is Emeritus Professor at College of DuPage, in suburban Chicago, where he taught creative writing and literature for thirty years. He's the author of six nonfiction books, including *Cabin Fever: A Suburban Father's Search for the Wild*, a nature memoir, and *The Long Way Home: Detours and Discoveries*, a travel memoir.

Margaret Finders is a retired professor from Augsburg University, Minneapolis. She has written extensively on the sociopolitical dimensions of literacy learning and teacher education. Her recent areas of inquiry are on equity and democratic practices for teacher education and higher education.

David Hamilton, the longtime editor of *The Iowa Review*, was before he retired a core member of the University of Iowa's Nonfiction Writing Program. He is the author of *Deep River: A Memoir of a Missouri Farm* and *A Certain Arc: Essays of Finding My Way*.

Douglas Hesse is Professor of English at the at the University of Denver, where he was founding Executive Director of Writing and where he has been named University Distinguished Scholar. He has been president of NCTE, chair of CCCC, and president of WPA, among other national leadership roles. Among his four books and 80 published essays are works both of and about creative nonfiction, including *Creating Nonfiction*, co-authored with Becky Bradway, with awards including the Donald Murray prize and "notable essay" mention in *The Best American Essays*.

Laura Julier edited *Fourth Genre: Explorations in Nonfiction* for ten years. At Michigan State University, she directed the Professional Writing Program, and taught courses in editing, publishing, and nonfiction. She lives and writes in Iowa City, where she is working on two memoirs.

Carl H. Klaus founded and directed the University of Iowa's Nonfiction Writing Program. His literary nonfiction includes *My Vegetable Love: A Journal of a Growing Season, Weathering Winter, Taking Retirement: A Beginner's Diary, Letters to Kate: Life after Life,* and *The Ninth Decade: An Octogenarian's Chronicle*, which was published shortly before his death in February 2022, just a few months before what would have been his 90th birthday. He was primarily an author of journals that chronicled significant personal experience in the form of essays rather than notes and jottings, though he also authored or co-edited several books on the craft of nonfiction.

John T. Price is Director of the Creative Nonfiction Writing Program at the University of Nebraska at Omaha. A recipient of a prose fellowship from the National Endowment for the Arts, he has authored four books of creative nonfiction, including *All is Leaf: Essays and Transformations*, and is editor of *The Tallgrass Prairie Reader*.

Kerry Reilly's writing has appeared in *The New York Times, The Gettysburg Review, The Threepenny Review* and a variety of literary and academic journals. She earned an M.F.A. from the University of Iowa's Nonfiction Writing Program. She serves as a teaching associate professor at the University of Colorado at Boulder.

Robert Root has written, edited, and co-edited twenty-two books, including *E. B. White: The Emergence of an Essayist, Happenstance,* and *The Fourth Genre*. His essays have been cited in the Best American Essays series. He is Emeritus Professor of English at Central Michigan University.

Jenny Spinner is Professor of English and Director of the Writing Center at St. Joseph's University, Philadelphia, where she teaches creative nonfiction and journalism. Her essays and scholarly work have appeared in *Fourth Genre, Assay, Essay Daily, Gateway Journalism Review,* the *Washington Post* and on NPR's *All Things Considered*, among others. She is author of *Of Women and the Essay*.

Ned Stuckey-French's publications include *The American Essay in the American Century, Essayists on the Essay: Montaigne to Our Time* (edited with Carl Klaus); and *Writing Fiction: A Guide to Narrative Craft* (co-authored with Janet

Burroway and Elizabeth Stuckey-French). His collection of personal essays, *One by One, the Stars*, was published by University of Georgia Press in 2022. He taught at Florida State University, and served for many years, before his death in 2019, as the review editor for *Fourth Genre*.

Nicole B. Wallack is Director of Columbia University's Undergraduate Writing Program and senior lecturer-in-discipline in the department of English and Comparative Literature. At Columbia, she teaches seminars in writing studies, essayism, educational history, American literature and film, and public intellectuals. She is a senior associate of the Institute for Writing and Thinking at Bard College and for the Modern Language Association has co-designed and leads sites of its Mellon-funded Reading and Writing Pedagogy Institute. Her articles, essays, and reviews have appeared in collections as well as *Public Books, Fourth Genre,* and *Essay Daily*. She is the author of *Crafting Presence: The American Essay and the Future of Writing Studies,* and co-editor, with Mario Aquilina and Bob Cowser, Jr., of *The Edinburgh Companion to the Essay*.

Kathleen Blake Yancey, the Kellogg W. Hunt Professor of English Emerita at Florida State University, has held leadership positions in CCCC, NCTE, and the Council of Writing Program Administrators. She has published extensively, often on issues surrounding writing curriculum, pedagogy, and assessment. Among her many books are *A Rhetoric of Reflection*, *Writing Across Contexts,* and *Assembling Composition*.